AF580894

ESSAYS: MODERN & ELIZABETHAN

a

ESSAYS MODERN AND ELIZABETHAN BY

EDWARD DOWDEN

Essay Index Reprint Series

BOOKS FOR LIBRARIES PRESS
FREEPORT, NEW YORK

First Published 1910
Reprinted 1970

STANDARD BOOK NUMBER:
8369-1647-6

LIBRARY OF CONGRESS CATALOG CARD NUMBER:
71-117784

PRINTED IN THE UNITED STATES OF AMERICA

CONTENTS

ESSAYS

MODERN AND ELIZABETHAN

WALTER PATER

LET us imagine to ourselves a boy born some ten years before the middle of the last century, of a family originally Dutch, a family with the home-loving, reserved temper of the Dutch, and that slow-moving mind of Holland which attaches itself so closely, so intimately to things real and concrete, not tempted away from its beloved interiors and limited prospects by any glories of mountain heights or wide-spreading and radiant horizons ; a family settled for long in the low-lying, slow-moving Olney of Buckinghamshire—Cowper's Olney, which we see in the delicate vignettes of *The Task*, and in the delightful letters, skilled in making so much out of so little, of the half-playful, half-pathetic correspondent of John Newton and Lady Hesketh. Dutch, but of mingled strains in matters of religion, the sons, we are told, always, until the tradition was broken in the case of Walter Pater, brought up as Roman Catholics, the daughters as members of the Anglican communion. Walter Pater's father had moved to the neighbourhood of London, and it was at Enfield, where Lamb, about whom the critic has written with penetrating sympathy, Lamb and his sister Mary, had lately dwelt, that Pater spent his boyhood. "Not precocious," writes his friend of later years, Mr. Gosse, "he was always meditative and serious." Yes, we cannot think of him at any time as other than serious ; withdrawn from the boisterous sports of boyhood; fed through little things by the sentiment of home—that sentiment which was nourished in Marius at White Nights by the duteous observances of the religion of Numa; in Gaston at the Château of Deux-Manoirs with its immemorial associations and its traditional Catholic pieties; in Emerald Uthwart at Chase Lodge, with its perfumes of sweet peas, the neighbouring fields so green and velvety, and the church where the ancient buried Uthwarts slept, that home to which Emerald came back to die, a broken man; in Florian Deleal by "the old house," its old staircase, its old furniture, its shadowy angles, its swallow's nest below the sill, its brown and golden wall-flowers, its pear tree in springtime, and the scent of lime-flowers floating in at the open window.

And with this nesting sense of home there comes to the boy from neighbouring London, from rumours of the outer world, from the face of some sad wayfarer on the road, an apprehension of the sorrow of the world, and the tears in mortal things, which disturbs him and must mingle henceforth with all his thoughts and dreams. He is recognised as "the clever one of the family," but it is not a vivacious cleverness, not a conscientious power of intellect, rather a shy, brooding faculty, slow to break its sheath, and expand into a blossom, a faculty of gradual and exact receptiveness, and one of which the eye is the special organ. This, indeed, is a central fact to remember. If Pater is a seeker for truth, he must seek for it with the eye, and with the imagination penetrating its way through things visible; or if truth comes to him in any other way, he must project the truth into colour and form, since otherwise it remains for him cold, loveless, and a tyranny of the intellect, like that which oppressed and almost crushed out of existence his Sebastian van Storck. We may turn elsewhere to read of "the conduct of the understanding." We learn much from Pater concerning the conduct of the eye. Whatever his religion may hereafter be, it cannot be that of Puritanism, which makes a breach between the visible and the invisible. It cannot be reached by purely intellectual processes; it cannot be embodied in a creed of dogmatic abstractions. The blessing which he may perhaps obtain can hardly be that of those who see not and yet have believed. The evidential value of a face made bright by some inner joy will count with him for more than any syllogism however correct in its premises and conclusions. A life made visibly gracious and comely will testify to him of some hidden truth more decisively than any supernatural witnessing known only by report. If he is impressed by any creed it will be by virtue of its living epistles, known and read of all men. He will be occupied during his whole life with a study not of ideas apart from their concrete embodiment, not of things concrete apart from their inward significance, but with a study of expression—expression as seen in the countenance of external nature, expression in Greek statue, mediæval cathedral, Renaissance altar-piece, expression in the ritual of various religions, and in the visible bearing of various types of manhood, in various exponents of tradition, of thought, and of faith.

His creed may partake somewhat of that natural or human catholicism of Wordsworth's poetry, which reveals the soul in things of sense, which is indeed, as Pater regards it, a kind of finer, spiritual sensuousness. But why stop where Wordsworth stopped in his earlier days? Why content ourselves with expression as seen in the face of hillside and cloud and stream, and the acts and words of simple men, through whom certain primitive elementary passions play? Why not also seek to discover the spirit in sense in its more complex and subtler incarnations—in the arts and crafts, in the shaping of a vase, the lines and colours of a tapestry, the carving of a capital, the movements of a celebrant in the rites of religion, in a relief of Della Robbia, in a Venus of Botticelli, in the mysterious Gioconda of Lionardo? Setting aside the mere dross of circumstances in human life, why not vivify all amidst which we live and move by translating sense into spirit, and spirit into sense, thus rendering opaque things luminous, so that if no pure white light of truth can reach us, at least each step we tread may be impregnated with the stains and dyes of those coloured morsels of glass, so deftly arranged, through which such light as we are able to endure has its access to our eyes?

If such thoughts as these lay in Pater's mind during early youth they lay unfolded and dormant. But we can hardly doubt that in the account of Emerald Uthwart's schooldays he is interpreting with full-grown and self-conscious imagination his experiences as a schoolboy at Canterbury, where the cathedral was the presiding element of the *genius loci:* "If at home there had been nothing great, here, to boyish sense, one seems diminished to nothing at all, amid the grand waves, wave upon wave, of patiently wrought stone; the daring height, the daring severity, of the innumerable long, upward ruled lines, rigidly bent just at last in one place into the reserved grace of the perfect Gothic arch." Happy Emerald Uthwart in those early days, and happy Walter Pater with such noble, though as yet half-conscious, discipline in the conduct of the eye! If Pater thought of a profession, the military profession of his imagined Emerald would have been the last to commend itself to his feelings. His father was a physician, but science had no call for the son's intellect, and we can hardly imagine him as an enthusiastic student in the school of anatomy. He felt the attractions of the life and work of an English clergyman, and when a little boy, Mr. Gosse tells us, he had seen the benign face of Keble during a visit to Hursley, and had welcomed Keble's paternal counsel and encouragement. Had Pater lived some years longer it is quite possible that his early dream might have been realised, but Oxford, as things were, dissolved the dream of Canterbury.

Two influences stood over against each other in the Oxford of Pater's undergraduate days. There was the High Church movement, with which the name of the University has been associated. The spell of Newman's personal charm and the echoes of his voice in the pulpit of St. Mary's were not yet forgotten. The High Church movement had made the face of religion more outwardly attractive to such a spirit as Pater's; there had been a revival, half serious, half dilettante, of ecclesiastical art. But the High Church movement was essentially dogmatic; the body of dogma had to some extent hardened into system, and Pater's mind was always prone to regard systems of thought—philosophical or theological—as works of art, to be examined and interpreted by the historical imagination; from which, when interpreted aright, something might be retained, perhaps, in a transposed form, but which could not be accepted and made one's own *en bloc*. On the other hand there was a stirring critical movement, opening new avenues for thought and imagination, promising a great enfranchisement of the intellect, and claiming possession of the future. Jowett was a nearer presence now at Oxford than Newman, and Pater had already come under the influence of German thinkers and had discovered in Goethe—greatest of critics—a master of the mind. Art, to which he had found access through the *Modern Painters* of an illustrious Oxford graduate, had passed beyond the bounds of the ecclesiastical revival, and, following a course like that of the mediæval drama, was rapidly secularising itself. We see the process at work in the firm of which William Morris was the directing manager, at first so much occupied with church decoration, and by-and-by extending its operations to the domestic interiors of the wealthier lay-folk of England. Pater's dream of occupying an Anglo-Catholic pulpit re-shaped itself into the dream of becoming an Unitarian minister, and by degrees it became evident that the only pulpit which he could occupy was that of the Essayist, who explores for truth, and ends his research not without a sense of insecurity in his own conclusions, or rather who concludes without a conclusion, and is content to be faithful through manifold suggestions.

We can imagine that with a somewhat different composition of the forces within him Pater's career might have borne some resemblance to that of Henri Amiel, "in wandering mazes lost." But the disputants in Amiel's nature were more numerous and could not be brought to a conciliation. One of them was for ever reaching out toward the indefinite, which Amiel called the infinite, and the Màya of the Genevan Buddhist threw him back in the end upon a world of *ennui*. Pater was saved by a certain "intellectual astringency," by a passion for the concrete, and by the fact that he lived much in and through the eye. He had perhaps learnt from Goethe that true expansion lies in limitation, and he never appreciated as highly as did Amiel the poetry of fog. His boyish faith, such as it was, had lapsed away. How was he to face life and make the best of it ? Something at least could be gained by truth to himself, by utter integrity, by living, and that intensely, in his best self and in the highest moments of his best self, by detaching from his intellectual force, as he says of Winckelmann, all flaccid interests. If there was in him any tendency to mystic passion and religious reverie this was checked, as with his own Marius, by a certain virility of intellect, by a feeling of the poetic beauty of mere clearness of mind. Is nothing permanent? Are all things melting under our feet ? Well, if it be so, we cannot alter the fact. But we need not therefore spend our few moments of life in listlessness. If all is passing away, let the knowledge of this be a stimulus toward intenser activity, let it excite within us the thirst for a full and perfect experience.

And remember that Pater's special gift, his unique power, lay in the eye and in the imagination using the eye as its organ. He could not disdain the things of sense, for there is a spirit in sense, and mind communes with mind through colour and through form. He notes in Marcus Aurelius, the pattern of Stoical morality, who would stand above and apart from the world of the senses, not, after all, an attainment of the highest humanity, but a mediocrity, though a mediocrity for once really golden. He writes of Pascal with adequate knowledge and with deep sympathy, but he qualifies his admiration for the great friend of Jansenism by observing that Pascal had little sense of the beauty even of holiness. In Pascal's " sombre, trenchant, precipitous philosophy," and his perverse asceticism, Pater finds evidence of a diseased spirit, a morbid tension like that of insomnia. Sebastian van Storck, with the warm life of a rich

Dutch interior around him, and all the play of light and colour in Dutch art to enrich his eye, turns away to seek some glacial Northwest passage to the lifeless, colourless Absolute. Spinoza appears to Pater not as a God-intoxicated man, but as climbing to the barren pinnacle of egoistic intellect. Such, at all events, could not possibly be his own way. There is something of the true wisdom of humility in modestly remembering that we are not pure intelligence, pure soul, and in accepting the aid of the senses. How reassuring Marius finds it to be, after assisting at a long debate about rival criteria of truth, "to fall back upon direct sensation, to limit one's aspiration after knowledge to that." To live intensely in the moment, "to burn with a gemlike flame," to maintain an ecstasy, is to live well, with the gain, at least for a moment, of wisdom and of joy. "America is here and now—here or nowhere," as Wilhelm Meister, and, after him, Marius the Epicurean discovered.

There is no hint in Pater's first volume of the fortifying thought which afterwards came to him, that some vast logic of change, some law or rhythm of evolution may underlie all that is transitory, all the pulsations of passing moments, and may bind them together in some hidden harmony. Looking back on the period of what he calls a new Cyrenaicism, he saw a most depressing theory coming in contact, in his own case as in that of Marius, with a happy temperament—happy though subject to moods of deep depression, and he saw that by virtue of this happy temperament he had converted his loss into a certain gain. Assuredly he never regarded that view of life which is expressed in the *Conclusion to Studies in the History of the Renaissance* as mere hedonism, as a mere abandonment to the lust of the eye, the lust of the flesh, and the pride of life. No : looking back, he perceived that his aim was not pleasure, but fulness and vividness of life, a perfection of being, an intense and, as far as may be, a complete experience ; that this was not to be attained without a discipline, involving some severity ; that it demanded a strenuous effort ; that here, too, the loins must be girt and the lamp lit ; that for success in his endeavour he needed before all else true insight, and that insight will not come by any easy way, or, as we say, by a royal road ; that on the contrary it must be sought by a culture, which may be, and ought to be, joyous, but which certainly must be strict. The precept, " Be perfect in regard to what is here and now," is one which may be interpreted, as he conceived it, into lofty meanings. A conduct of the intellect in accordance with this precept, in its rejection of many things which bring with them facile pleasures, may in a certain sense be called a form of asceticism. The eye itself must be purified from all grossness and dulness. " Such a manner of life," writes Pater of the new Cyrenaicism of his Marius, " might itself even come to seem a kind of religion. . . . The true ' æsthetic culture ' would be realisable as a new form of the ' contemplative life,' founding its claim on the essential ' blessedness ' of ' vision '—the vision of perfect men and things." At the lowest it is an impassioned ideal life.

Such is Pater's own *apologia pro vita sua*—that is, for life during his earlier years of authorship—as given in *Marius the Epicurean.* But the best apologia is, indeed, the outcome of that life, the volume of *Studies in the History of the Renaissance*, and later essays, which are essentially one with these in kind. The richness of colour and delicacy of carving in some of Pater's work have concealed from many readers its intellectual severity, its strictness of design, its essential veracity. A statue that is chryselephantine may be supposed to be less intellectual than the same statue if it were worked in marble; yet more of sheer brainwork perhaps is required for the design which has to calculate effects of colour. There are passages in Pater's writing which may be called, if you like, decorative, but the decoration is never incoherent ornament of *papier maché* laid on from without; it is, on the contrary, a genuine outgrowth of structure, always bringing into relief the central idea.

This central idea he arrives at only through the process of a steadfast and strenuous receptiveness, which has in it something of the nature of fortitude. Occasionally he gives it an express definition, naming it, not perhaps quite happily, the *formula* of the artist or author who is the subject of his study. Thus, the formula of Raphael's genius, if we must have one, is this: "The transformation of meek scholarship into genius—triumphant power of genius." The essay on Raphael is accordingly the record of a series of educations, from which at last emerge works showing a synoptic intellectual power, and large theoretic conceptions, but these are seen to act in perfect unison with the pictorial imagination and a magic power of the hand. The formula, to turn from pictorial art to literature, of Prosper Mérimée, who met the disillusion of the post-Revolution period by irony, is this: "The enthusiastic amateur of rude, crude, naked force in men and women wherever it could be found; himself carrying ever, as a mask, the conventional attire of the modern world—carrying it with an infinite contemptuous grace, as if that too were an all-sufficient end in itself." Nothing could be more triumphantly exact and complete than

Pater's brief formula of Mérimée. But perhaps his method is nowhere more convincingly shown than in the companion studies of two French churches, Notre Dame of Amiens, pre-eminently the church of a city, of a commune, and the Madeleine of Vézelay, which is typically the church of a monastery. Here the critic does not for a moment lose himself in details; in each case he holds, as it were, the key of the situation; he has grasped the central idea of each structure; and then with the aid of something like creative imagination, he assists the idea—the vital germ—to expand itself and grow before us into leaf and tendril and blossom.

In such studies as these we perceive that the eye is itself an intellectual power, or at least the organ and instrument of such a power. And this imaginative criticism is in truth constructive. But the creative work of imagination rises from a basis of adequate knowledge and exact perception. To see precisely what a thing is—what, before all else, it is to *me;* to feel with entire accuracy its unique quality; to find the absolutely right word in which to express the perception and the feeling—this indeed taxes the athletics of the mind. Sometimes, while still essentially a critic, Pater's power of construction and reconstruction takes the form of a highly intellectual fantasy. Thus *A Study of Dionysus* reads like a fantasia suggested by the life of the vine and the "spirit of sense" in the grape; yet the fantasia is in truth the tracing out, by a learned sympathy, of strange or beautiful sequences of feeling or imagination in the Greek mind. In *Denys l'Auxerrois* and *Apollo in Picardy*, which should be placed side by side as companion pieces, the fancy takes a freer range. They may be described as transpositions of the classical into the romantic. Apollo—now for mediæval contemporaries bearing the ill-omened name Apollyon—appears in a monkish frock and wears the tonsure ; yet he remains a true Apollo, but of the Middle Age, and, in a passage of singular romance, even does to death the mediæval Hyacinthus. Denys, that strange flaxen and flowery creature, the organ-builder of Auxerre, has all the mystic power and ecstatic rage of Dionysus. Are these two elder brothers of Goethe's Euphorion, earlier-born children of Faust and Helena ?

Even these fantasies are not without an intellectual basis. For Pater recognises in classical art and classical literature a considerable element of romance—strangeness allied with beauty ; and to re-fashion the myths of Dionysus and even of Apollo in the romantic spirit is an experiment in which there is more than mere fantasy. Very justly and admirably he protests in writing of Greek sculpture against a too intellectual or abstract view of classical art. Here also were colour and warmth and strange ventures of imaginative faith, and fears and hopes and ecstasies, which we are apt to forget in the motionless shadow or pallid light of our cold museums. Living himself at a time, as we say, of " transition," when new and old ideas were in conflict, and little interested in any form of action except that of thought and feeling, he came to take a special interest in the contention and also in the conciliation of rival ideals. Hence the period of the Renaissance—from the auroral Renaissance within the Middle Age to the days of Ronsard and Montaigne, with its new refinements of mediævalism—seen, for example, in the poetry of the *Pleiad*—its revival in an altered form of the classical temper, and the invasions of what may be summed up under the name of " the modern spirit "—had a peculiar attraction for him. His Gaston de Latour, as far as he is known to us through what is unhappily a fragment, seems almost created for no other purpose than to be a subject for the play of contending influences. The old pieties of the Middle Age survive within him, leaving a deep and abiding deposit in his spirit ; but he is caught by the new grace and delicate magic of Ronsard's verse, of Ronsard's personality ; he is exposed to all the enriching, and yet perhaps disintegrating forces of Montaigne's undulant philosophy—the philosophy of the relative ; and he is prepared to be lifted—lifted, shall we say, or lowered ?—from his state of suspended judgment by the ardent genius of that new knight of the Holy Ghost, Giordano Bruno, with his glowing exposition of the Lower Pantheism.

His Marius, again, cannot rest in the religion of Numa, which was the presiding influence of his boyhood. His Cyrenaicism is confronted by the doctrine of the Stoics—sad, grey, depressing, though presented with all possible amiability in the person of Marcus Aurelius. And in the Christian house of Cecilia, and among the shadowy catacombs of Rome, his eyes are touched by the radiance of a newer light, which thrills him with the sense of an unapprehended joy, a heroic—perhaps a divine—hope. In the eighteenth century Pater's Watteau, creating a new and delicate charm for the society of his own day, is yet ill at ease, half detached from that society, and even—saddening experience !—half detached from his own art, for he dreams, unlike his age, of a better world than the actual one ; and by an anachronism which is hardly pardonable (for it confuses the chronology of eighteenth-century moods of mind) the faithful and tender diarist of Valenciennes, whose more than sisterly interest in young Antoine has left us this Watteau myth, becomes acquainted—and through

Antoine himself—with the Manon Lescaut of many years later, in which the ardent passion of the period of Rousseau is anticipated. And, again, in that other myth of the eighteenth century, Duke Carl of Rosenmold—myth of a half-rococo Apollo—the old stiff mediævalism of German courts and the elegant *fadeurs* of French pseudo-classicism are exhibited in relation to a throng of fresher influences—the classical revival of which Winckelmann was the apostle, the revival of the Middle Age as a new and living force, the artistic patriotism which Lessing preached, the " return to nature " of which a little later the young Goethe—he, a true Apollo—was the herald, and that enfranchisement of passion and desire, which, now when Rousseau is somewhere in the world, brooding, kindling, about to burst into flame, seems no anachronism.

I cannot entirely go along with that enthusiastic admirer who declared—surely not without a smile of ironic intelligence—that the trumpet of doom ought to have sounded when the last page of *Studies in the History of the Renaissance* was completed. Several copies of the golden book in its first edition, containing the famous Conclusion, would probably have perished in the general conflagration ; and Pater was averse to noise. But a memorable volume it is, and one which testifies to the virtue of a happy temperament even when in the presence of a depressing philosophy. Too much attention has been centred on that Conclusion ; it has been taken by many persons as if it were Pater's ultimate confession of faith, whereas, in truth, the Conclusion was a prologue. Pater's early years had made a home for his spirit among Christian pieties and the old moralities. When Florian Deleal, quitting for the first time the house of his childhood, runs back to fetch the forgotten pet bird, and sees the warm familiar rooms "lying so pale, with a look of meekness in their denudation," a clinging to the cherished home comes over him. And had Pater in his haughty philosophy of manhood in like manner dismantled and desecrated the little white room of his early faith? The very question seemed to carry with it something of remorse; but Pater's integrity of mind, his intellectual virility, could not permit itself to melt in sentiment. In the essay on Aucassin and Nicolette, he had spoken of the rebellious antinomian spirit connected with the outbreak of the reason and imagination, with the assertion of the liberty of heart, in the Middle Age. "The perfection of culture," he knew, "is not rebellion, but peace;" yet on the way to that end, he thought, there is room for a noble antinomianism. Now, like his own Marius, he began to think that in such antinomianism there might be a taint, he began to question whether it might not be possible somehow to adjust his new intellectual scheme of things to the old morality. His culture had brought with it a certain sense of isolation, like that of a spectator detached from the movement of life and the great community of men. His Cyrenaic theory was one in keeping with the proud individualism of youth. From the Stoic Fronto his Marius hears of an august community, to which each of us may perchance belong, "humanity, an universal order, the great polity, its aristocracy of elect spirits, the mastery of their example over their successors." But where are these elect spirits? Where is this comely order? The Cyrenaic lover of beauty begins to feel that his conception of beauty has been too narrow, too exclusive; not positively unsound perhaps, for it enjoined the practice of an ideal temperance, and involved a seriousness of spirit almost religious, so that, as Marius reflects, "the saint and the Cyrenaic lover of beauty would at least understand each other better than either would understand the mere man of the world." His pursuit of perfection was surely not in itself illegitimate, but by its exclusiveness of a more complete ideal of perfection it might almost partake of the nature of a heresy. Without rejecting his own scheme of life, might it not be possible to adjust it to the old morality as a part to a whole? Viewed even from a purely egoistic standpoint had not such attainments as were his—and the attainments were unquestionably precious—been secured at a great sacrifice? Was it a true economy to forfeit perhaps a greater gain for the less? The Stoical ideal, which casts scorn upon the body, and that visible beauty in things which for Marius was indeed a portion of truth, as well as beauty, he must needs reject. But might there not be a divination of something real, an imperfect vision of a veritable possibility in the Stoical conception of an ordered society of men, a Celestial City, *Uranopolis, Callipolis?* And what if the belief of Marcus Aurelius in the presence of a divine companion, a secret Providence behind the veil, contained some elevating truth? What if the isolated seeker for a narrow perfection could attach himself to some venerable system of sentiment and ideas, and so "let in a great tide of experience, and make, as it were, with a single step, a great experience of his own; with a great consequent increase to his own mind, of colour, variety, and relief, in the spectacle of men and things"?

There are two passages of rare spiritual beauty in *Marius the Epicurean:* one is that which tells of Marius wandering forth with such thoughts as these—keeping all these things in his heart—to one of his favourite spots in the Alban or the Sabine hills; the other is the description of the sacred memorial celebration in the Christian house of Cecilia. After a night of perfect sleep Marius awakes in the morning sunlight, with almost the joyful waking of childhood. As he rides toward the hills his mood is, like the season's, one of flawless serenity ; a sense of gratitude—gratitude to what?—fills his heart, and must overflow ; he leans, as it were, toward that eternal, invisible Companion of whom the Stoic philosopher and emperor spoke. Might he not, he reflects, throw in the election of his will, though never faltering from the truth, on the side of his best thought, his best feeling, and perhaps receive in due course the justification, the confirmation of this venture of faith ? What if the eternal companion were really by his side ? What if his own spirit were but a moment, a pulse, in some great stream of spiritual energy ? What if this fair material universe were but a creation, a projection into sense of the perpetual mind ? What if the new city, let down from heaven, were also a reality included in the process of that divine intelligence ? Less through any sequence of argument than by a discovery of the spirit in sense, or rather of the imaginative reason, Marius seems to live and move in the presence of the Great Ideal, the Eternal Reason, nay, the Father of men. A larger conception assuredly of the reasonable Ideal than that of his Cyrenaic days has dawned for him, every trace or note of which it shall henceforth be his business to gather up. *Paratum cor meum, Deus! paratum cor meum!*

It is a criticism of little insight which represents Marius as subordinating truth to any form of ease or comfort or spiritual self-indulgence ; an erroneous criticism which represents him as only extending a refined hedonism so as to include within it new pleasures of the moral sense or the religious temper.

For Marius had never made pleasure his aim and end; his aim and end had been always perfection, but now he perceives that his ideal of perfection had been incomplete and inadequate. He discovers the larger truth, and the lesser falls into its due place. His experiences among the Sabine hills, which remind one of certain passages in Wordsworth's *Excursion*, may have little evidential value for any other mind than his own; even for himself they could hardly recur in like manner ever again. But that such phenomena—however we may interpret their significance—are real cannot be doubted by any disinterested student of human nature. What came to Marius was not a train of argument, but what we may call a revelation; it came as the last and culminating development, under favouring external conditions, of many obscure processes of thought and feeling. The seed had thrust up its stalk, which then had struggled through the soil; and at last sunlight touches the folded blossom, which opens to become a flower of light.

Marius had already seen in Cornelius the exemplar of a new knighthood, which he can but imperfectly understand. Entirely virile, Cornelius is yet governed by some strange hidden rule which obliges him to turn away from many things that are commonly regarded as the rights of manhood; he has a blitheness, which seems precisely the reverse of the temper of the Emperor, and yet some veiled severity underlies, perhaps supports, this blitheness. And in the gathering at Cecilia's house, where the company—and among them, children—are singing, Marius recognises the same glad expansion of a joyful soul, "in people upon whom some all-subduing experience had wrought heroically." A grave discretion; an intelligent seriousness about life; an exquisite courtesy ; all chaste affections of the family, and these under the most natural conditions ; a temperate beauty ; all are here ; the human body, which had been degraded by Pagan voluptuousness and dishonoured by Stoic asceticism, is here reverenced as something sacred, or as something sanctified ; and death itself is made beautiful through a new hope. Charity here is not painfully calculated, but joyous and chivalrous in its devotion ; peaceful labour is rehabilitated and illumined with some new light. A higher ideal than Marius had ever known before—higher and gladder—is operative here, ideal of woman, of the family, of industry, including all of life and death. And its effects are visible, addressing themselves even to the organ of sight, which with Marius is the special avenue for truth ; so that he has only to read backward from effects to causes in order to be assured that some truth of higher import and finer efficacy than any previously known to him must be working among the forces which have created this new beauty. What if this be the company of elect souls dreamed of by the rhetorician Fronto ? And with the tenderest charity in this company of men and women a heroic fortitude—the fortitude of the martyrs, like those of Lyons—is united. What if here be Uranopolis, Callipolis, the City let down from heaven ? For Marius in the house of Cecilia the argument is irrefragable—rather the experience is convincing. Possibly in the light of a more extended survey of history new doubts and questions may arise ; but these were days of purity and of love, the days of the minor peace of the church.

Yet even in the end Marius is brought only to his Pisgah—the mount of vision. He does not actually set foot within the promised land. Even that act of surrender, by which Cornelius is delivered and Marius goes to his death, is less an act of divine self-sacrifice than the result of an impulse, half careless, half generous, of comradeship. His spirit — *anima naturaliter Christiana*—departs less in assured hope than with the humble consolation of memory—*tristem neminem fecit;* he had at least not added any pang to the total sum of the world's pain.

And although the creator of Marius had arrived, by ways very different from those of Pascal, at some of Pascal's conclusions, and had expressed these with decisiveness in a review of Amiel's *Journal*, we cannot but remember that essentially his mind belonged to the same order as the mind of Montaigne rather than to the order of the mind of Pascal. We can imagine Pater, had he lived longer, asking himself, as part of that endless dialogue with self which constituted his life, whether the deepest community with his fellows could not be attained by a profound individuality without attaching himself to institutions. Whether, for example, the fact of holding a fellowship at Brasenose, or the fact of knowing Greek well, bound him the more intimately to the society of Greek scholars. We can imagine him questioning whether other truths might not be added to those truths which made radiant the faces in Cecilia's house. Whether even those same truths might not, in a later age, be capable of, might not even require, a different conception, and a largely altered expression.

While in the ways indicated in *Marius the Epicurean* Pater was departing from that doctrine of the perpetual flux—with ideals of conduct corresponding to that doctrine—or was at least subordinating this to a larger, really a more liberal view of things, his mind was also tending, and now partly under the influence of Plato, away from the brilliantly-coloured, versatile, centrifugal Ionian temper of his earlier days toward the simpler, graver, more strictly ordered, more athletic Dorian spirit.

Plato and Platonism, in noticing which I shall sometimes use Pater's own words, is distinguished less by colour than by a pervasive light. The demand on a reader's attention is great, but the demand is not so much from sentence to sentence as from chapter to chapter. If we may speak of the evolution or development of a theme by literary art, such evolution in this book is perhaps its highest merit. No attempt is made to fix a dogmatic creed, or to piece together an artificial unity of tessellated opinions. Philosophies are viewed very much as works of art, and the historical method is adopted, which endeavours to determine the conditions that render each philosophy, each work of art, and especially this particular work of art, the Platonic philosophy, possible. And there is something of autobiography, for those who can discern it, below the surface of the successive discussions of ideas, which yet are often seemingly remote from modern thought.

The doctrine of the Many, of the perpetual flux of things, which was so consonant to the mobile Ionian temper, is set over against the doctrine of the One, for which all that is phenomenal becomes null, and the sole reality is pure Being, colourless, formless, impalpable. It was Plato's work to break up the formless unity of the philosophy of the One into something multiple, and yet not transitory—the starry Platonic ideas, Justice, Temperance, Beauty, and their kindred luminaries of the intellectual heaven. Platonism in one sense is a witness for the unseen, the transcendental. Yet, austere as he sometimes appears, who can doubt that Plato's austerity, his temperance is attained only by the control of a richly sensuous nature? Before all else he was a lover; and now that he had come to love invisible things more than visible, the invisible things must be made, as it were, visible persons, capable of engaging his affections. The paradox is true that he had a sort of sensuous love of the unseen. And in setting forth his thoughts he is not a dogmatist but essentially an essayist—a questioning explorer for truth, who refines and idealises the manner of his master Socrates, and who, without the oscillating philosophy of Montaigne, anticipates something of Montaigne's method as a seeker for the knowledge of things.

At this point in Pater's long essay, a delightful turn is given to his treatment of the subject by that remarkable and characteristic chapter in which he attempts to revive for the eye, as well as for the mind, the life of old Lacedæmon—Lacedæmon, the highest concrete embodiment of that Dorian temper of Greece, that Dorian temper of which his own ideal Republic would have been a yet more complete development. Those conservative Lacedæmonians, "the people of memory pre-eminently," are made to live and move before us by creative imagination working among the records, too scanty, of historical research. There in hollow Laconia, a land of organised slavery under central military authority, the genius of conservatism was enthroned. The old bore sway; the young were under strict, but not unjoyous discipline. Every one, at every moment, must strive to be at his best, with all superfluities pruned away. "It was a type of the Dorian purpose in life—a sternness, like sea-water infused into wine, overtaking a matter naturally rich, at the moment when fulness may lose its savour and expression." There in clear air, on the bank of a mountain torrent, stands Lacedæmon; by no means a "growing" place, rather a solemn, ancient mountain village, with its sheltering plane trees, and its playing-fields for youthful athletes, all under discipline, who when robed might almost have seemed a company of young monks. A city not without many venerable and beautiful buildings, civic and religious, in a grave hieratic order of architecture, while its private abodes were simple and even rude. The whole of life is evidently conceived as matter of attention, patience, fidelity to detail, like that of good soldiers or musicians. The Helots, who pursue their trades and crafts from generation to generation in a kind of guild, may be indulged in some illiberal pleasures of abundant food and sleep ; but it is the mark of aristocracy to endure hardness. And from these half-military, half-monastic modes of life are born the most beautiful of all people in Greece, in the world. Everywhere one is conscious of reserved power, and the beauty of strength restrained —a male beauty, far remote from feminine tenderness. Silent these men can be, or, if need arise, can speak to the point, and with brevity. With them to read is almost a superfluity, for whatever is essential has become a part of memory, and is made actual in habit; but such culture in fact has the power to develop a vigorous imagination. Their music has in it a high moral stimulus; their dance is not mere form, but full of subject ; they dance a theme, and that with absolute correctness, a dance full of delight, yet with something of the character of a liturgical service, something of a military inspection. And these half-monastic people are also —as monks may be—a very cheerful people, devoted to a religion of sanity, worshippers of Apollo, sanest of the national gods ; strong in manly comradeship, of which those youthful demi-gods, the Dioscuri, are the patrons. Why all this strenuous task-work day after day ? An intelligent young Spartan might reply, " To the end that I myself may be a perfect work of art."

It is this Dorian spirit which inspires the Republic of Plato. He would, if possible, arrest the disintegration of Athenian society, or at least protest against the principle of flamboyancy in things and thoughts—protest against the fluxional, centrifugal, Ionian element in the Hellenic character. He conceives the State as one of those disciplined Spartan dancers, or as a well-known athlete ; he desires not that it shall be gay, or rich, or populous, but that it shall be strong, an organic unity, entirely self-harmonious, each individual occupying his exact place in the system ; and the State being thus harmoniously strong, it will also be of extreme æsthetic beauty—the beauty of a unity or harmony enforced on highly disparate elements, unity as of an army or an order of monks, unity as of liturgical music.

It could hardly happen that Pater's last word in this long study should be on any other subject than art. It is no false fragment of traditional Platonism which insists on the close connection between the æsthetic qualities of things and the formation of moral character ; on the building of character through the eye and ear. And this ethical influence of art resides even more in the form—its concision, simplicity, rhythm—than in the matter. In the ideal Republic the simplification of human nature is the chief affair ; therefore art must be simple and even austere. The community will be fervently æsthetic, but withal fervent renunciants as well, and, in the true sense of the word *ascetic*, will be fervently ascetic. " The proper art of the Perfect City is in fact the art of discipline." In art, in its narrower meaning, in literature, what the writer of the Republic would most desire is that quality which solicits an effort from the reader or spectator, " who is promised a great expressiveness on the part of the writer, the artist, if he for his part will bring with him a great attentiveness." Temperance superinduced on a nature originally rich and impassioned—this is the supreme beauty of the Dorian art. Plato's own prose is, indeed, a practical illustration of the value of intellectual astringency. He is before all else a lover, and infinite patience, quite as much as fire, is the mood of all true lovers. It is, indeed, this infinite patience of a lover which in large measure gives to Pater's own studies of art and literature their peculiar value. The bee, that has gone down the long neck of a blossom, is not more patient in collecting his drop of honey.

HENRIK IBSEN

SEVERAL of Ibsen's men and women are possessed with a highly reprehensible passion for exposing their lives to danger on perilous eminences. Halverd Solness, the master-builder, with trembling zeal achieves the impossible, ascends his ladders, and waves his hat for one triumphant moment from the top of his tower. It is among the high mountains and in the great waste places that little Eyolf's father discovers his mission which is no mission, and hears the call which is no call. Brand, bearing the banner with a strange device—not " Excelsior " but " All or Nothing "—perishes where the ice-church impales the blue, among the white wreaths and glacier-spines. John Gabriel Borkman struggles through snow to the plateau from which he sees the fiord below, and his imaginary kingdom of mountain-chains above, and there the ice-cold hand grips his heart. Professor Rubek and Irene reach an altitude from which unaided descent is impossible for them, and, as with Brand, the final stage direction introducing the *deus ex machina* might run " Enter Avalanche, who ingeniously saves the situation."

As we look back upon the series of Ibsen's works, to which the word " Finis " has now been appended, we feel that we, too, while our interest in them was still quick, were eager climbers, were perpetually on the strain, and never quite reached the point at which we could repose and enjoy in quietude a sure attainment. There are liberal fields of art in which the eye finds rest in horizontal lines, and this is no dull rest, for the lines may stretch away to the illimitable. In many great artists there is even a good bovine quality, which strangely may alternate with a winged joy, and which learns through tranquillity some of the deepest secrets of our Mother Earth. With Ibsen the lines are all precipitous and abrupt; we are forever scaling to the Viddes or above them; we hang over desperate fissures; we cling to jagged edges; we are enclosed in forlorn and shadowy chasms, or encounter some sudden spear-like shaft of light; we learn none of the deep lessons of tranquillity. Even in *Peer Gynt* fantasy brings no relief, for it is fantasy with all the energy of will behind it—fantasy with a purpose hidden in its flight. Yet in *Peer Gynt*, if anywhere, there is some hovering and circling on the wing, some smooth balance and curving poise of motion in the sea-gull fashion. For the most part, however, Ibsen's advance resembles rather the terribly business-like progress of the cormorant, bent upon attaining his point with a quite relentless resolve and with incessant beat of pinions.

If his end and aim as an artist were beauty and enjoyment in beauty, it could not have been thus with Ibsen. He must have found a place of rest. But though beauty comes incidentally in some startling form, which is half terror, or in some swift antagonism of brightness and gloom, beauty is not Ibsen's end. His end, even in his earlier romantic plays, even in plays that are historical or semi-historical, is to free, arouse, dilate. He desires to bring the reader or spectator to some point—a point attained by effort—from which things may be seen more clearly or more deeply, even though this may be only a moment's standing place in some ascent which does not here cease; he desires to raise questions, even if no entirely satisfactory answer can as yet be given to them, to awaken those who slumber on the easy pillow of traditional opinion and conventional morals, to startle them from the false dream of custom, and, if need be, to combat, to censure, to satirise. He was not pleased, indeed, to be regarded as a didactic poet; he asserted that his primary object was to see and to represent life, to create true and living men and women. But he did not deny that he attempted to attain and to express a philosophy of life, and undoubtedly his art suffered because that philosophy of life was not broad-based upon the attainments of the past, because it was not the inevitable growth of the national life surrounding him, because it was a philosophy of revolt, the protest of an individual, embodying only a fragment of truth, aggressive, polemical, revolutionary. Hence his art was often marred by over-emphasis. The little towns upon the fiords seemed to Ibsen to be buried in sleep, though morning was growing broad. He would steam up the fiord from the open sea, and try whether the hooting of the fog-horn would make them open their eyes. And certainly there followed wide-spreading reverberations, reverberations which passed across Europe.

"To realise oneself"—to bring into full being and action whatever force exists within us, this was Ibsen's chosen expression for what the Shorter Catechism terms "man's chief end." "So to conduct one's life as to realise oneself," he wrote to a friend in 1882, "seems to me the highest attainment possible to a human being." And again: "I believe that there is nothing else and nothing better for us all to do than in spirit and in truth to realise ourselves. This, in my opinion, constitutes real liberalism." He desired for his friend and critic, George Brandes, before all else "a genuine, full-blooded egoism," but he begged at the same time that this desire might not be taken as an evidence of something brutal in his nature. Being an artist, Ibsen found self-realisation to mean for him the putting forth of all that was best within him in and through his art. Dramatic art for him was not so much a delightful play as an inexorable duty. Work which may seem wholly detached from his own personality, wholly imaginative and objective, was in fact intensely personal; not indeed in the dramatic action, the sequence of incidents, but in the view of life which gave a meaning and a unity to the incidents. The whole man, as he was for the time being, pressed into his work; but, while certain general characteristics run through all that he wrote, and constitute the Ibsen *cachet*, it happened not seldom with him, as it happened with Goethe, that the view of life embodied in this play or in that was one which Ibsen desired to master, to place outside himself, to escape from and leave behind him in his advance. Lessons of warning for the dramatic critic who would discover the mind of a dramatist through his art may be read in Ibsen's correspondence. Thus while into the character of Brand he transposed certain things which he found in himself—things which he regarded as the best part of himself, discovered only in his highest moments—the poem *Brand* was partly written, as he declares to Laura Kieler, who attempted a continuation of the poem, because it became a necessity with him to free himself from something that his inner man had done with, by giving it a poetic form. A canon of criticism founded upon such a confession, or upon similar confessions made by Goethe, would play havoc with many of the crude attempts to infer the mind and moods of Shakespeare from his dramatic compositions. Precisely because he wrote *Hamlet* Shakespeare may have been delivered from the Hamlet mood and the Hamlet view of life, and may have lost interest in them for ever. Nothing can be created, in the true sense of that word, according to Ibsen, except it takes into itself some life-experience; but we see most clearly, he adds, at a distance; "we must get away from what we desire to judge; one describes summer best on a winter day." Soon after his own happy marriage in 1858 Ibsen was engaged upon his *Comedy of Love*, which, however, was not completed until four years later. Shall we say that his mockery of love-betrothals and love-marriages—or what are called so—and his pronouncement in the play in favour of a marriage of prudence and worldly wisdom expresses the whole of his mind at this time? Or may it not have been that his deeper sense of the worth of a true marriage of love urged him to take his revenge upon a state of society in which, with its half-heartedness and its feeble sentimentalities, the ideal marriage, as it seemed to him, had become almost impossible? Falk and Svanhild, with the terror before them of a Pastor Straamand and his Maren, a Styver and Miss Skjære, a Lind and Anna, are incapable of trusting their own hearts, and without such a confident venture of faith it is better that Svanhild should be the sensible bride of a kind and sensible Guldstad. A lower view of marriage is set forth and justified perhaps for the precise reason that Ibsen had come to value the true romance above the pseudo-romance of a sentimental convention.

With much of the strenuousness, if not the severity, of the Northern temper, Ibsen was yet a lover of brightness and joy. The southern sunshine and the colour of the south gave him a sense of happy expansion. But where could he find the joy of life in his earlier years ? Hardly anywhere except in his own consciousness of strength; and sometimes he lost heart and courage. He was poor and he was proud. He pounded drugs at Grimstad to earn a scanty living, stung his enemies and even his friends with epigram or lampoon, fashioned his youthful verses in stolen hours, and meditated in his *Catiline* on the discrepancy between our desires and our power of giving them their satisfaction. He repelled others and was in turn repelled. He retreated into himself and there he heard the " call," about which his poems in dramatic fashion tell us much. And his ambition, his egoism leaped up and responded to the call. There are men whom an unfavourable environment crushes and destroys. But Ibsen was not one of these. He grew stronger through opposition, and the surface of his mind, like the face of a sea-captain, hardened in the rough weather. Through resistance he came to understand his own powers, he came to attain self-definition.

Harder to bear than any direct opposition were the narrowness, the pettiness, the death-in-life of the society in which, " like a seven-sealed mystery," he moved. Storm for him was always inspiriting, but fog was stifling. The Vikings of elder days had been transformed into a grocer, an innkeeper, a barber, and he himself was pounding his drugs in an apothecary's shop. The common excitement which now and again may have stirred his eight hundred fellow-townsfolk was like the flurry in a very small ant-hill. They pried, and gossiped and slandered; they found their law in the artificial proprieties; they sentimentalised and had their ineffectual pseudo-passions. Religion was the mummy of ancient faith, eviscerated and swathed; the pastor was only a spiritual beadle. The State was represented by an official or two, who earned a salary by wearing the approved blinkers and pulling the old cart through the old rut. If liberalism existed, it spent its enthusiasm in vacuous words and high-sounding phrases. The best persons were no more than fragments of a whole man, who held together the fragments by some illogical compromise, and perhaps named this compromise "morality." Ibsen, the Norwegian poet, was never quite at home in the land of his birth. Long afterwards, when he had sunned himself among Italian vines and felt the stupendous life of Rome—life over which in those days there seemed to rest an indescribable peace—the *heimweh* that drew him back to Norway was not a desire to revive the sentiment of his early life, but his deep, unconquerable passion for the sea. Yet he tells his friend Björnson that when he sailed up the fjord he felt a weight settling down on his breast, a feeling of actual physical oppression: "And this feeling," he goes on, "lasted all the time I was at home; I was not myself"—not his own man, as we say—"under the gaze of all those cold, uncomprehending Norwegian eyes at the windows and in the streets." And in 1897 he writes to Brandes from Christiania: "Here all the sounds are closed in every acceptation of the word—and all the channels of intelligence are blocked. Oh, dear Brandes, it is not without consequence that a man lives for twenty-seven years in the wider, emancipated and emancipating spiritual conditions of the great world. Up here, by the fjords, is my native land. But—but—but! Where am I to find my home-land?"

It was natural that Ibsen should sigh for a revolution, or rather—since sighing was not his mode—that he should work towards it. But in the programme of political liberalism he took little interest. A people might—like that of Norway—be free, yet be no more than a congeries of *un*free persons. "Dear friend," he cried to Brandes in 1872, "the Liberals are freedom's worst enemies. Freedom of thought and spirit thrive best under absolutism; this was shown in France, afterwards in Germany, and now we see it in Russia." While Björnson, like a good member of the Liberal Party, said, "The majority is always right," Ibsen, an admirer, as was Edmund Burke, of the natural aristocracy, was ready to maintain that right is always with the minority. Dr. Stockmann, of the Baths, is in a minority of one; not only does officialdom hunt him down; the "compact majority" of middle-class citizens and the public Press turn against him; yet Stockmann—somewhat muddle-headed hero as he is—has the whole right and the whole truth upon his side. The rhetoric of a Stensgaard can always gather a party of so-called progress around him, yet Stensgaard, eloquent for freedom, has no conception of that wherein true freedom lies. The Mayor in *Brand* is busily employed in ameliorating the lot of his fellow-men by the prescribed methods of social "progress," only he has not yet conceived what a man and the life of a man truly mean. "Liberty," wrote Ibsen in 1882, "is the first and highest condition for me. At home they do not trouble much about liberty, but only about liberties—a few more or a few less, according to the standpoint of their party. I feel, too, most painfully affected by the crudity, the plebeian element in all our public discussions. The very praiseworthy attempt to make of our people a democratic community has inadvertently gone a good way towards making us a plebeian community." As for the peasantry, Ibsen found them in every country very much alive to their own interests; in no country did he find them liberal-minded or self-sacrificing.

The revolution for which he hoped was not a revolution of government. He desired, indeed, as immediate measures—so he writes to Björnson in 1884—a very wide extension of the suffrage, the statutory improvement of the position of women, and the emancipation of national education from all kinds of mediævalism; but these were valuable, he thought, only as means to an end. Governments, States, religions will pass away, but men will remain. As for the State, Ibsen regarded it sometimes with almost the hostility of an anarchist. He pointed to the Jewish people—"the nobility of the human race"—as a nation without a State, possessing an intense national consciousness and great individual freedom, but no organised government. Perhaps he overlooked the fact that the national consciousness is based upon the common faith and common observances of a unique and highly-organised religion. Ibsen's starting-point and his goal was the individual man or woman. The struggle for liberty which interested him was not the effort to obtain political "rights," but the constant, living assimilation by each individual of the idea of freedom. When December, 1870, came, he rejoiced that "the old, illusory France" had collapsed. "Up till now," he wrote, "we have been living on nothing but the crumbs from the revolution table of last century, a food out of which all nutriment has long been chewed. The old terms require to have a new meaning infused into them. Liberty, equality and fraternity are no longer the things they were in the days of the late-lamented guillotine. This is what the politicians will not understand; and therefore I hate them. They want only their own special revolutions in externals, in politics, etc. But all this is mere trifling. What is all-important is the revolution in the spirit of man." Like Maximus in *Emperor and Galilean*, Ibsen dreamed of the third empire.

The third empire will come when man ceases to be a fragment of himself, and attains, in complete self-realisation, the fulness of the stature of the perfect man. Julian, Emperor and apostate, as Ibsen conceives him, is a divided nature, living in a time of moral division. As a youth he has heard the terrible, unconditional, inexorable commands of the spirit, declared through the religion of Christ; but they have always been without and not within his heart; at every turn the merciless god-man has met him, stark and stern, with some uncompromising "Thou shalt" or "Thou shalt not," which never became the mandate of his own will. And the old pagan passion for the beauty and the joy of terrene life is in Julian's blood. He is pedant enough to seek for spiritual unity through the schools of philosophy, and man enough to find the shadows of truth exhibited in the schools vain and impotent. Christianity, as he sees it in Constantinople, is not a faith but an *un*faith—made up of greeds, ambition, treachery, distrust, worldly compromises, external shows of religion. "Do you not feel disgust and nausea," he cries to Basileus, "as on board ship in a windless swell, heaving to and fro between life, and written revelation, and heathen wisdom and beauty? There must come a new revelation. Or a revelation of something new." He can dream of the rapture of a martyr's death—but martyrdom for what? All that he had learnt in Athens can be summed up in one despairing word—"The old beauty is no longer beautiful, and the new truth is no longer true." But the need of action compels him, if not to make a choice in the full sense of that word, at least to take a side. The shouts of the soldiery at Vienna are ready to hail him as Emperor. On the one hand are life and the hope of a rehabilitation of beauty, the wisdom of Greece, the recovery of joy. On the other hand are the Nazarene, the cross, the remorseless demands of the spirit, and all for sake of what the Christianity of his time had proved to be a lie. The instinct of the blood decides for Julian that he shall be the apostate. Life is at least better than a lie.

There follows in Ibsen's second drama the record of Julian's failure, his illusions, his partial disillusioning, and the darkening of the light within him. The patron of free speculation is transformed into a persecutor. The philosopher grows greedy of the adulation of courtiers. He is led on before the close to the madness of self-divinisation. He will restore joy and beauty to the world; with the panther-skin upon his shoulders and the vine-wreath on his head he plays the part of Dionysus amid a troop of mummers and harlots, and he himself loathes this mockery of beauty and of joy. He will reform the world—for he has still the pride of pedantry—with a treatise. He takes his guidance in action from ambiguous oracles and the omens of priests. He dies with a dream of a triumphal entry into Babylon and a vision of beautiful garlanded youths and dancing maidens. Yet all the while Julian knows that he cannot revive what is long withered, and he is aware of some great power without him and above him which is using him for its own ends. The world-spirit, in truth, has made Julian its instrument. The old era of the flesh had passed away. The new era of the spirit had come. And to quicken it to true life, the spirit, incarnated in the religion of

Christ, needed the discipline of trial and suffering and martyrdom which Julian had devised for its destruction. "Christ, Christ," exclaims Basileus, "how could Thy people fail to see Thy manifest design? The Emperor Julian was a rod of chastisement—not unto death, but unto resurrection." And so the Galilean has conquered.

The Galilean, however, according to the mystic Maximus, through whom evidently Ibsen expresses his own thought, is not to rule for ever. From the empire of the flesh, through the empire of the spirit, the world must advance to the third empire, which does not destroy but rather includes both its predecessors. Both the Emperor and the Galilean—such is the prophecy of Maximus—must succumb; at what time he cannot tell; it will be on the day when the right man appears, who shall swallow up both Emperor and Galilean. The fulness of the perfect man must succeed the unconscious joy of childhood and the unqualified ideality of youth, and resume them both in itself. "You have tried," says Maximus, addressing Julian, "to make the youth a child again. The empire of the flesh is swallowed up in the empire of the spirit. But the empire of the spirit is not final any more than the youth is. You have tried to hinder the growth of the youth—to hinder him from becoming a man. Oh, fool, who have drawn your sword against that which is to be—against the third empire in which the twin-natured shall reign!"

For a time, at least, Ibsen regarded *Emperor and Galilean* as his chief work. That positive theory of life, which the critic had long demanded from him, might here, he believed, be found; "the play," he wrote to Brandes, "will be a kind of banner." Part of his own spiritual life went into this dramatic history; he laboured at the "Herculean task" of reviving a past age with a fierce diligence; while, at the same time, he held that the subject had "a much more intimate connection with the movements of our own time than might at first be imagined"; the establishment of such a connection—so he tells Mr. Gosse—he regarded as "imperative in any modern poetical treatment of such a remote subject, if it is to arouse interest at all." The great drama of the Franco-German war delivered Ibsen from his narrow Scandinavian nationalism, and gave him that wider conception of the march of events which he needed in dealing with historical matter of colossal dimensions.

With a clear perception of the leading ideas set forth in *Emperor and Galilean*, a reader of the earlier *Brand* can without difficulty assign to this poem its due position in the series of Ibsen's works. Brand is the hero of the second empire—the empire of the spirit. Ibsen had escaped from Christiania to Rome—the centre of the life of the world, yet for an artist brooded over by a great peace—and because Norway was distant, he seemed to see it all the more clearly, with its many infirmities and its conceivable heroisms. He could not but contrast the spirit of generous self-sacrifice which had resulted in the unification of Italy with the half-heartedness or downright selfishness of his own country during the Danish-German war. "How often we hear good people in Norway," he wrote to Magdalene Thoresen, "talk with the heartiest self-satisfaction about Norwegian discretion, which is really nothing more than a lukewarmness of blood that makes the respectable souls incapable of committing a grand piece of folly." As Ibsen conceived it, a grand piece of folly might be the test and the demonstration of a valiant soul; and such it is with the hero of that poem, to accomplish which he had laid aside the unfinished *Emperor and Galilean*. He was indescribably happy while he worked upon *Brand*. "I felt," he says, "the exaltation of a Crusader, and I don't know anything I should have lacked courage to face." He wanted to deliver the Brand within himself—that which was best in him—from the narrowness and the severity of the empire of the spirit, and the poem was a receptacle for what he desired to expel from his inner consciousness. On his desk, as he wrote, was a glass with a scorpion in it: "From time to time the little animal was ill. Then I used to give it a piece of soft fruit, upon which it fell furiously and emptied its poison into it—after which it was well again." The poet is surely thinking of himself when he describes this curative process of his little brother, the scorpion.

Brand is the hero of the empire of the spirit. As Julian was double-minded, with a life which essayed a vain return from the spirit to the flesh, so Brand is necessarily single-minded, a free servant of his stern, inexorable God, who is no grey-beard that may be haggled with, no dotard or dreamer, but young as Hercules, and terrible as he who stood on Mount Horeb when Moses heard the call from the burning bush. That Brand is a priest only deflects but does not alter the idea of the poem. That idea, as Ibsen says in one of his letters, might have been set forth, though with different circumstance, if Brand had been an artist, a statesman, or a man of science. He is not a fanatic, unless to be a strict logician under the empire of the spirit is to be a fanatic; granted his premises, all his action, if he be a man of single mind, necessarily follows.

Puritanism was named by Carlyle the last of the heroisms. Brand is a puritan and an idealist, but Ibsen dreams of a higher and saner heroism than that of Brand—the heroism of "the third empire," when the right man shall have come and swallowed up both Emperor and Galilean. To be a whole man, however, even under the rule of an incomplete conception of manhood, is a greater thing than to be a half man, and a whole man Brand is, according to his idea, which is an idea incomplete in itself, but on the way to a higher and truer idea. "How can I *will* the impossible?" asks Julian of the mystic Maximus, and Maximus replies by the question, "Is it worth while to *will* what is possible?" What Julian could not do is achieved by Brand—he wills the impossible, as every uncompromising idealist must, and he perishes in the act.

The absolute tendency in Brand's logic is stimulated and reinforced by the incoherence and inconsequence of the society in which he lives and moves. With the folk around him it is a little of this and a little of that—things out of which no consistency can be made—and therefore with him it must be "All or nothing," pushed even to the extreme issue. He is a man among fragments of men. Apart from Ibsen's satirical indictment of Norwegian society, such a condition of moral faint-heartedness and spiritual lethargy was needed to enhance by contrast the uncompromising valiancy of the hero and his fidelity to an idea. The Mayor, representative of the secular power, is only a petty wheel of the state machinery; his honest efforts in the ways of use and wont relieve the public conscience from all that might spur men to originality and individual effort. The Dean, representative of the spiritual power, is also no more than a state official, a moral drill-sergeant, a corporal who leads his troop at the regulation pace to church on one day of the week; as to the other days, they are not his affair, for faith and life must be kept discreetly apart. Neither mayor nor dean is an independent will, or an intelligence, or a soul; neither of them has a human personality in the true sense of that word.

Brand is at least an individual will, and therefore a man. Even in attempting to efface self, and to make his spirit a clean tablet on which God may write, he is in truth realising and affirming himself. And yet Brand's idea—that proper to the empire of the spirit—is a tyrannous idea, which starves his intelligence, chills his human affections, and conducts him to the icy and sterile region where he must perish. Something of human love he learns through Agnes and his boy, and, after he has lost Agnes, he feels in a pathetic way that without the wisdom of human love he must needs strive in vain. But the tyranny of the idea requires the martyrdom of all natural affections. He dreams of a church of humanity, and at least the virtue is in him of aspiration and desire. But the only church which he can attain is Svartetind, the "ice-church," where the distracted girl Gerd is the only votary. The avalanche thunders down, and the judgment—a judgment including mercy—on all Brand's endeavour is heard in the Voice which proclaims "He is a God of Love."

It was a daring experiment of Ibsen to present in a companion poem to *Brand*, as the chief person of the poem, an individual whose distinguishing characteristic is that he has no individuality. Peer Gynt is not like Julian a divided nature; he is not, like Brand, single and indivisible; like the women of Pope's satire, Peer Gynt has "no character at all." Will, intellect, love are needed, one or all, to constitute true personality. Peer has none of these; he is simply a bundle of appetites, desires, shadows of ideas thrown upon him from without, and fantasies which for him almost, but not quite, succeed in becoming facts. In his strange experiment Ibsen was singularly successful. Through all the Norwegian scenes Peer is a delightful person, worth a wilderness of heroic King Hakons or resolute Dr. Stockmanns. The cosmopolitan Peer of Morocco and elsewhere loses much of his attractiveness. Nowhere else is Ibsen so genial as in *Peer Gynt*, yet the faith that is in him compels him to be also stern. If Brand is a Norwegian Don Quixote, Peer is a charming, irresponsible Autolycus of the fells and fjords. Ibsen himself, being, despite his genius for fantasy, a desperately earnest person, gives warrant for heavy moralisings over his hero, if anyone is prone to indulge them; but the Norwegian Peer, if not his prosperous second self, full-blown in Yankee methods of business, leaps too lightly over the laws of morality, to be captured and indicted solemnly before an ethical tribunal. He compares himself happily to an onion, from which layer after layer may be peeled, which indeed is nothing but swathings with neither core nor kernel at the centre. But this in itself is a distinction and gives your onion its character—this, and a certain savour by which, with our eyes shut, we can recognise and name the bulb. And Peer has an atmosphere and aroma much more agreeable than that of an onion. "Tell me now," asked Peer's creator of his friend Björnson, "is not Peer Gynt a personality, complete and individual?" That he assuredly is. Like Mr. Kipling's Tomlinson of Berkeley Square, Peer may be rejected by the guardian of heaven's gate and the devil may refuse to waste good coal on such a phantasmal spirit. It can be proved from the text of the poem that Peer has no good ground for a stay of judgment when the Button-moulder demands his soul for the melting-ladle, unless it be that his true self has all the while existed in Solveig's heart. Peer has never put forth a substantial piece of virtue; he has never sinned a whole sin; he is neither true man nor true troll. Off with him, therefore, to the melting-pot! And yet Solveig here seems somewhat of an impertinence: we cannot exactly construe the metaphor of Peer's personality made substantial by Solveig's love. There is surely some Limbo of Vanities on the other side of the moon where Peer, in his own right, may be immortal and may still recount his incomparable feats of the Gendin-Edge. Or shall we say that the Limbo of Vanities is that of literature in which Ibsen has placed Peer, and where he has in truth obtained immortality?

Intellect seizing and holding a truth, love expounding the significance and the relations of that truth, will satisfied with nothing less than incarnating the truth in a deed—these, as Ibsen conceives it, constitute a complete human personality. For such a complete man or woman the whole of morality is comprised in the words, "Man, be thyself." The law for such a one is that of self-realisation; he acts with his entire nature fused into unity, by virtue of what Ibsen names a "free necessity"; the compulsion is no external constraint; it is within the man, and therefore he is absolutely free. Hence the problems of the complete or the incomplete human being, the single or the divided nature, are profoundly interesting to Ibsen; and hence, too, the problems of the life founded upon the rock of truth and the lives built upon the sands of illusion, the illusions of ignoble self-interest, which leaves out of consideration all that really constitutes "self," the illusions of conventional morality, social responsibility, mere use and wont, and that kind of pseudo-religion which is only a form of postponed self-interest. The life erected upon a lie and the life established upon the truth are themes which he is drawn again and again to contemplate and, in dramatic fashion, to discuss with the most searching and eager insistence. He bores and mines underneath the surface of life into passions and motives, where the light is faint or where thick darkness dwells, in the hope that he may strike upon the ultimate, incontrovertible fact. The crisis in his plays often corresponds to what in another order of ideas and experience would be named religious conversion. But conversion in Ibsen's plays means simply being brought face to face with a truth of life and "realising" its power and virtue in some act which gives a death-blow to the lie. Sometimes the unwrapping of the swathe-bands of self-deception is a long and laborious process; sometimes this is effected swiftly in an hour or in a moment. Then for the first time genuine "self-realisation" becomes possible; intelligence, love and will coalesce in some act of "free necessity." It must be remembered, however, that while these three are the elements from which character is formed, there may exist in a human being certain deep, uncontrollable forces, emerging into consciousness from some subconscious region. A man or woman possessing, or rather possessed by, these would have been termed by Goethe "dæmonic"; the phrase of Ibsen is that there is a little, or perhaps much, in him of the troll.

The troll element is a source of danger; its action is incalculable and irresponsible, except as other elements of character may arrest or control its progress. But if it is a source of danger, it is also a source of power. Had King Skule even a little of the troll within him, the history of Norway might have been other than it was.

For setting forth his ideas, for the conduct of the action of his plays, and for the exposition of his *dramatis personæ*, Ibsen forged a remarkable instrument in his prose dialogue. He has taken with singular fidelity the mould of actual, living converse between two minds at play upon, and into, and through each other, in which the thought or feeling evolved belongs to neither alone, and is not so much communicated from mind to mind as produced by the swift interaction of the pair. The shuttle plies incessantly to and fro, and the pattern of the web grows before our eyes. Question, reply, suggestion, development, pause, anticipation, hesitancy—these, and all else of which conversation is made up, are most ingeniously reproduced. The conventions of the stage are ignored; there are no asides and no soliloquies. And yet in striving to be real Ibsen has missed a part of reality. The dialogue, in its manner, seems like the type or the abstract of a hundred conversations to which we have listened, or in which we have borne a part. But although the matter varies with this person of the drama and with that, the manner lacks variety and individuality, a lack which is not really disguised by the recurrence of some catchword or phrase on the lips of this or the other speaker. Ibsen, aiming at reality, in truth narrowed the range of dramatic dialogue. His speakers are never rhetorical, except when they are born rhetoricians, like Stensgaard, or born sentimentalists like Hialmar Ekdal; when passion grows tense, the speech is ordinarily most concentrated and simple. The dialogue seldom errs by excess of brilliancy, seldom glitters with epigram or flashes with paradox. But in reality we are all at times rhetoricians, and often poor ones, when we would express a passion that only half possesses us; we are ill-trained actors—the best of us—faultily rendering an emotion that may be genuine, and Ibsen has missed this fact. And even your dullard will on occasion make his brilliant rapier-thrust of speech; while your epigram-maker may stumble on occasions into a simple and natural utterance. The range of varying levels of dramatic dialogue in Shakespeare is incomparably wider than it is in Ibsen; there is in Shakespeare incomparably more variety and individuality in the modes of speech. His verse is often nearer to the required realism of the stage—which is never literal reality—than is Ibsen's prose.

In passing from the dramas which deal with historical and romantic matter—*Lady Inger*, *The Vikings* and *The Pretenders*—to the plays of modern life, Ibsen gradually came to connect and to define his leading ideas. In Lady Inger of Oestraat he presents rather a conflict of motives—maternal passion at war with the passion of patriotism—than a divided nature essentially at odds with itself. It is the circumstances of her life and her time which bring division into Fru Inger's spirit and produce the tragedy. The idea of the havoc wrought for two lives by even a generous suppression of the truth is a leading motive in *The Vikings*, but Ibsen's chief joy in writing that noble play must have been in the mere presentation of the Valkyrie woman, Hjördis, possessed by a single consuming desire which glorifies and which destroys her. For

The Pretenders we might find a motto in the words " faith and unfaith can ne'er be equal powers." King Hakon, the whole man, called by God and the people to his throne, confident in his call, possessed of a great and generous thought—the unity of the nation—single in will and resolute in act, is set over against the divided man, God's step-child on earth, Earl Skule, who questions his own claim, who doubts even to the point of doubting his doubt, who has no great thought of his own, but would filch that of his rival, whose good and evil instincts trammel and trip each the other, whose faltering ambition needs the support of that faith given by another which he cannot find in himself, yet who dies at the last in the joy of an expiation and an atonement.

King Hakon, whole and at one with himself, is the man of good fortune—" he whom the cravings of his time seize like a passion, begetting thoughts he himself cannot fathom, and pointing to paths which lead he knows not whither, but which he follows and must follow until he hears the people shout for joy." He puts his total self into every act, impelled by the free necessity of his complete manhood. This idea of " free necessity " receives its most luminous illustration in the *dénouement* of a much later drama, *The Lady from the Sea.* In matrimonial advertisements the candidate wife—as if woman were naturally a creature of the wild—commonly announces that she is " thoroughly domesticated." This merit certainly could not have been claimed for herself by the second Mrs Wangel. She pines for the unattainable freedom of which the sea is the symbol; it affrights her, but it allures her even more than it affrights; and the stranger from the sea is to Ellida the promise of this freedom. Such a deep, instinctive longing for freedom cannot be overmastered by external restraint; it can be met and controlled only by a higher freedom. The physician has at all times been the victim of raillery with writers of comedy; but the physicians of Ibsen's plays, with scarcely an exception, are either wise or shrewd, or, in their own fashion, heroic. Dr. Wangel, having diagnosed the case, discovers the nature of his wife's strange malady; by a supreme act of self-surrendering love, which is also an act of the finest discretion, he releases Ellida from every restraint; she is absolutely free to make her choice between the sea and her home, between the stranger and himself. What is best and highest in Ellida is awakened by the sudden recognition of her husband's love, by the remembrance of an affectionate word of her stepdaughter, Boletta, and by a new sense of responsibility. Her whole nature—brain and heart, conscience and will—is instantly fused into unity, and on the moment declares itself in an act of free and final election, which delivers her from the sick yearning for the lower kind of freedom that had made her home a prisoner's cage. By no preaching of moralities, by no fear of social disrepute, by no bonds of legal right or ecclesiastical control, the Lady from the Sea is converted, reclaimed, and, in the matrimonial formula, "thoroughly domesticated." Ellida has never been a shrew who needed taming; her ailment, however, was harder to deal with than Kate's; and by a different and a more courageous treatment the good Dr. Wangel has been as successful as was Petruchio. Ellida desires freedom, but she also desires love and the work which issues from love. A lighter nature desiring freedom alone might have followed the mysterious stranger. So Maia, in *When We Dead Awaken*, who neither sought nor found love in the sculptor's luxurious villa, is beguiled by the lower freedom, even when the promise of it is made by a vigorous brute who hunts alike bears and women, and her triumphant song is heard at the moment when her sculptor and his spiritual bride are conveniently disposed of by a benevolent avalanche.

Ibsen advanced to his modern social plays through a comedy which was also a satirical study of political parties in Norway, *The League of Youth.* While engaged upon its composition he called it a " peaceable " play, but the hisses, the cat-calls, and the applause in the theatre, when it was first represented at Christiania, must have undeceived him. It placed for a time Ibsen and his friend Björnson in hostile camps. The unmasking of an adventurer, half-deceiver, half self-deceived, is a not infrequent theme of comedy. What is proper to Ibsen in the character of his political adventurer is the conception of moral disintegration —" soul, disposition, will, talents, all pulling in different ways "—the jarring elements being yet bound together by a fierce and ruthless egoism. Stensgaard is himself intoxicated by the enthusiasm of his liberal sentiments and his effusive rhetoric; and behind the goodly show lurks a sordid soul, as small and hard as it is mean, which waits till the fifth act to be stripped naked and exposed to the general view.

Such is the pseudo-democratic leader and the pretended reformer of established society. But the representatives of constituted authority may be just as pretentious and just as hollow. In the title of his play, *The Pillars of Society*, Ibsen concentrates an indignant irony. It tells the story of a life that has been erected upon a lie, a structure specious but desperately insecure, and it exhibits the social environment, with its vulgar pietisms and conventional morals and manners, which gives opportunity to the architect of such a structure. Consul Bernick, the virtuous husband, has had his disgraceful adventure with an actress, and has transferred the shame which should be his to an innocent man; he has sacrificed the honest passion of his youth for a mercenary marriage; he has saved the credit of the house of Bernick by a lie. Consul Bernick, the public-spirited citizen, has engineered his great railway project merely with a view to private greed; and he, whose mission it is to be an example to his townsfolk, will send *The Indian Girl* to sea with rotten timbers and sham repairs. By the side of this worthy pillar of Society stands another, Rector Rörlund, whose edifying readings and self-gratulatory moral comments instruct the ladies who sacrifice themselves by plain-stitching on behalf of the Lapsed and Lost, and fill the intervals of reading and moral discourse with scandals, slanders and spites. "Oh! if I could only get far away!" cries that child of Nature, Dina Dorf, "I could get on well enough by myself, if only the people I lived amongst weren't so—so—so proper and moral." As her last possible service to the man whom she had loved, that flouter of the proprieties, Lona, would get firm ground under Bernick's feet. But firm ground can be won only by a public confession of his iniquities and by righting the generous man who had been his scapegoat. Such a confession is wrung from him by the agony of joy at the recovery of the lost son who—it seemed—had perished as the victim of the father's crime. And with the attainment of firm ground a new life may begin. "For many years," exclaims Bernick's wife, just before the curtain is rung down, "I have believed that you had once been mine, and I had lost you. Now I know that you never were mine; but I shall win you." In *The Pillars of Society* there is nothing fine or subtle. Ibsen's pleading for rectitude is written with a broad-nibbed pen. But stage-effect and stage-ethics are not always enhanced by subtlety.

The same expression, "Life erected upon a lie," is the formula for both *A Doll's House* and *Ghosts*. But in these plays Ibsen turns from the life of Society to domestic life. In the words of Mrs. Bernick just quoted, and in a speech of Selma in *The League of Youth* the germ of *A Doll's House* may be discovered. The truth of married life can be found only when the woman is seen not as an adjunct or appendage, formed for the ease or pleasure of her husband, but as herself a complete individual, who has entered into an alliance of mutual help. The charming Nora is a sweet little song-bird, a little lark, a pretty squirrel—anything graceful and petted, but not a reasonable and responsible woman. She is an exquisite toy in her husband's hands, and he would be to her a conscience and a will. He has found his doll-wife, who plays such delightful tricks, amusing, but loved her, in the true sense of the word, he has not. And she has never known him; she has been living with "a strange man" for eight years and borne him three children. Her whole married life has been a lie; now suddenly the truth breaks in upon her; and she must be alone in order to see things clearly and to think things out aright. Husband and children have no claim upon her; she must understand and in some measure realise herself before she can render any true service to others. Inquiries should be set on foot to ascertain whether a manuscript may not lurk in some house in Christiania entitled "Nora Helmer's Reflections in Solitude"; it would be a document of singular interest, and probably would conclude with the words, "To-morrow I return to Torvald; have been exactly a week away; shall insist on a free woman's right to unlimited macaroons as test of his reform." The last scene of the play, in which Nora quits her husband's house, did not at first commend itself to Eleonora Duse, though in the end she accepted it. The prompt instinct of a great actress is perhaps more to be trusted than her later judgment—or perhaps submission. To that scene Ibsen attached the highest importance; for its sake, he declares, "I may almost say the whole play was written." Yet, hearing that it might suffer alteration on the German stage, he did what he calls an act of barbaric violence to his idea; an alternative scene was provided in which Nora is led by her husband to the door of the children's bedroom, and there sinks down before the curtain falls. The uncompromising author had condescended to a compromise; it was as if Brand had come to terms with the Dean.

Whatever may have been Nora's final decision, the unhappier Mrs. Alving pulled the heavy door behind her with loud reverberations. It was her error that she did not seek solitude, in which to study the wreck of her life and think things clear. The shadows projected on the present from our own or our parents' past are not the only "ghosts"; dead ideas and lifeless old beliefs are ghosts as formidable, which, like the great Boyg of *Peer Gynt*, conquer but do not fight. And for Mrs. Alving the ghost-leader is the prudently pious Pastor Manders. From that discreet counsellor she learns the duty of a wife to an erring husband; she takes up the burden of her sorrow and tries to hide its shame. Not to conceal any wrong-doing of her own, but through a false idea of duty and a false idea of honour, she converts her life into one long, elaborate and piteous fraud. The recoil from Pastor Manders's ghosts carries her to the opposite order of ideas, pushed perhaps—for she is a woman—to an extreme; yet still she acts out her lie and will canonise Captain Alving's saintly memory with her orphanage. At last a terrible necessity demands a full disclosure of the truth to her son; but it has no healing efficacy for him or for her. The terrible ghosts of heredity take the place of the ghosts which she had exorcised, and she sinks the victim of the veritable Furies of an age of science.

The public howled and the critics flung their heaviest stones at the author of *Ghosts*. The author faced round upon his pursuers and shook his fist at them in *An Enemy of the People*. The formula of the play is no longer "a life erected on a lie," but "a life founded on the truth," and Ibsen—only for dramatic purposes a less perspicacious Ibsen—is his own hero. It is not he who has made the water of the Baths poisonous and the whole place pestilential. He has only submitted the water to scientific tests, and announced the fact that it swarms with infusoria. True, the representatives of law and order, the Press, the middle-class liberal majority, the Householders' Association, are all united against him; but what of that? The majority are always in the wrong; "the Liberals are the worst foes of free men," and "party programmes wring the necks of all young and vital truths." Ibsen, as Dr. Stockmann, ends with his word of defiance—"The strongest man upon earth is he who stands most alone." Dr. Stockmann, of the Baths, is an *Athanasius contra mundum;* a Galileo with his *E pur si muove*. And yet Ibsen does not deny that the champion of truth must suffer in the cause; beside other calamities patent to the doctor and his excellent family, it is discovered that his foes have torn a hole in his black trousers. No critic of *An Enemy of the People* can spare his readers the sentence beginning with "The strongest man upon earth" as the heroic moral of the play; but perhaps, for a full statement of the truth, it should be conjoined with another sentence: "One should never put on one's best trousers to go out to battle for freedom and truth."

Ibsen's biographer, Henrik Jæger, represents *The Wild Duck* as the outcome of a mood of despondency, and almost of pessimism, following upon the excitement of self-defence which produced *An Enemy of the People.* This surely is a misconception. Having shaken his fist at the hostile crowd, Ibsen parleys with them. He begs to inform them that everything they have alleged against him and his doctrine is better known to himself than to them. They have cried aloud that his teaching is dangerous, and he repeats the words—Yes, certainly it is dangerous. Every new and every true doctrine of life is an edged tool. Children and fools ought not to play with tools that may cut to the bone. And who will deny that a man's worst foes may be found among his own disciples, when they happen to be fools? "Caricature, if you please, the principles which I have maintained," cries Ibsen, and he proceeds to show in *The Wild Duck* that he takes no responsibility for the caricatures of his own professed followers, whose abuse of true principles he understands only too well. This is no outcome of despondency on his part; it is a mode of bringing into action his second line of defence. We do well to present the claims of the ideal; but "when crazy people," as the good, ignorant Gina shrewdly says, "go about presenting the claims of the what-do-you-call-it," who can answer for the consequences? If a Gregers Werle elects himself to a "mission," we know what must follow. And who with a grain of common sense would try to put firm ground under the feet of a Hialmar Ekdal, when the man himself is so fashioned as to convert inevitably every truth presented to him into a lie? There is virtue in the humble common sense and practical energy of poor Gina. Dr. Relling, though his theory of life may be false, at least perceives the fact that Hialmar is compounded of self-indulgence, vanity and sentimental folly. Mrs. Sörby is not perhaps a perfect woman nobly planned, but she can conduct her affairs with some honesty and good judgment. Each of these is capable of handling a truth or the fragment of a truth to useful ends. But the edged tool of truth—even though it be an admirable instrument in itself—can only work mischief in the hands of a Gregers, and the highest of truths with a Hialmar can only fold him in some new delusion. Meanwhile the innocent may be the victim; little Hedvig lies dead; and before long her death will supply her supposed father with a pretty theme for sentimental declamation.

Life erected upon a lie, life established upon the truth, had occupied Ibsen long. In *Rosmersholm* there is a terrible concealment of truth followed by a terrible disclosure, but the problem of the true life and the false is here complicated with the problem of a divided nature. Rebecca West is in her intellect, as Kroll names her, an emancipated woman. She has read herself into a number of new ideas and opinions: "You have got a sort of smattering of recent discoveries in various fields"—so discourses the astute Kroll—"discoveries that appear to overturn certain principles that have hitherto been held impregnable and unassailable." But, he adds, and Rebecca cannot deny that he speaks with justice, "all this has been only a matter of the intellect, Miss West—only knowledge. It has not passed into your blood." She sees Rosmer bound in the trammels of the old faith, and languishing in his union with an ailing, hysterical wife. She imagines him freed from the ghosts of beliefs that have had their day, freed from the servitude of a weary marriage, and advancing joyously by her side to struggle and victory. Her passion for Rosmer, her emancipated intellect, and something of the Viking spirit co-operate within her, and she resolves that he shall be hers. She wins him over to her new ideas, and while maintaining the appearance of being the unhappy Beata's devoted friend and attendant, by a system of slow torture she drives Rosmer's wife to the mill-race. A year of what seems pure and disinterested friendship follows, and during this year, under Rosmer's influence, her heart in its gentler feelings, and her conscience, which had lagged behind her intellect, are awakened to activity. Rest descends on her soul, "a stillness as of one of our northern bird-cliffs under the midnight sun." The wild desire within her dies and self-denying love is born. She renounces joy, makes frank confession of her extinct Viking passion and her sin; and since death is the test which alone can restore his lost faith in her to Rosmer, she prepares to execute justice on herself. But now the pair are in truth united; they have become one in spirit; for Rosmer true life is gained in the moment when life is to be lost; and thus in their death the spiritual husband and wife are not divided. The composition of forces resulting from emancipated ideas and the old faith in the blood has its tragic issue in the mill-race.

The theme of *Hedda Gabler* can be expressed in a word; it is neither the life founded on truth, nor the life erected on a lie; it is the baseless life. The beautiful Hedda knows neither love nor duty, nor is she possessed even by a passionate egoism; she is capable of no real joy, no beneficent sorrow; she simply alternates between prolonged boredom and brief excitements. She seems to arise out of nothing and to tend nowhither. Had her luck been better than to be the wife of a rather stout, blond, spectacled, young aspirant professor, who is entirely happy when he can stuff his bag with transcripts concerning the domestic industries of Brabant during the Middle Ages, her existence would not have been essentially changed. She comes from the void, and into the void she goes. Her death was not an act of courage, whatever Judge Brack may say; it was only the last note struck of her wild dance-music, and has at best an æsthetic propriety. There is not substance enough in her even to go into the melting-ladle of Peer Gynt's button-moulder; she cannot be re-cast; she is extinguished, and that is all. Judge Brack will find place in another triple alliance and perhaps be cock of another walk. George Tesman will assist Mrs. Elvsted in her pious labours, may throw from her inspiring mind a pallid illumination on the industries of Brabant, and will transcribe many more invaluable documents. The whole of Hedda's story is summed up in the fact that she has pulled her dear friend Thea's irritating hair and effectually scorched the curls. She has had her entrance and has had her exit.

As Ibsen felt his hold grow stronger on his public, he became more venturesome and experimental in his art. He had early left romantic art behind him and had advanced to his own peculiar kind of realism; now he would appropriate something from what has chosen to name itself symbolism. In Ibsen's plays symbolism means that an act, while intelligible as an act, is also a metaphor, which gives the act a wider meaning, or that words tending to action have a secondary and fuller significance over and above their direct import. Some lives, says a speaker in *Peer Gynt*, are fiddles which can be patched and repaired, some are bells which, if cracked, cannot be mended. This is a metaphor. But if the action of the play showed us a man vainly endeavouring to mend a cracked bell, we should at once surmise the presence of a secondary and symbolic intention on the part of the writer. When such symbolism in any degree diverts the action of the play from what is real and natural, it becomes illegitimate; the secondary meaning does not then lie in the action, but is forced upon it. It cannot be said that Ibsen always avoids this danger. Both the action and the dialogue of *The Master-Builder*, which may serve as an example of his latest group of plays, are denaturalised by the symbolic intentions. It is a drama in which thought-transference and hypnotic suggestion play a part. That excellent critic, Mr. William Archer, to whom, with his fellow-labourers, we are indebted for a translation of Ibsen's works as spirited as it is faithful, was so far hypnotised by the writer's genius as to maintain that we can give imaginative credence to both the action and the dialogue of *The Master-Builder*, considered apart from their double meanings. His friend, Mr. Walkley, had been protected by some fine non-conducting medium from the hypnotic spell. Mr. Archer in his trance uttered ingenious words in defence of the play, but to one who remained awake they were not quite convincing.

The Master-Builder, more perhaps than any other work of Ibsen's, swarms with ideas, and to catch at these ideas and bring them under their law is a fascinating exercise in gymnastics. The action has all the consequence and logic which a dream seems to have while we are still dreaming, and all the inconsequence and absurdity which we perceive in our dream when we awake. The arrival of Hilda, the story of the church-tower, the three nurseries, the nine beautiful dolls, the climbing of ladders are the coinage of Queen Mab; with the catastrophe we start, are open-eyed, and behold it was a dream. Halverd Solness, the master-builder, has erected his fortunes on the ruin of the lives of others, and, among them, of his own wife. Yet with all his greed of ambition he possesses little of the true Viking-spirit, and his conscience is the reverse of "robust." It is, once again, the problem of the divided nature. A day comes when he decides that he will build no more churches for God; he will build only homes wherein men may be happy. But his own home has been made unhappy by his fierce ambition and its consequences. He can no longer believe in happy homes. What then remains for him to build? Only castles in the air, for in these alone can human happiness reside. And to such a pursuit of unattainable ideals the younger generation which he had feared, yet towards which he had yearned, now represented by a woman, who is to him like a sunrise, pricks him on. He will build with her—his fairy princess—his beautiful castle in the air. But the test of his capacity for such an achievement is that he shall for once do the impossible—mount to the dizzy summit of his tower, and there hold commune with the Powers above.

He mounts, stands for an instant triumphant, totters, falls, and is dead. All this hangs together coherently enough as the shadowing-forth of an idea. As a sequence of real incidents in this real world of ours it does not rebuke that critic who called it "a bewildering farrago of rubbish."

It would be entertaining to extract some drops of the quintessence of Ibsenism from other plays—*Little Eyolf*, *John Gabriel Borkman*, *When We Dead Awaken*. But the fate of the master-builder suggests the prudence of leaving a few rungs of the ladder unscaled. Happily a literary critic is not obliged to take as his word of order, "All or nothing."

HEINRICH HEINE

A CENTENARY RETROSPECT

"I LOVE Napoleon Bonaparte beyond all limit," wrote Heine, "up to the 18th Brumaire—when he betrayed freedom." On that day, when the legislature was forcibly closed, Heine was not, as his biographers commonly give us to understand, an unborn infant; he was a blue-eyed, chestnut-haired boy of nearly two years old. He came into the household of Düsseldorf, not in the year of Napoleon's "betrayal of freedom," but (13th December 1797) in that of the treaty of Campo-Formio, which gave to France the boundary of the Rhine. His contemporary in babyhood, born in the far South as Heine was in the far North, was afterwards an illustrious enlarger of the Napoleonic legend, "the Goethe of Politics"—so Heine named him—first President of the later Republic, Adolphe Thiers, who faced the spectre of Communism, which Heine, earlier than others, descried with alarm in the distance. When the dead poet lay at last freed from torture on his mattress-grave in February 1856, the finely-chiselled mask of marble, described by the friend of his closing days, was the face of a man whom a few more months would have carried into his sixtieth year.

To be born with diverse souls is embarrassing, but it was Heine's distinction. It signifies that life is to be no steadfast progress, directed by some guiding light, but a wavering advance through a countless series of attractions passing into repulsions, and of repulsions transformed into attractions. To belong to the past and to the future, to be romanticist and realist, to mingle Mephistopheles with Faust, to be an aristocrat and a revolutionary, to be of a tribe and of a nation, to be a patriot and cosmopolitan, to be a monotheist through the emotions, a polytheist through the imagination, a pantheist through the intellect, to see Jerusalem through the atmosphere of Hamburg, to sit at the feet of Moses and of Aristophanes, to reckon Brother Martin Luther and the Patriarch Voltaire among one's ancestry—all this makes fidelity to one's true self a difficult and intricate affair. What is each of us, asked Matthew Arnold, in his poem on "Heine's Grave," but a single mood of the World-spirit in whom we exist? One of these moods, bitter and strange, constituted Heine's life; a sardonic smile wandered for one short moment over the Spirit's lips—"that smile was Heine." A graceful fantasy, but no true criticism; it is Heine's special characteristic that he expressed a multiplicity of the moods of the World-spirit. His genius will not submit to be condensed into an epigram.

There have been men whose character has had the integrity of a diamond, and whose talents have been as variously directed as the diamond's facets. Others exhibit stratum superimposed on stratum, but we can pierce to some central granite. Or mood may melt into mood, and yet the total effect be harmonious, like that of an iridescent wave. Heine was not so fashioned, and to image his total being we labour after a metaphor in vain. With Heine unity did not underlie diversity, but, as far as it existed, rose out of diversity as a last result. No urchin crew of sprites and kobolds possessed him in his cradle, but when his parents named him "Harry," one is surprised that the baby did not smile ironically and protest—" My name is Legion, for we are many."

Shall we say that the deepest thing within him was the inheritance of race, which could be detected, one observer declared, in his gait, though not in his countenance? When he loved a French grisette he advised a friend to read the Canticles of King Solomon, so to understand the new joy that had overtaken him. When the mattress-grave grew narrow, the faith of his fathers seemed to draw back the curtains of the heavens and reveal Jehovah. We think of young Rabbi Abraham of Bacharach, pure, pious, serious, and of the beautiful Sara for whom he served seven years, in Spain. We think of the enchanted Prince changed to the unclean form of a dog, but as each Friday evening comes round entering his royal father's halls—tents of Jacob—in his true shape for a renewed espousal with the Princess Sabbath. We think of Jehuda ben Halevy, the troubadour of a desolate lady-love, afflicted Jerusalem. We think of that impressive passage in the *Confessions*, where Heine speaks of the resurrection of religious sentiment within him through the influence of the Bible. He had danced like a butterfly over all possible systems, but now he knelt by the side of Uncle Tom, the devout negro, before the sacred book. He had not greatly loved Moses, who was somewhat defective in his connoisseurship in the fine arts. Yet, after all, was not Moses a true artist, intent, like his Egyptian compatriots, on colossal and indestructible erections? Only it was not in brick or granite that the genius of Moses worked; no, he too constructed pyramids, but they were pyramids of human beings; " he created Israel." The Greeks were no more than beautiful youths; the Jews were always men, powerful and unsubduable; such they were in the past, such they are even in the present day, still the " Swiss Guards of Jehovah," notwithstanding eighteen centuries of persecution and misery.

But what Heine inherited from his father, besides his delicate senses and the refined hands of an artist, was not the Hebrew rigour ; it was rather an unquenchable thirst for life, an insatiable appetite for pleasure. His mother's god was less the legislator of Sinai than the amiable eighteenth-century Deity worshipped by the Savoyard Vicar. In the group of *Hebrew Melodies*, which appears in company with Heine's last poems, the " Princess Sabbath " and " Jehuda ben Halevy " are immediately followed by the extravaganza named " Disputation." A spiritual tournament between Christian monks and Jewish Rabbis is enacted in the presence of King Pedro and Queen Blanche of Spain ; fast and furious grows the mêlée of theologians, with fierce scholastic charges, rallies, and recoils ; for twelve hours the combat has lasted and the result is still undecided ; at length the Queen pronounces judgment ; which party is right she does not profess to know, the only thing indisputable is

> " Dass der Rabbi und der Mönch
> Dass sie alle Beide stinken."

There were times when Heine's own sentiment was not far removed from that expressed by Herr Hyacinth at the pleasant Baths of Lucca—" I tell you Judaism is not a religion, but a misfortune." It came forth from Egypt—so he informs Matilda—from Egypt, land of the crocodile and of priestcraft ; and what is the race of Israel now but a mummy, which wanders over the world wrapped in swathing-bands of the letter, a petrified fragment of the history of the world, a spectre that lives by trading in bills of exchange and old pantaloons. The prophet upon Mount Sinai jostles with the old clothes' man of the Judengasse in Heine's imagination; Prince Israel is the brother of Moses Lump. The worst offence of Börne in Heine's eyes was his narrow, Jewish spiritualism, his Nazarene limitation of mind—and a Nazarene may be either Christian or Jewish—which made him hate the great Greek, Goethe. All men, Heine explains to us, are born either of the Hebrew or the Hellenic family, men of ascetic instincts, hostile to form, prone to spiritualise, or men who rejoice in living, lovers of self-development, grasping reality: to the latter alone, who are conscious of their divinity, is the majesty of true enjoyment known.[1]

Heine's militant Hellenism lacks the Hellenic happy spontaneity. It was a passionate effort to restore a lost ideal. There were times when he revolted against Christianity as a religion of sorrow, with the atmosphere of the hospital hanging about it. He was a nightingale that had made a nest in the old periwig of Voltaire, and neither the nest nor the bird was dear to Christian hearts. When the ecclesiastics of the Council of Basle, wandering one day in a wood near the city, had suddenly been surprised by a nightingale's song, they stood still for a moment in ravishment, but a learned father, recovering himself, ob-

[1] Börne's criticism of Heine's representation of Christianity as a religion of sorrow, the central idea of which is the opposition between the flesh and the spirit, is worth quoting. "Christianity did not abolish the rights of the flesh, it never required the sacrifice of the delights of the senses, it only subjected those pleasures to the tutelage of the spirit, so to render them purer and more enduring. No religion ever had so much indulgence for human infirmity as the Christian religion. Catholicism, far from having enervated the nations, restored to them the force and energy which they had lost under the Roman domination. . . . Catholicism is not a gloomy and colourless religion as M. Heine has said; it is the most serene, the most joyous religion that has ever existed." (*Gesammelte Schriften*, vii. 264).

served that the notes were not very canonical; the bird might be a demon in disguise alluring them to pleasure, and when the formula of exorcism was pronounced, "Adjuro te per eum qui venturus est judicare vivos et mortuos," such indeed it proved to be; the nightingale confessed itself a fiend, and flew away with mocking laughter. Heine's half-understood Hegelian philosophy placed him upon the incline to pantheism, that old religion, as he held, of the North, and he was ready to adventure the glissade. Must it end in a gulf of indifference, where all things are levelled in the identity of universal being? Heine held that such need not be the final issue—"Alles ist nicht Gott, sondern Gott ist Alles"; God manifests himself in different degrees through different things; but all things partake of divinity. Before he came into relation with the Saint Simonian School, Heine was prepared by his temperament and by his philosophy to accept as an emancipating truth the doctrine of the rehabilitation of the flesh.

Yet Heine maintained that the Christian religion during eighteen centuries had been a blessing to the human race. If it was the religion of sorrow, it was also the religion of consolation. Its idea, its inward essence is indestructible. Voltaire, with his sarcasms and epigrams, had touched only the body of Christianity; its mortal envelope had been reached by his poisoned darts; its soul remained immortal. Heine had indeed within him—at least, in his imagination—something of the spirit of Catholicism; in separating himself from the Christian tradition he was parting with a portion of himself. His education had been conducted by Catholic priests. Rector Schallmeyer had advised his mother to devote her son to the service of the Church, and Heine in his *Confessions* humorously imagines what he might have been as a

Roman *abbate*, ministering at once to the Church of Christ and to Apollo and the Muses ; from *abbate* he might have climbed to *monsignore*, to the cardinal's hat, even to the triple crown, when, seated with careless elegance in the chair of St. Peter, he would have extended his foot for the kiss of the faithful, or, borne in triumph and profoundly serious (" for I can be very serious when it is absolutely necessary ") have given his blessing to the universal Christian world.

This is a jest of the invalid's chamber, a play of light in the gloom ; but Heine was not in his mood of mockery when he wrote as follows : " I was always a poet, and therefore that poetry which blooms and flames in the symbolism of Catholic dogma and worship revealed itself to me more deeply than any other " ; and he goes on to say how overpowering had been its charm, how he had often lost himself in enthusiasm for the blessed Queen of Heaven, and had celebrated her graciousness in the verses of his " Madonna period," many of which in his later collections were rejected with ironical laughter. The Queen of Heaven was replaced by " our blessed Lady of Melos " in his later worship ; it was at her feet that Heine lay and wept on that day in May 1848, the last on which he felt the sunshine of the Paris street ; and the goddess looked down upon her afflicted votary with pity, but with no power to comfort him, as if she would say, " Do you not see that I have no arms, and so I cannot help you? "

Heine viewed Catholicism and feudalism, not as constituting the essential genius of the romantic art, which was always dear to him, but as the means through which that art had manifested itself in the past. There is a romantic art—we see it in Shelley and in Hugo—which looks to the future. But this also connected Heine with Christian ideas and Christian sentiment. He was cosmopolitan; he had tried to persuade himself that there are no longer nations in Europe, but only two great parties—the party of progress and the party of retrogression. The great cosmopolitan, he thought, was Jesus Christ. Moses legislated for a nation, the idea of Jesus was world-wide and universal; "how circumscribed in comparison with Him appears the hero of the Old Testament! Moses loved his people with sincere affection, he cared for the future of that people like a mother. Christ loved all mankind; that Sun illumined the whole earth with the warming beams of His charity."

But Jesus was not only cosmopolitan; He was, Heine maintained, a spiritual democrat, a God more attaching than the gods of Greece, who, in the form of a gentle youth wandered under the palms of Palestine, preaching those doctrines of freedom, fraternity, equality, which as a French gospel inspired the nineteenth century. "Christ is the God whom I love best, not because He is a legitimate God, whose Father since time immemorial ruled the world, but because He, though a born Dauphin of Heaven, has democratic sympathies, and cares not for courtly ceremonies; because He is no God of an aristocracy of crop-headed theological pedants and bedizened warriors, but a modest God of the people, a citizen-God, *un bon dieu citoyen.*" So Heine wrote in one of the later volumes of the *Reisebilder*, and the idea remained with him to the close of his life. It is sunrise at Paderborn, and, as the morning mists grow thin, the poet of *Deutschland; ein Wintermärchen* sees by the roadside a cross on which the figure of the Saviour hangs. Unhappy enthusiast! poor, crucified kinsman in the war of liberation, who spoke so inconsiderately of Church and State! Pity it was that the art of printing had not been invented in the first century; then the young reformer would have written a book on questions in theology; the licensers of the press, Scribes and Pharisees, would have struck out the objectionable passages, and, thanks to the censure, the author would have escaped the cross.

And thus Heine, when with an inward sense of shame he submitted to the rite of baptism, must needs profess himself, notwithstanding his imaginative sympathies with the Roman communion, a Lutheran; for Protestantism was the form of Christianity most in accord with liberal thought. He felt that it was bleak and chilly for the sensuous imagination. "And how do you like the Protestant religion?" Herr Hyacinth, once Herr Hirsch of Hamburg, lottery-agent, corn-cutter, and dealer in jewellery, is asked, and that devout convert to Christianity confesses that it would not suit him, for it is much too reasonable a religion; indeed, if the Protestant churches had not their organs it would be no religion at all; "between ourselves this religion does no harm, and is as pure as a glass of water, but at the same time it is of no earthly use"—"Sie hilft auch Nichts."

Protestantism in its idea, Heine held, was a revolt of spiritualism against the system of accommodation between the senses and the spirit, which had grown up in the Catholic Church of the Middle Ages. But our dear master, Martin Luther, most German of the Germans, lover of Eimbeck beer, lover of wine, woman and song, was no pallid devotee of the spirit. He was a complete human being, a child of nature as well as of grace, a mystic and a man of action, an autochthonic birth, a champion of freedom, a leader of religious democracy, a reformer of morals, the liberator of the Bible, the creator of the German speech. From him proceed the Deism of the eighteenth century, the enlightened criticism of Lessing, the "Critique of the Pure Reason"—that axe of Kant the deicide—the pantheism of modern German philosophy, which restored the old national faith of the people, and even the Saint Simonian gospel with its rehabilitation of the flesh. "Glory to Luther! eternal honour to that illustrious man, to whom we owe the safety of our dearest possessions, and by whose gifts even now we live. It little becomes us to complain of the narrowness of his views. The dwarf perched on the giant's shoulder may see more than the giant, especially when he has the aid of spectacles; but to such a wide survey are wanting the lofty feeling, the giant heart, to which we can lay no claim. . . . Luther's failings have profited us more than the virtues of a thousand others. Neither the subtlety of Erasmus nor the benignity of Melancthon could ever have advanced us so far as the divine brutality of Brother Martin."

Jew and Greek and Christian, Protestant and Catholic, monotheist, polytheist, pantheist, Heine named himself in that confession of faith, in which he plays the part of Faust to the miner's daughter of Clausthal, his Gretchen of the moment, a "Knight of the Holy Ghost." Not indeed of the third Person of the Trinity, for Heine thought that the multiplication table should not be printed in children's school books after the Catechism or the Creed. "The Third Person of the Trinity," said his acquaintance, the free-thinking scoffer of Königsberg, "is much like the third horse when we travel post with a leader—one has always to pay, and yet one never gets a sight of it, this third horse." The flick of Heine's irreverent wit has in it more than a touch of inhumanity. The Spirit to which he swore allegiance was that which inspired the " war for the emancipation of mankind," and his day of Pentecost occurred in 1789. " I honour the real holiness of every religion," he writes ; " . . . I do not hate the altar, but I hate the serpents which lurk amid the loose stones of the old altar." To religious thought, though it occupied him much, he contributed nothing positive ; he only showed by an example—one of many in our age—that a vague religiosity may exist independently of definite forms of faith. The people, indeed, need a religion of forms ; he would indulge them, as he indulged his wife with the play-things of childlike piety. As for himself, he would contemplate with interest all the mythologies of the Unknowable, and fetter himself to none. In making the recantation of his *Confessions*, while acknowledging the divine nostalgia of the invalid's couch, he expressly announces that he remains unattached, as in past times, to any of the various positive religions. Indeed, his recoil to a vague theism was aided by the fact that he had seen atheism grow dogmatic, and even vulgarly dogmatic. Heine could still fling back a jest to the heavenly Aristophanes, who had been so cruelly sarcastic at the expense of his poor imitator, the *soi-disant* German Aristophanes. But when barbers' assistants and tailors' apprentices denied the existence of God, when atheism had grown grimy, and acquired an odour of schnapps and tobacco, it was time for a well-bred sceptic to part company with disbelief.

" Lay on my coffin a sword, for I was a brave soldier in the War of Freedom for mankind." Yes, Heine fought courageously, and by the uncompromising utterance of his opinions succeeded in giving offence equally to friend and foe. Like the tranquil French sceptic of the sixteenth century, for the Guelph he was a Ghibelline, for the Ghibelline he was a Guelph. Born in Düsseldorf of a persecuted race, to whom the military representative of the Revolution had come as a deliverer, Heine was inevitably attracted by the great words inscribed on the Revolutionary banner. He loved them indeed all his life, whether he interpreted them into detailed meanings or not. A brave soldier—but hardly a leader, for he was not a coherent thinker in politics, he lacked persistent ideas, though a swarm of ideas played through his mind, and he had not the organising genius which devises a campaign. A brave soldier—but undisciplined, ready in a moment to discharge a musket at his neighbour in the ranks, and therefore ill fitted for regular service. A brilliant guerilla chief, at most, who harassed the enemy, and sometimes disturbed the encampment of his friends.

It has been observed by one of Heine's critics that, though he wrote a multitude of exquisite lyrics of love, and can express delight and despair, desire and regret, it was not until his last days, when that young consoler whom he named "la Mouche" visited his sick-room, that he filled the abstract idea of love with definite meanings. "There is a certain vacuity in Heine's conception of love; it has no actual contents, no spiritual significance." The criticism is in a large measure just, and the observation might be extended to Heine's feeling for political liberty. Freedom was dear to him; he was ready to run certain risks in its cause; but his conception of freedom was not filled in with positive contents. It was in a great degree negative; he hated a state religion; he hated the licensers of the press; he hated the tyranny of petty rulers. As for the rest, its positive elements were few. He regarded Goethe, who had contributed so much to the intellectual liberation of Germany, who had even created a spiritual basis for German unity, as a political quietist. He regarded Börne as a literary demagogue. He had no sympathy with the English method of building up free institutions bit by bit. That slow, inductive method of securing a right here, and securing another right there, without shouting aloud any transcendent words or waving the universal banner, had little in it to captivate the imagination. "The Englishman is contented with that liberty which secures his most personal rights and guards his body, his property, his wedlock, his religion, and even his whims." Well, supposing that this is all, it is a considerable attainment, and such a conception of liberty is far from being vacuous and barren.

Heine was more attracted by the deductive method in politics, which starts with comprehensive principles or phrases, but he lacked the reflective power and the patience of hope which fills those phrases with meaning. And the danger is great that one who soars aloft in the airy heights, if he has not great staying power of wing, may drop into the vulgar slough of disillusion. When in July 1830 the Gallic cock crowed the second time, Heine hailed the dawn and was dazzled by the risen light of freedom. "Flowers! flowers! I will crown my head for the death-struggle! And the lyre, too, reach me the lyre, that I may sing a battle-song! Words are like flaming constellations, which shoot headlong from on high, and burn down the palaces, and illumine the hovels, words like bright javelins, which whirl upward to the seventh heaven, and strike the pious hypocrites who sneak into the Holy of Holies. I am mere joy and song, mere sword and flame." Lafayette, the tricolour, the Marseillaise! To see Lafayette riding through the Paris streets, the citizen of both worlds, the godlike old man, his silver locks flowing down upon his sacred shoulders! O, to see the brave dog Medor! And Heine would not be Heine if, when he arrived in Paris, he did not enjoy the incongruity of finding that the silver hair of the hero of both worlds was changed to a brown wig scantily covering a scanty head, and that the place of Medor in the court of the Louvre was taken by a vulgar impostor, a mongrel brute over-canopied with tri-coloured banners, while the true Medor, as commonly happens with the heroes of revolution, had retired into a modest obscurity. Heine's irony is directed against himself as much as against the illusions of mankind.

In truth Heine, though he waged war against German aristocratic pride and privilege, was himself an intellectual aristocrat. The French were the chosen people and Paris was the New Jerusalem; but in July it was for the *bourgeoisie* that the people carried the day, a *bourgeoisie* more deprived of ideas than the *noblesse* whom they replaced. The citizen king, who lately with his umbrella under his arm had strolled the streets, and squeezed the hand of every grocer, now preferred the company of intriguing financiers. A Jesuit citizen-king! "It has become apparent that there is something more deplorable than a government by mistresses; in the boudoir of a *dame galante* more honour is always to be found than on the counter of a banker." If Heine at a later time came to tolerate the middle-class rule, it was because he regarded it as the last frail defence against the fiercer materialism of the masses.

For the people Heine had the sympathy, the pity of an aristocrat; and he had at the same time an aristocrat's alienation, an aristocrat's alarms. "I love the people," he wrote in the *Confession*, "but I love them at a distance; I have always fought for their emancipation; it was the great affair of my life; yet in the most ardent moments of the strife I avoided the slightest contact with the masses." He was never, he declares, the sycophant of his Majesty, King Mob. How beautiful is the People! how good is the People! how intelligent is this good and beautiful People!—so cry the foot-lickers of the royal Caliban. No—Heine replies—the poor sovereign People is not beautiful; on the contrary, it is very ugly; but the day may come when his Majesty will wash himself gratis in the public baths. The People is not good; it is often as wicked as other potentates; but the sovereign People is hungry, and one day it may have wherewithal to eat. The People is certainly not very intelligent; perhaps it is even less intelligent than other monarchs; it would now, as eighteen hundred years ago, cry, "Give us not Christ, but Barabbas"; but one day it may attend free schools and get bread and butter free along with schooling.

Such were Heine's democratic hopes; his fears as an intellectual aristocrat outweighed them. The future, he thought, belongs to the monster Communism. He looked forward with dread and horror to a reign of gloomy iconoclasts. Our Lady of Melos, Queen of Beauty, would soon be dust under the blows of their brutal hammers; groves of laurel would be hewn down to extend the potato-bed; the lilies would be instructed how to spin; the idle nightingales would be banished with the roses; and Heine's own book of songs would serve grocers as paper bags for old women's snuff or coffee. Yet all men have a right to eat, and logic can draw diabolical conclusions from that major premiss. And one comfort lies in the fact that a cosmopolitan Communism will at least make short work with the Teutomaniacs, those patriotic owls of Germany, whose love for their native land resides solely in idiotic aversion to all neighbouring peoples.

Heine's alienation from Börne, which developed into hostility, was the inevitable result of a deep-seated contrariety of natures leading to adverse positions and a conflict of opinions. Both were children of Germany; both were of the persecuted Jewish race; both were soldiers in the war of liberation; both had wit to use as a weapon of their warfare; each had sought a refuge in Paris. But Börne was a man of rigid republican convictions, eager for the immediate application of his ideas to life, caring less for spiritual enfranchisement than for a reorganisation of the machinery of society, one who could let literature and art bide their time, if only the popular rights were secured, one who cherished the idea of nationality. Heine ridiculed the distinction that was made between character and talents; the worthy folk who flattered themselves on possessing character were deplorably bad musicians, while the good musicians were often anything but worthy folk. What of that? the chief thing is character, not music. The epitaph which honoured Atta Troll, that bear with "a tendency," admitted proudly that he danced ill, but he was a bear, whose character shone forth through his vacuity of talents—"Kein Talent, doch ein Charakter." The distinction, however, which Heine ridiculed, is a just distinction; and Börne's talents, inferior to those of Heine, were supported by a stronger character. His conception of freedom was narrow, and wanted depth; but at least it was definite and coherent.

Heine's detachment from system and his incessant mobility of mind were to Börne a bewilderment and an offence. "The most agile criticism, the most stealthy and catlike," he wrote in his review of

De l'Allemagne, "will never succeed in catching M. Heine, who is more a mouse than criticism is a cat. He has contrived mouse-holes for his uses in every corner of the moral, intellectual, religious and social world, and these holes have subterranean communications, one with another; you see M. Heine peep out from one of his small opinions; you pounce upon him, and he is in his hole again; you lay siege to him, and he escapes by a wholly opposite opinion." A grimy democracy, which would have gone far to satisfy Börne, excited Heine's abhorrence. Börne was a slave to Nazarene abstinence, who hated Goethe and held the fine arts to be frivolous luxuries. In Börne's room was to be found a menagerie of Republican animals, such as could scarcely be seen in the Jardin des Plantes—German polar bears, who smoked and swore; Polish wolves, who howled the banalities of revolution; a French ape, who varied his grimaces in order that one might select the least repulsive of many. And there was Börne himself, appearing amid clouds of bad tobacco to instruct his menagerie that only a republic can save us, and that all good things come from the German side of the Rhine.

The truth is that, while Börne acknowledged no allegiance to Goethe, Heine was a son of that great liberator, though a prodigal son who had wasted some of his portion in journalism and the politics of a *littérateur*. He valued highly political and social freedom, which, he held, could exist under a monarchy as truly as in a republic, and he mocked those German quietists who were content with an inward or intellectual emancipation without incarnating freedom in institutions. The man of an idea is followed, he tells us, at no great distance by the lictor who bears the axe:

> "Ich bin dein Liktor, und ich geh'
> Beständig mid dem blanken
> Richterbeile hinter dir—ich bin
> Die That von deinem Gedanken."

He would turn Germany from dreams—dreams of philosophy, dreams of mediævalism, dreams of classic art—to the modern and the practical. But Heine did not attach supreme importance to political machinery. He retained something from that large ideal of humanism and that cosmopolitan culture which had been developed in the period of Goethe and Schiller. Hence his deep dissatisfaction with England, ever present, though he afterwards regretted the extravagance of its expression, and with America. In England, that vile country of weary toil and dense *ennui*, the machines act like men, the men like machines. America is one vast prison-house of liberty, " where," said Heine, " the invisible chains would hang more heavily upon me than the visible ones at home, and where the most repulsive of all tyrants, the mob, exercises its rough dominion." Thus, with what survived in him of the richer and more concrete humanism of Goethe, he partly filled the abstract conception of liberty. It was well, as a protest against over-valuing the apparatus of government, and as a protest against mere materialism, that Heine should have presented even in a fragmentary and an intermittent way a humanist ideal.

An aristocrat in things of the mind, a humanist, even though a superficial humanist, Heine was naturally an admirer of great personalities. From Goethe he was partly detached because Goethe would postpone the social and political revolution until inward freedom had been attained, and also, as he confesses, because he was envious of Goethe ; but he would reserve for himself the privilege of being impertinent in the presence of intellectual greatness; his mockery was the inevitable foil to his reverence. For Napoleon, who seemed to him to lift the principles of the Revolution into the light of genius, and to concentrate the passions of a people in a single mind, he could beat the Marseillaise or Ça Ira with as much enthusiasm as that of the eloquent performer, Monsieur Le Grand. A captive at St. Helena, Napoleon was the Titan Prometheus, who stole fire from the gods, and whose heart was gnawed by the ignoble kites of Britain. Heine was capable of representing to himself the Tsar Nicholas as no less than the *gonfalonier* of freedom. It was not without reason that Börne suspected such a champion of the cause dear to him, one who avoided contact with the people, and applauded a despot. And in truth an enlightened despotism, animated by ideas, adorned with art, and graceful in its luxuries, would have gone far towards satisfying Heine's political aspirations.

Yet, amid the errors of one who was a combatant in a bewildering battle, and who saw only fragments of the strife, he showed on occasions remarkable powers of observation, and uttered some political prophecies which time has not belied. Right or wrong, he profoundly distrusted the liberalism of Prussia, that "long hypocritical hero in gaiters, with his big stomach, his huge mouth, and his corporal's cudgel, which he dips in holy water before he strikes." He warned France of the dangers that were to come from without in a united Germany, and from within in the uprising of the proletariat. In the closing poem of his *Lazarus* he names himself the "Enfant perdu" of the war of emancipation; he is a sentinel who has held his post for thirty years, and never will return home alive; night and day he watched, and even in the tent the heavy snoring of his friends kept him from sleep ; many a fiery bullet has he sent home into the paunches of the dullards ; but, alas ! a dullard may also know how to shoot, and his own wounds gape :

> " Ein Posten ist vakant ! Die Wunden klaffen—
> Der Eine fällt, die Andern rücken nach—
> Doch fall' ich unbesiegt, und meine Waffen
> Sind nicht gebrochen—Nur mein Herze brach."

And in the dying combatant's *fanfaronnade* there is more than a touch of true pathos.

But when looking Godwards Heine confessed himself " a poor dying Jew " ; looking towards his fellows he thought of himself as " nothing—nothing save a poet." Recovering himself he adds : " But no ; I will not abandon myself to a hypocritical humility, and undervalue this noble name of a poet. One who is a poet is much, and especially if one is a great lyric poet of Germany, the poet of the people which in two things, philosophy and lyric verse, has surpassed all other nations. I will not, with that mock modesty discovered by beggar-knaves, renounce my glory." And it is certainly, as Matthew Arnold said, with the emblem of the laurel rather than with the emblem of the sword that posterity will decorate Heine's tomb—with the laurel, into which may be woven a lotus flower from the Ganges, and some Western blossoms, sharp-scented and pungent.

Atta Troll was described by its author as the last wood-notes wild of the romantic school. It was in the house of his maternal uncle, Simon von Geldern—the Noah's Ark of Düsseldorf—that Heine as a child was initiated into romance. In the attic of Noah's Ark, where the spider spun his web, and the fat Angora cat looked on with the eyes of an enchanted princess, the boy spent hours of mystery and delight ;

there were his mother's mouldering cradle, his grandfather's sword and wig, his grandmother's stuffed parrot, half plumeless and turned from green to grey, the broken porcelain dog, much respected by the enchanted princess, an ancient flute, faded manuscripts on the occult sciences, dusty volumes of Paracelsus and Van Helmont; above all, his great-uncle's notes of travel in the East—records of the wandering Orientalist, who had seen Jerusalem, and had been chosen sheik of a Bedouin tribe. In his imagination the boy identified himself with the legendary traveller, and had the singular experience of being for a time his own great-uncle. It was doubtless from Simon von Geldern's library that he bore away that book of romance and irony—the first which he read after attaining a boy's years of discretion—*The Life and Deeds of the Sagacious Knight Don Quixote de la Mancha*, his world of delight and pity from spring till autumn, while day after day he sat on the old mossy stone bench in the Court Garden. Its chivalry he understood, its irony lay in reserve to be discovered at a later time.

Some childish premonitions of love were followed by that deep impression, made on his imagination if not on his heart, by the pale marmoreal beauty of Josepha—niece of the old witch who sold love-philtres and (having the advantage of a husband who had been public executioner) dead men's fingers, the possession of which magically enriched the flavour of German beer. Josepha's marble face shone under torrents of blood-red hair; her voice, commonly muffled in tone, broke forth with a metallic resonance when she sang the old folk-songs, which did much to awaken Heine's dormant genius. "Beyond all doubt she exerted the greatest influence on the poet now stirring within me. My first poems, which I wrote soon after, are of a cruel and sombre colour, akin to that attraction which threw its crimson shadow over my young life and mind."

From the *Wunderhorn*, from A. W. Schlegel, Hoffmann, Brentano, and Wilhelm Müller, he derived much. The romantic movement in Germany, a reaction in sentiment from the spirit of the eighteenth century, a reaction in art from the objectivity of Goethe, " the great Greek," was at once a reversion to mediævalism and an assertion of the rights of the *ego* in literature. A work of art was no longer to be tested by its truth to nature, and its accordance with reason ; it was all the more admirable if it rendered the cry of individual passion, the measureless sigh of individual regret or desire, the sensibility, the phantasy, the caprice of a solitary soul. As far as the individualism of romantic art was controlled or held in check, that control came from the artist's superiority to his own creation betrayed in the irony taught by the critics, if not always practised by the poets, and from a common tendency towards the sentiment and the imaginative forms of the age of faith. The romantic influence is present in Heine's poetry from first to last ; the writer even of *Atta Troll*, and of *Deutschland ; ein Wintermärchen* —his most mature, his most characteristic creations—was a romantic poet, though a romantic poet unfrocked.

Heine never escaped from the individualism of the poetic generation to which he belonged. But the control of his artistic egoism came not from the past, but from the present and the future. He would be at once romantic and realist, romantic and revolutionary. The Middle Ages he viewed as a domain in which his fantasy might disport itself ; there he was free to indulge every caprice and every humour ; anti-clerical and anti-Catholic through his intelligence, he could gratify his imagination with the sentiment of Catholicism. His genuine hopes, his serious fears were all connected with the nineteenth century. He had seen the great Emperor, riding his white palfrey in the avenue of the Court Garden at Düsseldorf, his face of chiselled marble, his eye reading the souls of men, a smile upon those lips which had but to whistle *et la Prusse n'existait plus*, which had but to whistle and the entire body of clerics would have stopped their ringing and singing, the entire Holy Roman Empire would have danced. There was the true hero of modern romance; there was the veritable incarnation of the new idea.

A second check upon Heine's romantic egoism was of a wholly artistic kind. He had learnt from Goethe the virtue that lies in definite form. He saw no reason why exact conceptions, precise and vivid imagery, verse close-knit and succinct should not belong to the romantic as well as to the classical poet. "The images, by means of which romantic feeling may be evoked," so Heine wrote as early as 1820, "should be drawn as clearly and with as well-defined outlines as the images of plastic poetry." Vague and wandering sentiment, he felt, must yield to the boundary of art; the floating fragrance must be condensed to an essence, and be imprisoned in a tiny phial. In other lyrists we may study the methods of evolving and expanding a theme; from Heine we learn innumerable devices of lyrical condensation. A sudden tug of the bearing rein checks the lyrical career, and we halt with more of the sense of motion in our blood than if Pegasus had cantered or ambled for a league. Sometimes indeed, Heine's feats of equitation are those of the circus, ending with a violence of surprise, and we see the performer expecting his applause. Sometimes the close is what Wordsworth calls " a shock of mild surprise," which carries far into our hearts all that is expressed, and all that is vitally present and unexpressed. So much of spontaneity has rarely been united with so much of calculation.

But the chief control of Heine's romantic egoism came from within—" my name is Legion, for we are many." He plays off one faculty against another, and often in a manner which enhances the power of each. Serious and edifying German critics have preached on the text of Heine's self-mockery as if they would rebuke the offence of spiritual suicide. A true German poet should never suspect his own sentimentality; a true German poet should be unalterably virtuous, loyal, domestic, pathetic, patriotic. If he weeps, he should draw down the blinds in the chamber of weeping; if he laughs, he should do so with Teutonic uproariousness in a remote chamber of laughter. O wicked Heine, who sapped the foundations of heavy sentiment with irony, who withered his own linden flowers with the desolating breath of scepticism! " No," cried Nannerl, the comely barmaid in the *Reisebilder*, " we haven't got irony, but you can have any other sort of beer."

Heine confessed that he was not one of the great poets, sound and integral, proper to an age of faith. But irony, in an age of doubt and conflict, may be preservative of such sanity as is possible. " Dear reader," Heine asks in *The Baths of Lucca*, " do you by chance belong to the flock of pious fowl who have joined in that song of ' Byronic disintegration,' which for ten years in every variety of piping and twittering has sounded in my ears? Ah, dear reader, if you would complain of discordancy, let your complaint be that the world is rent in pieces.

For, as the heart of the poet is the central point of the world, it must in times like these be miserably divided and torn. He who boasts of his heart that it remains whole, only confesses that it is no more than a prosaic, isolated cornerheart (Winkelherz). But through this heart of mine went the great rift of the world, and hence I know that the high gods have given me grace above many others, and have counted me worthy of the poet's martyrdom." Heine's apology may be accepted in all seriousness as expressing a portion of the truth. An age of dissonance gives an opportunity to the poet of many moods, who might be wholly silent or might sing a single penetrating strain in an age at one with itself.

If Faust declaims and Mephistopheles derides, it is too readily assumed that the result is wholly negative; or it is assumed that Mephistopheles necessarily has the last word. But perhaps the last word and the best of the argument remain with Faust. It is demonstrated at least—and this is something positive—that each has a right to exist, that each has a case to state on his own behalf, and against the other. In many instances Heine does not desire to bring things to an issue; he mocks his own exalted sentiment, but it survives to rebuke or to mock his mockery. In *Die Nacht am Strande*, one of the North Sea poems, the Byronic stranger, after his wanderings by night on a desolate shore, enters the fisher's cottage where the fisher's daughter, lovely and wondrous, sits listening to the "sweet domestic prophecies of the kettle"; for a moment he declaims as a deity who has descended from heaven to embrace one of the daughters of men; but the deity has a mortal body, night airs may induce catarrh in his god-ship's head, and hot tea with rum is an excellent prophylactic. Surely both sides of the fact deserve to be stated, and the romance is not so timid as to fear the touch of realism. The poetic motive of the piece is not attacked by a prosaic conclusion; the heroics and the jest of the heroics play their part in a duel, and are reconciled by poetic art; each has received satisfaction, and neither can triumph over the other. Don Quixote on Rosinante is accompanied by Sancho on his ass, and Sancho Panza, with all his shrewd good sense, has a touching fidelity to his master; the hero of the piece is neither master nor squire alone, but the double personality of the immortal pair of adventurers.

Heine had neither the nobility of character nor the moral sanity of the great epic inventor of Spain. Some of the dissonances which his poetry expresses were not those abiding incongruities of human nature which form the basis of Cervantes' humour; they were dissonances of the time, or dissonances which rose from his own infirmities of character; yet even these are delivered from much of their baser matter by the imagination, and find what we may term their "katharsis" in irony. His purest joy conceals a pain; his passion of love is half despair; his intoxication of life ends in a galliard of skeleton dancers; his jests are keenest when the jester lies stretched upon the rack; his tears are repressed with bitter laughter; beauty weds grotesqueness in his verse; what is noble holds hands with what is mean; the flesh and the spirit encounter or embrace; faith and unfaith interpenetrate each the other; he leans towards the future while he turns and gazes at the past. Nothing is concluded, no complete solution is attained; but it is something to state facts and to raise questions; it is something to be discontented with shallow or partial solutions; it is something to disturb a demure self-complacency; it is something to delay the answers to our problems until the conditions of an adequate answer have been considered.

Thus out of the diversities which lay in Heine's nature there rises at last a certain unity, and the conciliation of his contending powers and tendencies is effected by an irony which detaches him from each of his inward moods and from each of his views of things external. He belongs to the race of sceptics, but he is a sceptic who inquires, a sceptic who hopes. He felt the need of a religion of joy, and also of a religion of sorrow, and he states the case on behalf of each. He felt that the political future belongs to the populace—they have, fortunately or unfortunately, a right to eat; but he would preserve the higher rights of an aristocracy of intellect. He swam with the current of romantic art, and he headed round and swam more vigorously against the current, so anticipating the movement of realism which was to meet and turn the tide; but Heine's ideal of art, at once realistic and romantic, is still unattained. He smiles at his own enthusiasm, and the sceptic is an enthusiast to the end: "I used formerly to suppose," he writes in the introduction to an illustrated edition of his beloved *Don Quixote*, "that the laughable character of Quixotry lay in the fact that the noble knight wished to recall to life a long-buried past, and that his poor limbs, or rather his back, came into painful collision with the actualities of the present. Alas, I have learnt since then that it is just as thankless a piece of folly to try to bring the future prematurely into the present, and that any such antagonism to the substantial interests of the day is mounted on an exceedingly sorry nag and is provided with very rusty armour and a body as easily shattered. A wiseacre will shake his head over one form of Quixotry as much as over the other.

Yet, all the same, Dulcinea del Tobosa is the fairest woman in the world; and, though I lie miserable on the ground, never will I recant this profession. I cannot do otherwise—so thrust in with your lances, you silver knights of the Moon, you disguised barbers' apprentices."

One feeling rich in virtue, and perhaps only one, lay during all his life in Heine's heart pure and unmingled. Not the love he bore his wife; children were always dear to him, and Heine had much joy in the spoilt child who was his wife; but a child who is a woman, who puts no control upon her tempers, and has an incurable mania for flinging money out of windows, causes some vexations. His one unmingled felicity was in his affection for his mother. It was for her he wrote in youth those sonnets which tell how he had wandered far and fruitlessly in search of love, and had found it at last in her dear eyes. It was for her sake long afterwards that he concealed the terrible ravages of his malady, and wrote those letters, cheering and caressing, which brought her bright news of Paris and of her son. "Take good care of my poor old mother," he implores his sister, "she is indeed the pearl of women." "I cover the face and two hands of my dear mother with kisses." "I embrace my dear little mother five-and-twenty times, and love her better than all the cats in the world." If the old days of Hebrew miracle were not departed, we might cast this green tree of filial piety into the bitter waters of Heine's passion and wit, and hope to make them sweet. But at best the waters must remain brackish to our lips.

GOETHE'S WEST-EASTERN DIVAN

"Men of genius," said Goethe to Eckermann, "may experience a renewed puberty, while other people are young but once"; having expounded his thought he presently qualified it—"aber jung ist jung"—still youth is youth. The last word is the true one. The flush of what seems new life which may come to a sexagenarian is not that of spring-time, it is the Indian summer:

> "What visionary tints the year puts on
> When falling leaves falter through motionless air!"

In the greeting of the season there is a touch of farewell. The sun is still warm at noon, but at morning and evening there is an edge upon the air which is not the freshness of spring. There is a strange and wide stillness in the land, or sounds reach us from far away—horns of Elfland faintly blowing. The atmosphere is sometimes singularly pellucid, and sometimes it becomes a luminous mist. The time is one of joy, but in such joy there is something of pathos. Goethe's Indian summer came when he was sixty-five. Its record is to be found in his last important body of lyrical poetry, the *West-Eastern Divan*. Even in Germany the *Divan*, as a whole, is much less known than it deserves to be. In England many persons who are familiar with *Faust* and *Iphigenie* and the ballads have never opened this collection of verse. There are excuses which may be pleaded for such neglect. The Indian summer has not the mighty ravishment of spring. The marks of old age in thought and feeling, in style and diction, are evident. Few poems are quite equal individually to the most enchanting of Goethe's earlier lyrics. Some are obscure even to German commentators; some are over-ingenious in their symbolism; some require for their comprehension an acquaintance with Goethe's scientific ideas; the play at sexagenarian love-making in the *Book of Zuleika* may be easily misunderstood. Yet certain lines and phrases are on all our lips from time to time. We all remember that characterisation in five words of a primitive condition of the human mind—"broad faith and narrow thought." We all remember the poet's plea for admission as a warrior to Paradise:

> "For I have been a man, and that
> Means I have been a combatant."

The book as a whole has had worthy lovers and diligent students. From the standpoint of "spiritual freedom" and "inner depth of fantasy," Hegel placed it in the forefront of modern poetry. Heine learnt from it something of his lyrical manner, and wondered how such ethereal lightness as that of certain poems of the *Divan* was possible in the German language. Charlotte von Schiller writes happily: "We find ever new results the more we read it." It was the subject—but what work of Goethe was not?—of Düntzer's laborious scholarship. It was carefully edited by Loeper. But no one has done so much to further a true appreciation of the *Divan* as Konrad Burdach, who has reproduced the text in its earliest form, edited, with introduction and notes, the received text in the Jubiläums-Aufgabe of Goethe's works, superintended the volume containing it and a complete critical apparatus for the great Weimar edition still in progress, and made it the subject of the *Festvortrag* delivered at the general meeting of the German Goethe Society in June 1896.

I cannot go astray if I follow the guidance of this excellent scholar and borrow from him what may seem needful. As Hafiz could recite the Koran page by page without an error, so this editor of the *Divan* has doubtless taken on heart and brain the image of his chosen book; and as Goethe dared to place himself, through his devotion to the sacred writings of Christendom, almost by the side of Hafiz, so, from the inferior position of an English student of the *West-Eastern Divan*, I would aspire to come, with a long interval, after Konrad Burdach. Having previously known the poems well, I took with me last summer Loeper's edition to Cornwall, and found that the game of translating Goethe's poetry into what aimed at being English verse could be played on wind-blown cliffs of the Lizard or in the shadow of some fantastic cave of serpentine to the accompaniment of the western waves. Even to fail in such a game was to enter into the joy of *l'amour de l'impossible*. By slow degrees the whole of Goethe's silver arabesque work was transmuted into Cornish or British tin. But the foiled translator had at least to scrutinise every line of the original and encounter every difficulty. And there were some things so wise, so humane, so large in their serene benignity, that they could not be wholly spoilt even by a *traduttore*, who, at least as regards the sense of each poem, strove not to be a *traditore*.

From his early years Goethe had taken an interest in the poetry of the East. The patriarchal life presented in the Old Testament had even in boyhood stirred his imagination. In the period of his youthful Titanism he had chosen Mohammed as the central figure of a dramatic poem, and had prepared himself for the task, never to be accomplished, by a study of the Koran. In 1774 he informed his friend Merck that he had translated Solomon's *Song of Songs*—" the most glorious collection of love songs ever fashioned by God." Partly through Herder's influence, he came to set special store by all that was primitive in the life and literature of the East, all that seemed to spring from nature and from the heart of a people, as conceived by the romantic and humanitarian eighteenth century. At Weimar he had translated one of the pre-Islamic poems from the Mu'allakât, Sir William Jones having opened up the way. He had been charmed by that pearl of Indian drama, *Sakuntala*. Some of the roses from Saadi's garden and Jami's *Loves of Laila and Majnun* had introduced him to Persian poetry. But it was not until after the publication of Joseph von Hammer's celebrated translation of the *Divan* of Hafiz in 1812 that the great German poet became, as it pleased him to imagine himself, a wandering merchant in the East, trucking his wares for those of Persian singers. " The author of the preceding poems," he writes in the opening of the dissertation which follows the verse of the *West-Eastern Divan*, " would choose to be regarded as a traveller who is applauded if he accommodates himself to the customs of foreign countries, tries to appropriate their ways of speech, to share their sentiments and adopt their manners. He is excused if his effort is successful only to a certain point, if, by virtue of a peculiar accent and an unconquerable rigidity proper to his nationality, he can still and always be recognised as a foreigner." And to gratify his own folk, such a traveller will return home with his lading of Oriental merchandise.

Is Goethe, then, only assuming an Eastern garb and disguise ? Is he only playing with the turban wound around his head? No, for he is interpreting in his own way a tendency of the time. The dominating classical influence, Greek and Roman, seen in the *Iphigenie* and the *Roman Elegies*, had waned. He was again free to be eclectic or as universal as his genius of unparalleled flexibility would permit. And the new Romantic literature was turning towards the East. In England Southey's *Thalaba* had presented the life of the Arabian desert and the fantastic marvels of Oriental mythology; but the moral idealism of the poem was the immediate offspring of Southey's own character. The Fairy Mab conducts the spirit of Shelley's Ianthe to gaze on "Palmyra's ruined palaces," and when a little later he attempted a huge epic of revolution and reaction, it took the form of a *Revolt of Islam*. For Byron the East was the land of entrancing visible beauty and of boundless human passion:

> "Where the rage of the vulture, the love of the turtle,
> Now melt into sorrow, now madden to crime."

The East of Goethe's imagination was as remote as possible from Byron's East. If he was a Romantic poet again it was in his own original and incomparable fashion. Although, partly through the influence of Sulpiz Boisserée and his collections, Goethe's interest in Gothic architecture and old German painting received a new development, he felt profoundly hostile—for one so liberal in his sympathies bitterly hostile—to the neo-Catholic party in the Romantic school, and in the *Divan* some shrewd thrusts are delivered against them by the old Pagan. Yet the spirit of the old Pagan was in truth religious, not less, but rather more, than theirs. Like Hafiz, he had found the secret of being blessed—*selig*—without being *fromm*, a *dévote*, and this was a fact they could never admit or understand. He turned to the East as to a refuge from the strife of tongues, as well as from the public strife of European swords. There the heavens were cloudless, and God—the one God—seemed to preside over even the sand-waste. There Islam, submission to God's will, seemed to be the very rule of life. And within the circuit of this all-embracing piety, it was permissible even for an old man to be innocently gay. The cumbrous baggage—intellectual and material—of Western civilisation was no longer a necessity. A wine-cup and a little book of song, upon some strip of herbage that just divides the desert from the sown, would suffice. Or in the wine-tavern the cup-bearer, a boy with all the charm of youth, might fill the old poet's goblet and receive his reward in the form of wisest counsel and a kiss upon the forehead. Before all else the merchandise which Goethe sought to purchase in the East was wisdom and piety and peace.

These Hafiz had somehow found; he was gay, but he was also wise; "it is through the Koran," he said, "that I have done everything that ever succeeded with me"; and yet he wrote these Anacreontic ghazels of love and wine, and, possessed of inward piety, did not pursue with zeal the outward practices of religion. He had his grave studies, too, the lessons in grammar, and even in theology, which he gave to his disciples. In like manner Goethe had occupied himself ardently with botany, with comparative anatomy, with optics. The special quality, as Goethe perceived, of the poet Hafiz was his spontaneity, though he often wrote in elaborate forms; he was a true poetic fount, "wave welling after wave"; and Goethe could not but remember the lyrical impulses of his own earlier days, described in his autobiography, when song seemed rather to possess him than to be held in possession. There was another circumstance in common with them. Hafiz, a contemporary of our own Chaucer, had seen that scourge of God, Timur the Tatar, sweep over Persia with his hordes and spread his conquests from Delhi to Damascus. Another Timur had arisen in Europe of the nineteenth century, whose name was Napoleon. Hafiz could not stay the conqueror's career; but at least he could teach grammar well, and he could give the world the joy of his ghazels. Had those songs of love and wine a spiritual significance? Was more meant by them than meets the ear? Hafiz had been named "the mystical tongue"; the learned commentators, scholars in words who had no notion of the sense of the word "mystic," had read into the poems, says Goethe in his verse, every silly notion of their own; they, like sorry tapsters, had retailed as true Hafiz their thin and insipid vintage; yes, for them he was a mystical tongue; how could they ever get a glimpse of the real import of the utterances of one who was *selig* without being *fromm*. But presently second thoughts come to Goethe. Perhaps he recalled the symbolism of some of his own West-Eastern poems; when he sang the praises of wine, it was not always the juice of the grape that he meant; when he spoke of the kiss of the houri, in the Mussulman's Paradise, he meant something more than the seal of earthly love. Those commentators whom he had blamed, after all, have right on their side; words may play a double part:

> "A word 's a fan ! a glance is shot
> Between the sticks from eyes divine ;
> The fan 's a veil, no more, whose fine
> Substance may keep the face in shade,
> But cannot hide from me the maid,

Since her prime loveliness, the eyes,
Flash into mine some swift surprise."

In this, too, the expression, almost in an inevitable way, of spiritual mysteries through material imagery —were not he and Hafiz alike ?

With a strange and happy return upon him of the creative impulse of youth, urging him as of old to swift and spontaneous jets of song, Goethe, in the early morning of 25th July 1814, started in his carriage from Weimar for the Rhine, Frankfurt and Wiesbaden. It was seventeen years since he had visited the scenes of his childhood and youth. Something of enchantment was added by this revival of the past to the Indian summer of Goethe's sixty-fifth year. With a rearrangement of certain pieces of the *West-Eastern Divan*, such as is indicated by Burdach in his *Festvortrag* (which here I gladly follow), we can make out a kind of diary in verse of these days of travel. As the carriage left Weimar a white bow was visible upon the July mist ; it was a sign of promise, though not radiant with colour as it should be for a youthful wanderer :

"Greybeard, with clouds in sight,
Blithe shouldst thou prove ;
What if thy hair be white,
Yet thou shalt love."

The summer mist still hung over the landscape when Erfurt seemed coming nearer, and a vision of lovely mingled colour upon a slope caught Goethe's gaze, and at first failed to expound itself to the eye. The record and explanation of the incident will be found in the poem entitled "Liebliches" :

"What motley shows are those that bind
The heavens with yonder height,
Through mists of morning ill-defined,
That half defeat the sight ?

Are they the Vizier's tents displayed,
  Where his loved women bide?
Are they the festal carpets laid
  For footing of the bride?

Scarlet and white, mixed, freckled, streaked,
  Vision of perfect worth!
Hafiz, how came thy Shiraz thus
  To greet the cloudy North?

Yes, neighbour poppies spreading far,
  A cordial, various band,
As if to scorn the god of war
  Kindly they robe the land.

So let the sage who serves our earth,
  With flowers still make it gay,
And, as this morn, the sun shine forth
  To light them on my way."

In the early Weimar days, when the Duke was still untamed, and he himself was overflowing with the spirit of youth, Goethe had known Erfurt well. The old man—if we may trust a poem included after the writer's death among those of the *Divan*—was now recognised and welcomed; it was all dreamlike, and yet the past had been so real:

"And when old dames from stall and booth
  Me—old like them—would gladly greet,
I thought I saw those days of youth
  We each for other made so sweet."

She yonder was a baker's daughter, but, whatever the distracted Ophelia may have said, certainly no "owl," and by her side stands the once fair shoe-vamper, who knew, in addition to her trade, the art of living:

"Hafiz, thy rival I would be
    In this, and may the humour last,
  To take the present joyously,
    And share my gladness in the past."

To Erfurt succeeded Eisenach, with more awakened memories—Eisenach, from which he had long ago addressed ardent letters to Charlotte von Stein; Eisenach, the scene of hunting expeditions of Karl August. Seen in the dewy dawn, the garden seemed to be the very same that once it was; lily and rose blossomed as long ago:

"And every air some odour brings
As when love ached in those old days,
Those dawnings when my psaltery strings
Contended with the morning's rays;
There where from greenwood shades would start
Rounded and full, the hunter's chant,
To quicken and to fire the heart,
Accordant to its wish or want.

Ever the woods fresh leaves unfold!
With these your soul rejoicing fill;
Pleasures that were your own of old
May be enjoyed through others still;
No man will then complain of us
Care for ourselves was all we had;
Through all life's process various
You must have virtue to be glad!"

And thus, as the name of the poem suggests, the Past may still survive in the Present. In the evening of the same day, at Fulda, Goethe added the closing lines, which, as Burdach says, refer also to the evening of our life:

"And with such winding of my lay,
Hafiz, once more we hear thy voice;
'Tis meet in each concluded day
With the rejoicing to rejoice."

A charming lyric of these days of travel, expressing the poetry of motion, the lyric first named "Vision," and finally "The New Copernicus," was excluded from the *Divan*, because, though in many respects the collection was Western, the imaginary wanderer of the East, Hatem, who was also Goethe, might be supposed to know the back of a camel better than the interior of a comfortably-fitted German chaise. The chaise is a charming little house, a shelter from the July sun, provided with every convenience of travel. And, O wonder! the woods come striding towards this house; the distant fields are in motion; mountains, grown large, dance past; nothing is wanting but the joyous cries of the awakened dwarfs; and all this commotion brings no disturbance to the quiet of a July morning. Can it be that the Copernican theory has here also its application, and that mountains and woods stand still while the occupant of the little house is himself borne onward? In this joyous spirit, as he advanced, song after song rose spontaneously to Goethe's lips; the exultation of life and something like the delightful arrogance of youth possessed him, but such arrogance was more profitable than a self-distrustful modesty:

> "Song is a certain arrogance,
> Let none find fault with me;
> But bravely let the warm blood dance,
> Be gay as I, and free.
>
> . . . . .
>
> When round the poet's mill-wheel turns,
> Stop not his whirl of rhymes;
> For who once understands us learns
> To pardon us betimes."

"The drive to Wiesbaden, on the warm night of 29th July," writes Düntzer, "has its monument in the beautiful poem, 'Universal Life.'" A thunderstorm had overtaken the traveller; the dry and dusty roads were drenched. And then he thought of those poems of Hafiz in which the praise of dust is sung—the dust on the threshold of the beloved, preferred by the lover to that carpet on whose gold-wrought flowers kneel Mahmud's favourites, the dust whirled from her door, which is sweeter to breathe than musk or attar of the rose. And again Goethe's thoughts wander to Italy, the dusty South, which he loved so much, and for the sight of which he still pined. Yet even without Italy there is the Universal Life of nature, and this storm of rain and thunder will quicken that life to a fresh putting forth of power

"Loved doors upon your hinges long
Sounded no sweet recoil,
Come heal me, ye tempestuous rains,
And scent of breathing soil!

For now if all the thunders roll,
Wide heaven with leven glow,
The wind's wild dust, rain-saturate,
Will fall to earth below.

Straightway life leaps, a sacred force
And secret strives in birth;
Fresh mists exhale, green things arise,
O'er all the bounds of earth."

This yearning towards the Universal Life may assume a mystical form; the intensity of the joy of individual life may pass on to an aspiration for the loss of the personal in the universal, which, as all mystical spirits, Christian, Mohammedan and Buddhist, will affirm, is not loss, but a higher life. Such is the feeling embodied in a poem written on 31st July 1814, "Selige Sehnsucht," of which Loeper and Burdach speak in such terms of unqualified admiration that to quote their words would be to ensure disappointment for any reader of an imperfect English version:

"Tell it the wise alone, for when
Will the crowd cease from mockery?
Him would I laud of living men
Who longs a fiery death to die.

In coolness of those nights of love
  Which thee begat, bade thee beget,
Strange promptings wake in thee and move
  While the calm taper glimmers yet.

No more in darkness canst thou rest,
  Waited upon by shadows blind,
A new desire has thee possessed
  For procreant joys of loftier kind.

Distance can hinder not thy flight;
  Exiled, thou seek'st a point illumed,
And last enamoured of the light,
  A moth art in the flame consumed.

And while thou spurnest at the hest
  Whose word is 'Die, and be new-born!'
Thou bidest but a cloudy guest
  Upon an earth that knows not morn."

Deeper words assuredly than ever came from a pagan spirit.

In a poem placed near the opening of the *Divan* Goethe enumerates the elements from which song derives its nutriment. First, and chief, is love; wine and war follow; and the fourth element is hatred:

"Last, hate is indispensable;
  Ay, many a thing true poets hate;
Shall he who beauty loves as well
  Foul things and loathsome tolerate?"

There is not much of hatred in these poems of an illuminated old age, which remained unpublished until the writer's seventieth year. But as a lady requires a boudoir to which she can retire, in order, as the derivation of the word boudoir suggests, to sulk or pout alone, whence she returns smiling to her guests, so Goethe, that he might show a gracious face to his friends, made one short book of the *Divan* the depository of his indignations and chagrins—*The*

Book of Ill Humour. No one reaches even middle life entirely free from dissatisfactions with things as they are. Shakespeare could write a *Timon* and a *Troilus and Cressida*. If to consume our own smoke ends in darkening our countenance, it may be wiser to run up a narrow shaft high in the air, by which our smoke may find a harmless vent. Goethe had been an emancipator, and now here were these neo-Catholic Romantics striving to undo his work. He had tasked his powers in service to his age, and now he was regarded by some as an obstructive, a self-centred egoist. There were folk who flattered him prodigiously, and regarded him with bitter, though secret, enmity. There were those who collect big subscriptions to erect a monument to any dead prophet, and who would gladly stone the living prophet. There were the sentimental or self-interested patriots—most often both in one—who had discovered that Goethe was no true German. There were those who knew much better than he knew himself how his work as an artist or as a man of science should be done. And there are always cribbed and cabined spirits, " half-men," who cannot away with any liberal interpretation of human life. Finally, there were the downright base, and, whatever men may say, baseness is a power in this world. These last are not to be contended with :

> " Wanderer ! thy strength would'st try
>   'Gainst what will be, and must ?
> Whirlwind and filth that's dry
>   Let spin and mount in dust ! "

Against those who would amend his work he has only the domineering word—If there be virtue in you, push on in your own pursuit ; but as for mine, learn that thus I willed it should be made. To the flattery of malice he replies with menaces equal to the flattery. But he will not spend his wrath on individuals; prompt hatred he has, if needed, but only for some collective mass. And then he reviews his own career, not without a touch of proud and warranted self-satisfaction:

> "To ape, re-shape, mis-shape me each in turn,
> Now for at least full fifty years they have sought;
> None the less what your worth may be, I thought,
> In your own native fields you best may learn;
> You in your time have played the madcap rude
> With a wild, young, demonic-genial crew;
> Then softly year by year you closer drew
> To wise men of divine mansuetude."

Mohammed himself had not contented all parties, and the Prophet's suggestion of a mode by which a wrathful spirit may be cooled is excellent:

> "Irks it some man that God in his high place
> Should grant Mohammed guardianship and grace?
> Let him his roof-tree's sturdiest timber choose,
> Let him make fast thereto a proper noose,
> Let him adjust his neck. Is it stoutly made?
> So shall he feel his anger is allayed."

But Goethe is not often moved to tender the advice, "Go, hang!"

The central motive of the poems is, in truth, love; first, there is a benignant charity extended to man as man; secondly, there is the charming relation of the old sage, poet, and toper of wine to the boy cup-bearer, blooming in beauty, eager, as a boy may be, for wisdom, a relation which is lightly touched with humour; and, last, there is the passionate love of man and woman exhibited in that ideal pair, Hatem and Zuleika.

Matthew Arnold conjectures that it was Heine whom Goethe described when he spoke of an unnamed poet who "had every other gift, but wanted love." Such a judgment pronounced on Heine, whether by Goethe or Arnold, was not just; but assuredly no one who knows Goethe himself aright could thus pronounce judgment on him. There is a melancholy poem by Matthew Arnold, "Growing Old," telling of all the sad concessions made by old age to time, which contrasts, on the one hand, with the exultant rapture of Browning's "Rabbi Ben Ezra," and on the other with the wise and luminous temperance of Emerson's admirable "Terminus." Goethe, in the *Divan*, also enumerates an old man's losses, but his tone is not one of depression, for something—and that the most precious thing of all—remains:

> "'The years,' thou sayest, 'take so much away:
> The proper pleasure of the senses' play,
> The sweet recall of loveliest wiles and words
> Last eve; nor vantage true it now affords
> To sweep from land to land; no princely token
> Of merit recognised, no praises spoken,
> Once welcome, now delight; no more avails
> Action for joy; thy courage quails and fails.
> Remains one special thing I know not of?'
>
> Enough remains! Illumined thought and love!"

Goethe, if ever any man, was not lacking in aspiration and effort toward intellectual attainment; but he makes his confession of faith that there is another door of knowledge than that which is entered by the intellect—(the "markets" of the opening line are doubtless all the various marts where learning may be purchased):

> "Markets stir the buyer's greed;
> But knowledge puffeth up indeed.
> Who looks around with quiet eye
> Learns how love doth edify.

Didst day and night thy pains bestow
Much to hear and much to know,
Now hearken at another door,
How to learn a wiser lore.
Shall Justice dwell in thee, thou must
Feel in God something that is just;
Who flames with some pure love alone
Will by the loving God be known."

There are charming poems, in the same book of the *Divan* from which this is taken, pleading for generous treatment of the poor—a poet's pleading that pictures the grace and speechless eloquence of the suppliant's attitude—and for that large charity consisting in a gift of self, "To whom thou givest thyself indeed, him as thine own self thou wilt love," a memorable word of counsel borrowed from the Pend-Nameh.

From a volume of lyrics designed, in part, to render for readers of the West something of the spirit of Hafiz and of Eastern poetry, "the immoderate passion for wine, half forbidden," could not, as Goethe says, be omitted, nor the delight inspired in old age by the grace of youth, with the answering feeling of reverence for illuminated old age and its heights of wisdom felt by the young. "The passionate attachment," he writes, "of a child for an old man is not a rare phenomenon. . . . But nothing is more touching than the aspirations of the boy, who, impressed by the lofty spirit of one who is old, experiences an inward amazement and a certain presentiment that something of like kind may develop within himself." Such is the motive—wholly spiritual—which determines Goethe's conception of the cup-bearer in the ninth Book of the *Divan*, and his relation to the aged poet for whom he serves the wine. Goethe had found models for his cup-bearer in a son of Professor Paulus, of Heidelberg, and a young waiter who attended him at Wiesbaden. The great poet of the East loves his half-forbidden wine as Goethe loves his flask of Eilfer—wine of the great vintage of the year eleven—placed before him "by Rhine and Main, in Neckar vale," and to join him over which he invites Hafiz to quit the cups of Paradise. Though he sits often silent and apart, the poet of the *Divan* loves the shifting, stirring, sounding, multitudinous tavern-life, so rich in a various humanity. It has in it something of the iridescence and of the rumours of the sea. Even that wild tumult at earliest morning, when torches flared, flutes shrilled, tabors rattled and insults flew, brought him a fuller sense of life and of the love of life. What if folk declare that he has never rightly learnt the proprieties of manners and morals! At least he wisely keeps far from certain other fiercer disputes—the wrangling of the doctors and the schools.

But the poet, by the very fact that he is a poet, often errs through indiscretion; the boy who bears the beaker is in some ways more prudent than he, and may even become guardian and counsellor of the sage whom he regards with so much reverence. Song in itself is a betrayal; and when the wine mounts to his head, and he smites the table with his fist, what rash words escape him, while in corners sit shavelings with cowled heads, who lurk and spy upon his infirmities! True, the wine he drinks is old and sound, and if the Prophet's prohibition must be disregarded it is better to sin for this than for a paltry and insipid liquor:

> "Damned for poor stuff that turns you sick
> Were to be twice a heretic."

And which of us can escape some intoxication?

Youth itself is drunkenness without the grape; love, poetry, the passion for knowledge, the enthusiasm of religion—in each of these a heady element lies hidden. Still it cannot be denied that the poet sometimes exceeds measure in his cups, and next morning, troubled by what the Persians name "Bidamag buden," and the Germans "caterwauling," comes late and with a languid step from his room. Then it is the part of the faithful boy to endeavour to restore the Master, whom he reveres in spite of his lapses from wisdom, to his better self:

"There on the terrace I would steep
  Your sense in the reviving air,
And in your eyes gaze long and deep,
  Till you shall kiss the cup-bearer.

Earth's not the cavern you suppose,
  With brood and nest 'tis ever gay,
Rose-wafts and attar of the rose,
  And bulbul sings as yesterday."

The people in the market-place hail the Master as the great poet; but the boy, into whose heart his wisdom has sunk, can commune with him even when words are few or none:

"They have their worth, the rhymes which throng;
  Hushed thought is better and more dear;
Give, then, to other folk your song,
  Give silence to the cup-bearer."

Most ennobling communion of all is that of the midsummer night, when the twilight of evening almost meets the uprise of the dawn, when Aurora burns with love for Hesperus, and yet in the Eastern midnight heavens the constellations flame. The boy's heart is full of the lore which he has learnt from the Master, while they both gaze at the vast procession of the planets:

"I know that this o'erhanging sky,
This infinite, you love to view,
While yonder cressets magnify
Each one the other in the blue;

And who flames brightest will but say—
'Here in my allotted place I shine;
Willed God that you a broader ray
Should cast, your lamps were bright as mine.'"

Presently it is great morning, and the worn-out boy murmurs to himself in drowsy tones:

"Me thy long hoped-for gift at last contents—
God's presence known in all the elements;
How lovingly thou givest it! yet above
All other things the loveliest is thy love."

And over the fair young sleeper the Master bends:

"Sweetly he sleeps, and sleep is fairly earned!
Dear boy, who hast poured the wine the Master drinks,
From friend and teacher thou, so young, hast learned,
Unforced, unpunished all the old man thinks.
Now the delicious tide of health is flush
In every limb; new life comes momently;
I drink once more, but not a sound! hush, hush!
That, wakening not, I may have joy in thee."

With these words, which sum up the spirit of the whole, the *Book of the Cup-bearer* closes.

During his visit to Frankfurt, in the autumn of 1814, Goethe had the pleasure of personal intercourse with his friend and correspondent, the banker Willemer, a man of generous heart and cultured intelligence. Willemer was in his fifty-fifth year, more than ten years younger than Goethe. In his house lived his widowed daughter by a first wife, and Maria Anna Jung, whom Willemer had removed from the temptations of the stage when she was sixteen years old, and brought to his house to be the companion of his younger daughters. She was now thirty, and before the close of Goethe's visit to the South she became Willemer's third wife. Marianne's pleasant, ringleted face is a witness to her good humour and her good sense. She had bright social gifts, sang admirably, wrote graceful verses, and had an enthusiastic veneration for the genius of Goethe, her husband's friend. That she became the model for the Zuleika of the *West-Eastern Divan* is certain; that a few beautiful poems in the collection are substantially hers cannot be doubted. She accepted her part as Zuleika with pride and pleasure, and played up to the part with spirit and not without a sense of humour. The poems are poems of passionate love; but to squander sentiment and romance on the relation of Goethe and the good Marianne is to turn to waste what should be reserved for better uses. The relation was absolutely honest; the passion was born for the imagination from a friendship which was of the happiest kind, and which endured without interruption, though after 1815 they never met, up to Goethe's last days. The secret of Marianne's contributions to the *Divan* was well kept; but it was noticed, of course, that in the following stanza of one of Hatem's poems the rhyme of the original text where "Hatem" stands must have been supplied by the name of Goethe:

> "As sombre mountain walls the beauty
> Of morn will flush, you bring me shame,
> And once more is known to *Hatem*
> Springtime's breath and summer's flame."

Marianne Willemer disclosed the facts not long before her tranquil death at the age of seventy-six.

The incidents and accidents which gave rise to several of these poems are known; they are interesting —interesting especially to the anecdote-monger; but they were unknown to the earlier readers who enjoyed the *Divan*, and in truth the actual incidents are the shadows, while the poems themselves—creatures of imaginative moods—are the realities. It adds a certain pleasure to the verses beginning:

> "Come, dearest, come, wind round my brow this band!
> Thy fingers only make the turban fair,"

to learn that on Goethe's sixty-sixth birthday, spent with the Willemers at their delightful country house, the Gerbermühle, he received from Marianne the gift of a muslin turban with a laurel wreath. At the Frankfurt fair she bought a Turkish Order of the Sun and Moon, and suddenly came upon her husband and Goethe, for whom the purchase was meant, and there were happy smiles, followed a little later by Hatem's interpretation of the symbolism of his new possession:

> "Be this an image of the joy we have won!
> Herein I see refigured me and thee;
> Me, my beloved, thou hast named thy Sun;
> Come, give it proof, sweet Moon, enclasping me."

From Frankfurt he sent her a leaf of the Indian plant, the Gingo Biloba, emblem of perfect friendship; but the poem seems to have been transmitted through her step-daughter, Rosette Städel. When she sang for him from Mozart's opera she was Goethe's "little Don Juan"; when she bustled and overbore in household affairs she was his "little Blücher." They played at letters in cypher to be read by references to page and line of Hammer's translation of Hafiz, and Goethe, in his verse, commended to the diplomatists of Europe the use of such a cypher. They agreed as Eastern lovers to think of each other in absence when the moon orbed to the full, and so the charming lyric, *Vollmondnacht*, came into being. The terrace of the poem, which tells of the ring dreamed of as lost in the Euphrates, is the terrace of the Gerbermühle. The visit of Willemer and his wife to Heidelberg suggested the great lyric, with its cosmic theory of love and Goethe's theory of colours involved, *Wiederfinden*. The chestnut trees of the Heidelberg Castle gardens inspired the exquisite song, "An vollen Büschelzweigen." At Darmstadt Zuleika wrote her address to the East Wind, and again at Darmstadt, some days later, her lovelier song to the West Wind. All these details are interesting to the literary student, and especially to the literary anecdote-monger.

I will confess that it was the beauty of two lines in the *Zuleika Book* that indentured me to the busy idle task of trying to translate what cannot be translated—the last two lines of a quatrain by Hatem:

"Is it possible, sweet Love, I hold thee close,
Hear the divine voice pealing musical?
Always impossible doth seem the rose,
And inconceivable the nightingale!"

Those two lines went straight from German into English. It might be possible also to make Bagdad, with its sometime population of a million and a half, subservient to the use of a solitary lover:

"Are your love and you apart
Far as East from West. The heart,
Swift runner, o'er the waste will start:
'Tis its own guide, go where it may;
Bagdad for lovers lies not far away."

And then there was Hudhud, the crested hoopoe, that served, according to Oriental legend, as go-between for Solomon and the Queen of Sheba; might not such a bird be captured for the uses of those who need her? Goethe was geologising when Hudhud ran along the path:

"Shells of the ancient sea
I sought in stones, shells turned to stone ;
Hudhud with stately pace,
Spreading abroad her crown,
Flaunted with drollest air ;
It was life's raillery
That mocked at death."

But Hudhud learnt such wisdom from Solomon that she can serve as page and envoy not to geologists alone, but to representatives of all the arts and faculties.

It is difficult to represent by examples these love-poems of Goethe's elder years, for the collection has much variety in feeling, manner and metre, and many of the lyrics have a special beauty which cannot be found in others. The following poem was probably at first designed to find a place in the *Book of Zuleika*, but, the *Book of Timur* needing an addition to that piece which tells of Napoleon's campaign in Russia, a fourth stanza was appended, and a new idea—the tyrannous egoism of lovers—was introduced to fit it to its altered position.

To Zuleika.

To flatter thee with incensed air,
Thy mounting pleasure to complete,
A thousand rosebuds opening fair
Must shrink and shrivel in the heat.

One little phial, at whose lips
Age-long the snared scent lies enfurled,
And slender as thy finger tips
—To compass this demands a world ;

A world of living motions fine,
Which, in their passionate press and throng,
The bulbul's coming notes divine,
And all his soul-awakening song.

GOETHE'S WEST-EASTERN DIVAN

Why with their griefs be overgloomed
 If joy through perished things soar free?
Were not a myriad souls consumed
 To 'stablish Timur's tyranny?

Just forty years previously, when Goethe was a wonderful young man of five-and-twenty, Lili—the daughter of a Frankfurt banker—had been his love, and some of his most charming early lyrics had been addressed to her. It may be that here, in Frankfurt, Marianne had mischievously mocked the old poet for his facility and versatility in finding appropriate objects for the gifts of song that lay in him. On a glorious morning of September 1815, in view of the Castle at Heidelberg, he either made his apology or anticipated her playful satire:

"*Zuleika:* Much have you sung, be it confessed,
 And here or there the verse addressed,
 Penned in your own rare charactery,
 With pomp of binding, marge of gold,
 Faultless each point and stroke inscrolled,
 Ay, many a tome to allure the eye;
 Say, did not each such missive prove,
 Wherever sent, a pledge of love?

Hatem: Yes, and in sweet and potent eyes,
 Wreathed smiles foretelling extasies,
 In dazzling teeth of youthful pride,
 In eyelash-dart and snaky tress
 Fallen o'er a bosom's loveliness,
 Thousandfold dangers may be spied:
 Think then how long since, think and guess,
 Zuleika has been prophesied!"

But an attempt must be made, though much of the grace of the original may be lost, to exhibit Marianne herself as a poetess, and what better example can be chosen than her song to the West Wind, which every German singer knows in a beautiful musical arrangement? It may be noted that in the second stanza there is a doubtful reading; the whole weight of external evidence is against the reading "fields" (*auen*) and in favour of "eyes" (*augen*), which yet, after all, may be a printer's error:

"Ah, West Wind, for thy dewy wing
How sorely do I envy thee,
For tidings thou to him canst bring
Of grief his absence lays on me!

The waving of thy pinions light
Wakes silent yearning in the heart;
From flowers and fields, from wood and height
Breathed on by thee the quick tears start.

Yet these soft wanderings of thy breath
Cool the hurt eyelids and restore;
Ah, I should faint with pain to death,
Hoped I not sight of him once more.

Haste then to my beloved, haste,
Speak to his heart in gentlest strain;
No shade across his spirit cast,
And hide, ah, hide from him my pain!

Tell him, but tell with lips discreet,
His love's the life by which I live;
Glad sense where life with love shall meet
His nearness to my heart will give."

To confess the truth, the songs of Marianne have more of the direct, simple lyrical cry, or lyrical sigh, in them than certain of Goethe's more ingenious or more elaborate poems of these elder years.

My last specimen from the *Zuleika Book* must, however, be a poem by Hatem. It is that which tells of the origin of rhyme, and has special reference to the interchange of verses between Goethe and Marianne:

"Behramgur first discovered rhyme, men say;
Stress of pure joy through speech deliverance found;
Dilaram, she his hours' sweet friend, straightway
Replied with kindred word and echoing sound.

So, dearest, you were parted from my side,
  That rhyme's glad usage should become my own;
Unenvious I even of the Sassanide,
  Behramgur; mine the art has also grown.

This book you awaked; it is a gift from you;
  My full heart spake, for joy was at its prime;
From your sweet life rang back the answer true,
  As glance to glance so rhyme replied to rhyme.

Now let these accents reach you from afar;
  The word arrives, though tone and sound disperse;
Is it not the mantle sown with many a star?
  Is it not love's high-transfigured Universe?"

The attention of readers of the *Zuleika Book* may be specially directed to the beautiful unrhymed poem beginning with the words, "Die schön geschriebenen" (No. 18 of Loeper's edition), and, as an example of the ghazel, to the fascinating litany of love with which the Book closes.

The *West-Eastern Divan* consists of twelve Books. The Parables of the East form so distinctive a part of Oriental literature that Goethe could not pass them by. In his prose study which concludes the volume he tries to classify these parables—the ethical, the ascetic, the mystical, and others; but he leaves it to the intelligent reader to place each of his own parables under whatever rubric may seem right. Some are devout, some are moral, some embody a fragment of humorous wisdom. The last of the series, entitled "It is good," may serve as an example:

"In Paradise, where moonbeams played,
Jehovah found in slumber deep
Adam far sunk, and lightly laid
By him a little Eve asleep;
In earthly bounds lay there at rest
Two of God's thoughts, the loveliest!
'Good!' guerdoning Himself, He cried,
And passed with lingering look aside.

No wonder at our glad amaze
When eye meets eye in quickening gaze,
As if we had flown from regions far
Near Him to be, whose thoughts we are.
If He should call us, be it so,
Let but the summons be for two.
These arms thy bounds be, thy abode,
Dearest of all the thoughts of God!"

The *Book of the Parsees* is mainly occupied with the noble "Legacy of the Old Persian Faith," uttered to his disciples by a poor and pious brother now about to depart from earth. The worship of the sun and of fire, seemingly so abstracted, is regarded by Goethe as profoundly practical. The dying saint enthusiastically aspires towards the light, but his lesson for his brethren is wholly concerned with conduct; "daily fulfilment of hard services"—such is his legacy in a word; their part it will be to keep pure, as far as human effort can, the soil, the air, the water of the canal, and their own hearts and lives through devoted service, in order that these may be worthy to receive the divine and vivifying rays of the sun. And, as the sun rises above the peaks of Darnavend, the old man's spirit ascends from earth to be gathered from gyre to gyre of the heavens.

The *Book of Paradise* is almost purely Mohammedan; but it is at the same time West-Eastern, for, though Goethe in one poem justifies the use of sensible imagery as a symbolism, accommodated to our weakness, for the representation of ineffable things (Richard Baxter did the same), yet now and again his lips are wreathed with smiles at the material joys imagined for the heaven of Mohammed's followers. Under the starry heavens Mohammed himself stands and announces to the survivors after the battle of Bedr the glories of that Paradise which his slain warriors have already entered. The lot of women is less assured; we only know for certain of four who have passed the gate—Zuleika, who had loved Yussuf, the mother of the Christian Saviour, the wife of Mohammed, and Fatima the Fair:

"Spouse, daughter, spotless-souled,
Pure spirit with her angelic air,
In body of honey-gold."

Yet the faith and devotion of other women forbids us to despair. And, indeed, certain specially favoured beasts have been admitted—the ass on which Jesus entered the City of Prophets, the wolf, schooled in the duties of a wolf by Mohammed, the little dog that slept long centuries in the cave with the Seven Sleepers, and last, Abuherrira's cat, now purring at the master's knee, and formerly caressed by the Prophet's hand. If Zuleika the Second should be excluded from Paradise, at least an obliging Houri—and here Goethe's smile is broad—in obedience to the command of the Prophet can assume her form, and when questioned as to her identity can give such explanation as she pleases.

The poem, "Admission," records the dialogue between a Houri, warder of the gate, and a poet—assuredly a German poet—who craves for entrance:

"*Houri:* To-day I stand, a warder true,
Before the gate of Paradise,
And scarce I know what I should do,
Thou comest in such a doubtful guise.

Art thou in very truth allied
To these our folk, the Moslem race?
What combats keen, what service tried,
Commend thee to the heavenly place?

With those heroic souls dost dare
To number thee? Thy wounds display!
For they will glorious things declare,
And I shall lead thee on thy way.

Poet: Why all this nice punctilio? What!
Promptly my right of entrance grant;
For I have been a man, and that
Means I have been a combatant.

Keen-visioned thou, but look more near,
Traverse this breast with piercing sight;
Wounds of life's perfidy, see here,
See here the wounds of love's delight!

And yet I sang in credulous wise
My love's pure faith inviolate,
And that the world, which whirls and flies,
Is gracious nor can be ingrate.

I wrought with men of rarest worth,
And this attained, that round my name
Love from the fairest hearts on earth
Shone like an aureole of flame.

No mean man hast thou chosen. Nay,
Give me thy hand, for I devise
On these slight fingers day by day
To reckon the eternities."

Much of the spirit of the whole collection of lyrics is expressed in the opening poem, with which we may bring our quotations to an end:

Hejira.

North and West and South upbreaking,
Thrones are shattering, empires quaking!
Fly thou to the untroubled East,
There the patriarchs' air to taste;
What with love and wine and song
Chiser's fount will make thee young.

There, 'mid things pure and just and true,
The race of men I would pursue
Back to the well-head primitive,
Where still from God did they receive
Heavenly lore in earthly speech,
Nor beat the brain to pass their reach.

GOETHE'S WEST-EASTERN DIVAN

Where ancestors were held in awe,
Each alien worship banned by law ;
In nonage bounds I am gladly caught,
Broad faith be mine and narrow thought,
As when the word held sway, and stirred
Because it was a spoken word.

Where shepherds haunt would I be seen,
And rest me in oases green ;
When with the caravan I fare,
Shawl, coffee, musk, my chapman's ware,
No pathway would I leave untraced
To the city from the waste.

And up and down the rough rock ways,
My comfort, Hafiz, be thy lays,
When the guide enchantingly,
From his mule-back seat on high,
Sings, to rouse the stars or scare
The lurking robber in his lair.

In bath or inn my thought would be,
Holy Hafiz, still of thee ;
Or when the veil a sweetheart lifts
From amber locks in odorous drifts ;
Ay, whispered loves of poets fire
Even the Houris to desire !

Would you envy him for this,
Or bring despite upon his bliss,
Know that words of poets rise
To the gate of Paradise,
Hover round, knock light, implore
Heavenly life for evermore.

GOETHE'S HERMANN AND DOROTHEA

GOETHE had little sympathy—at least in its application to his own poems—with that kind of curiosity which traces a work of art back to its sources. He thought that when guests are invited to a feast they may be content to enjoy the good cheer set before them without visiting the kitchen, calling upon the cook to enumerate the ingredients, and proceeding to inspect the garden where the pot-herbs grew. He himself never connected *Hermann und Dorothea* with the narrative of the exiles from Salzburg, in which it had its origin; when that narrative was pointed out as his source in the *Morgenblatt* of the year 1809 (No. 138) he uttered neither affirmation nor denial.

ON 31st October 1731, Leopold, Archbishop of Salzburg, Legate of the Holy See and Primate of Germany, issued a decree directed against his Protestant subjects, by which they were required to depart from their country, some within eight days, some after a period less terribly brief, and were forbidden ever again to enter it, upon pain, if deemed expedient, of death. Snows had already fallen. The expulsion of the Protestants during the late autumn and winter months was attended with many acts of extreme severity. In February 1732 the exiles received an invitation from Friedrich Wilhelm of Prussia to settle in his territory; Protestant princes threatened reprisals against their Roman Catholic subjects; and at length some check was placed upon the Archbishop's violence. All Protestant Europe was interested in the misfortunes of the expatriated fugitives. A pamphlet giving an account of their sufferings was published in London in 1732; it sets down the number of exiles from ten districts of the Archbishopric as 20,678; it closes with an announcement that subscriptions for their relief would be received and transmitted by certain gentlemen, lay and clerical, who are named in a list which includes among others the rector of Lambeth and the preacher in the German chapel at St. James's.

This English pamphlet does not contain the story on which Goethe's poem is founded. But in a German pamphlet of the same year it is found, and again in 1732 in a large quarto entitled *Ausführliche Historie derer Emigranten oder vertriebenen Lutheraner aus dem Erzbisthum Salzburg*. Two years later the story was repeated, as one of the evidences of providential care extended to the exiles, in Göcking's *Vollkommene Emigrationsgeschichte*. The following is the version given in the *Ausführliche Historie*:—

"In Alt-Mühl, a town lying in the Oettingen district, a worthy and well-to-do citizen had a son whom he had often—but without success—urged to marry. As the Salzburg emigrants were passing through this little town, among them was a maiden who so attracted the youth that he resolved in his heart to make her his wife, if this might be brought about. He made inquiry of the other Salzburgers respecting the girl's conduct and family, and was informed that she was the child of good honest folk, and was always well conducted, but had separated from her parents on the ground of religion, and had left them behind. Thereupon the young man went to his father, and told him that, as he had so often been urged to marry, he had now made choice of a person, if his father would allow him to have her.

When the father desired to know who this person might be, he was told that a Salzburg maiden had won his son's heart, and that if she were not to be his bride he would never marry. At this the father took alarm, and tried to dissuade him from the match. Certain friends were called in, and a pastor, in the hope that by their means his son might be brought to another way of thinking; but all was in vain. At last it seemed to the pastor that God might design some special providence in this affair, and that hence it might be for the best, in regard both to the son and to the emigrant girl; whereupon consent was finally given, and the youth was permitted to do as he pleased. Off then went the young man to his Salzburg maiden, and asked her how she liked things in this neighbourhood. 'Well indeed, sir,' answered she. 'And would you'—he went on—'be willing to act as servant in my father's house?' 'With entire content,' she replied, 'and, if he will take me, I mean to serve him faithfully and diligently'; and then she proceeded to enumerate her various accomplishments, how she could fodder cattle, milk cows, work in the fields, make hay, with much more of a like kind. Upon this the youth took her with him and presented her to his father. He asked her whether she liked his son, and would marry him. But she, knowing nothing of the matter, thought that he meant to tease her, and answered that they had no right to jeer at her: the young man had sought a servant for his father, and, if he desired to have her, she meant to serve him in all faithfulness, and honestly to earn her bread. But when the father stuck to it, and the son moreover showed his serious longing for her, she declared that if their purpose was earnest she could be well content, and she would cherish the youth as the apple of her eye. And when the son presented her with a wedding gift she placed her hand in her bosom, saying, 'I, too, must give a marriage-portion,' and handed to him a little purse in which were found two hundred ducats."

Böttiger, who held close relations with Goethe while the poem was in process of development, and who helped to negotiate its sale, states that Goethe discovered the story in 1794, and that at first he thought of converting it into a drama. The incidents were enough to form a nucleus from which other incidents might be evolved as soon as imagination came to quicken them. The personages—the youth, the maiden, the father, the pastor—were already in existence; only the mother of the young man, the apothecary, and the judge, had no prototypes in the tale of the Salzburg exiles. But Goethe, who held himself aloof from theological and ecclesiastical partisanship, could hardly have accepted with pleasure the background of this idyllic love-story—the strife of Catholic against Protestant, which drove forth the heroine from her native home. Trusting to the power of art to confer ideality upon the theme, he resolved to give it more immediate actuality by placing the incidents and characters in the present time. It was a time when events of epic proportion were occupying the attention of Europe; and behind the events lay an epic combat between great ideas respecting the life of society. The French Revolution and the upheavals which it caused in neighbouring countries provided a background of wider historical extent and of deeper ethical significance than that of the religious strife of Salzburg some sixty years previously. The interval between the composition of *Hermann und Dorothea* and the supposed time of the action was measured not by years but by months; Goethe himself, in a letter to Meyer

(5th December 1796), places the events of the poem in the preceding August. The war of France against Prussia and Austria had fluctuated to and fro in its earlier years. In 1796 the advance of the French armies under Moreau and Jourdan, after some important successes, was checked by the vigorous action of the Archduke Karl, and the French retreat which followed was marked by those cruelties which are common to a soldiery rendered desperate. The imagined scene of Goethe's poem lies near the right bank of the Rhine, perhaps in the region of Hesse-Darmstadt.

Goethe himself had witnessed and even experienced some of the hardships caused by war. In 1792 he accompanied the Grand Duke of Weimar on that disastrous campaign—led by the Duke of Brunswick—against the French Revolutionary forces which closed with the cannonade of Valmy, and a retreat rendered inexpressibly miserable by insufficiency of provisions and the torrents of autumnal rain. In Goethe's account of his experiences, *Campagne in Frankreich*, will be found the origin of several incidents and reflections in *Hermann und Dorothea*. He had himself seen a young woman who, like Dorothea's companion, had given birth to an infant during her flight ; an old female camp-follower made imperious requisitions on behalf of the mother and new-born child, and, as she knew no French, Goethe himself expounded in words her passionate gestures. At Etain, on the retreat, the master and mistress of the house in which he found shelter were filled with alarm on behalf of a son, who like Dorothea's betrothed had been carried away by the passions of the time, and had been hurried into the vortex of the revolutionary maelstrom in Paris ; at his parents' request he had returned home, deserting the party to which his feelings had bound him, and, now that he was inscribed in the list of traitors, he found his new allies overwhelmed with defeat. Thus through Goethe's personal experiences and through the excitement of his own day a new life and energy were infused into the story derived from the earlier years of the eighteenth century.

" *Hermann und Dorothea*," said Goethe to Eckermann in the year 1825, " is almost the only one of my larger poems that still gives me pleasure ; I can never read it without deep interest. I love it best in the Latin translation ; there it seems to me nobler, as if, as regards the form, it had reverted to its source." The poem was the creation of the best period of Goethe's maturity, a period when he had escaped from the storm and stress of his earlier years, when he was delivered from the excessive pressure of public business that had proved alien to his genius, when the influences of classical art in Italy had sunk deep into his spirit, when the Revolutionary wars had animated in his heart the love of his own country, when, above all, he enjoyed the stimulus and the support of Schiller's comradeship.

Some of Goethe's larger works suffered from the way in which they came to be written. A fragment was produced ; there followed a long interval during which rival interests drew the poet away in other directions ; and when he resumed his work it was perhaps in an altered spirit or a different mood. Or, again, he first adopted the medium of prose, and at a later date recast his work in verse. The process by which *Hermann und Dorothea* was brought into being certainly tended to give the poem that harmony, or rather that unity, by which it is pre-eminently characterised. The germ dropped into Goethe's mind and lay there for a considerable time ; it was borne about and nourished in silence; although the creative energy lapsed away when some two-thirds of the poem had been swiftly set down in writing, the capacity for careful and sympathetic revision remained, and a second creative impulse, which carried the work to a close, followed after a brief interval. There were few perplexing knots to untie, or tangles to unravel. Goethe's interest in his work never really waned during the period of creation. Some seven or eight months—from August 1796 to March 1797—sufficed for creation and in great part for exact revision. "It is in fact remarkable," wrote Schiller, in a letter of 18th April 1797, "how swiftly Nature gave birth to this work and how carefully and considerately Art has perfected it."

During a visit to Jena, from 8th August to 5th October, while Goethe resided in the old ducal castle, the first four cantos of *Hermann und Dorothea*, according to the original arrangement, were written. The whole poem was to be comprised in six cantos; the first four correspond to the first six as we have them in the final arrangement, according to which each of the nine cantos bears the name of one of the nine Muses. It was not until 11th September that Goethe actually "began to versify the idyl." "The execution," wrote Schiller to Körner (28th October 1796), "which, as it were, took place under my eyes, has been achieved with a lightness and swiftness incomprehensible to me; he has written over one hundred and fifty hexameters daily for nine successive days." The days from 11th September to 19th September are probably those to which Schiller refers.

The idyll, as the poem had been at first conceived, now expanded in Goethe's mind into an idyllic epic. At the close of October he found himself obliged to go to Ilmenau for a few days. "It would be a great piece of good luck," he wrote to Schiller, "if I could manage to write a portion of my epic poem while in Ilmenau; the perfect solitude of the place seems to promise something." And Schiller, two days later (31st October), sends his greeting to the lonely valley, with a wish that the fairest of the Muses may encounter his friend: "you may, at all events, there find your Hermann's little town, and probably also an apothecary and a greenhouse with stucco work." But the wind bloweth where it listeth, and no fresh inspiration came at Ilmenau. "I did not even touch the garment's hem of any one of the Muses," Goethe confesses to Schiller on his return to Weimar; all he could with advantage attempt was revision and correction. It was not, indeed, until the days of travel to Leipzig and Dessau, at the close of the year 1796 and the opening of the new year (28th December to 10th January), that the plan of the unfinished portion of the poem was fully considered and elaborated. At last, during another residence at Jena—from February 20th to the end of March 1797—the creative impulse returned, and that at a time when Goethe was confined to his room by a cold. "My work is progressing," he informed Schiller on 4th March. . . "In two more days I shall have raised the treasure, and when it is once above ground the polishing process will come of itself. It is remarkable how, towards the end, the poem inclines to its idyllic origin." The work advanced quickly to the close; the task of revision followed and was deliberately pursued. On 8th April Goethe refers to the "double headings" of the cantos, indicating that the distribution of the text into nine books, named both after the Muses and the subject-matter of each canto, was then in contemplation if not completely carried into effect. Three weeks later he writes to Meyer: "My poem is ready; it consists of 2000 hexameters, and is divided into nine cantos." *Hermann und Dorothea* was published in the *Taschenbuch für 1798*, which was issued in the late autumn of the preceding year. In the labour of revision Wilhelm von Humboldt—one of the earliest critics of the poem[1]—was ever ready with thoughtful counsel and suggestion. In 1804 a later revision was begun in conjunction with Heinrich Voss the younger, with a special view to metrical improvements. The MS., showing these emendations, remains among the Goethe archives; the alterations were not embodied in any printed text, nor can ground for real regret be found in this circumstance.

Among the forces which helped to mould the poem of *Hermann und Dorothea* Goethe's feeling towards the French Revolution was not the least important. The influences in society which make for change and the influences which make for conservation and stability are both recognised in the poem and are both justified. Goethe would not and does not deny that social progress and amelioration are themselves essential elements of true order; but he insists more strongly on the duty of preserving and maintaining the good that has already been realised in the well-being of a nation, for in the appalling danger of the time that truth seemed to be the one chiefly needed by his own country. It is possible to study Goethe's view of the Revolutionary movement in several works written under its immediate pressure—The *German Emigrants*, the *Venetian Epigrams*, the *Travels of the Sons of Megaprazon*, the *Natural Daughter*, the *Grosskophta*, the

[1] Aesthetische Versuche über Goethe's *Hermann und Dorothea*, by Wilhelm von Humboldt, 1799.

Bürgergeneral, the *Aufgeregten*, and *Reynard the Fox*; his matured wisdom will be found summarised in a conversation with Eckermann of 4th January 1824. He was no friend, he declares, of arbitrary rule. He was convinced that a great revolution is never a fault of the people; it is, on the contrary, always the consequence of faults of the government. If there exists a real necessity for a great reform among a people, "God is with it, and it prospers." God, he went on to say, was visibly with Christ and His first adherents He was also visibly with Luther: neither of these "was a friend of the established system; much more were both of them convinced that the old leaven must be got rid of, and that it would be impossible to go on and remain in the untrue, inequitable, and defective way."

But while Goethe is just to the influences that make for change, and even for revolutionary change, while, too, his sympathies were popular as much as aristocratic, he could not, he admits, be a friend to the French Revolution in the days of its power: "its horrors were too near me, and shocked me daily and hourly, whilst its beneficial results were not then to be discovered." He revolted especially from the efforts made in Germany to reproduce artificially such a state of things as had in France arisen from a great necessity:

> "Nicht dem Deutschen geziemt es, die fürchterliche Bewegung
> Fortzuleiten und auch zu wanken hierhin und dorthin."

So, through the mouth of his Hermann, the poet utters a warning against the factitious cultivation of Revolutionary sentiment by some of his own countrymen. And to Eckermann, more than a quarter of a century later, he expresses himself in the same spirit: "Nothing is good for a nation but that which arises from its own core and its own general wants; . . . All endeavours to introduce any foreign innovation, the necessity for which is not rooted in the core of the nation itself, are therefore foolish; and all premeditated revolutions of the kind are unsuccessful, for they are without God, who keeps aloof from such bungling."

Goethe could not forget that in his younger days he was himself a leader of revolution in things of the mind. *Götz von Berlichingen* was a cry for freedom; both in substance and form it revolted against eighteenth-century conventions. In *Prometheus* he asserted in the boldest spirit the independence and individuality of the artist. But the years of public service at Weimar had taught him that freedom is to be attained only through wise limitation, through intellectual clearness and order, through purity of feeling and through activity within a definite sphere. His scientific studies had taught him to expect much from a gradual evolution; he had come to believe that the way of development is not a way of violent cataclysms. His studies in art led him to value simplicity and repose as the elements from which beauty arises rather than the turbulence of passion or the straining of immoderate desire. In Italy, in the presence of the masterpieces of classical sculpture, he felt that intellectual sanity and obedience to law produce nobler results in art than are attained by emotional violence or unmeasured caprices of the imagination. In such a poem as *Hermann und Dorothea* Goethe was really assisting in the work of the European revolution of the eighteenth century, for he was delivering the ideal man—true manhood, true womanhood—from the faded conventions of the earlier art of the century, and also from the violences and sentimentalities of his own younger days. But the spirit in which he attempted this was far removed from the spirit which sought for freedom through the machinery of brand-new constitutions or the machinery of the guillotine. His word to the German people was that for them at least there was a better way—to preserve, to maintain, to develop what was good; to work for humanity through those limitations imposed by the love of things that are near and real, the home, the little vineyard, the little town with its kindly neighbours, father and mother, and wife and child; and, when need arises, the country and the nation which include all that is nearest and dearest, all that is best and most real:

"'All the firmer amidst this universal disruption
Be Dorothea the tie! And thus we will hold and continue
True to each other, and still maintain the good that is given us;
For the man who in wavering times has a mind ever wavering
Only increases the evil and spreads it wider and wider;
But who firmly stands, he moulds the world to his posture.
Not the German's work should it be, this fearful commotion
Onward to urge, or to reel in his courses this way and that way.
'Here we take our stand!' Such be our word and our action."[1]

Readers of *Hermann und Dorothea* have expressed surprise at the union effected by the poet between German life and manners, German thought and sentiment, on the one hand, and on the other a Greek feeling for art and Greek artistic methods. To admirers of the poem this has seemed an achievement almost miraculous. One excellent French critic, however, Edmond Scherer—and his words were quoted apparently with approval by Matthew Arnold—found something inharmonious, something even ludicrous in what he styled "the antico-modern and heroico-middle-class idyll of Goethe." For him the poem was at best a feat, and not quite a successful

[1] In the above paragraph I have used some sentences from *Goethe and the French Revolution*, an Address to the English Goethe Society, published in my volume, *New Studies in Literature*.

feat, of ingenuity. Goethe's manner of proceeding, he declared, is at bottom "that of parody," and the turn of a straw "would set the reader laughing at these farm-horses transformed into coursers, these village innkeepers and apothecaries who speak with the magniloquence of a Ulysses or a Nestor." This, according to Scherer, is not sincere poetry at all, but a factitious work, "the product of an exquisite dilettantism."

It ought to have been perceived that a genuine Hellenism is in no respect opposed to truth of observation and sincerity of feeling. Because Goethe was Greek he must—when dealing with a German theme—be genuinely and profoundly German. His earlier conception, indeed, of Greek art led him to some extent away from reality towards a factitious ideal. That earlier conception had in it certain elements of the eighteenth-century conventional feeling for classical art. It was supposed that ideality and the repose of classical art were attained by a process of abstraction, which thinned away details, and regarded with indifference, if not with a lofty disdain, whatever is individual. From this error of the pseudo-classical school Goethe did not wholly escape; but an inborn realism in general saved his work, even at its worst, from lifelessness or insipidity. Before *Hermann und Dorothea* was written he had visited Italy, and his eyes had carried into his imagination and his soul the life and the lesson of Greek sculpture. Here was the human body presented not in an abstraction, but in its essential truth; and the ideal was attained not by turning away from reality, but by seizing some moment of the highest physical and moral life, in action or in dignified repose, and by enabling that life at its fullest to declare and manifest itself; for which manifestation it uses every means that aids a deploying of the inward forces, omitting only—and that not so much by deliberation as by instinct—such dross of accident as rather obscures than interprets the vital energy. And now, having chosen a little German town as the scene of his epic-idyll, and German men and women as his actors, Goethe was constrained by the very principles of Greek art to manifest our common humanity through its German presentment, and to do this with such a profound truth of feeling that in and through reality the ideal should emerge.

The Homeric poems filled Goethe with inexhaustible delight; but the speculations of Wolf had led him at this time to feel that the path to modern poetry of an epic character is not barred by the vast figure of Homer, with whom contention or competition were hopeless. Many singers—he now held—had contributed to the material from which arose the *Iliad* and the *Odyssey*. Why should not a modern man also sing in a kindred spirit concerning modern life and action and suffering? Are not the elementary and primitive wants and desires and sufferings and joys and actions of man and woman extant in the world still as in the days of the singers of Greece? And if a modern poet should deal with the world that lies around him in a spirit akin to that of Homer, is there anything incongruous in a certain general resemblance to the Homeric manner? If in a few passages there should be actual reminiscence of the style and the language of Homer, can this rightly be regarded, to use Scherer's word, as "parody"? Or ought we not rather to view such passages as a suggestion to the reader that, although the Homeric *naïveté* (if there is, indeed, such a thing) no longer is possible and self-consciousness has come in its place, yet, if men will but lift up their eyes and look at the world aright, there are things to be seen in it like those of which Homer sang ? The horses which Hermann tackles are in reality spirited, majestic creatures, and Hermann himself is a noble and vigorous youth. Let us no longer be blinded by what is familiar and customary, let us envisage the reality, and we shall perceive a youth who can bear comparison with any Grecian charioteer, and steeds as strong and graceful as those that whirled the chariots on the fields of Troy. A sculptor walking along the countryside to-day may discover in the pose of a sower, or a reaper, or a woman drawing water at a well, the attitudes of heroes or of gods. It is the dulness of our wearied vision which hides the fact ; and may not the poet remind us once or twice—with a slightly ironic smile upon his lips—that nature is still Homeric ?

Goethe's epic idyll was not without a parentage in eighteenth-century German literature. Here it is enough to note that its immediate predecessors was the *Luise* of Johann Heinrich Voss. Both in contents and in form the poem of Voss exerted an influence on *Hermann und Dorothea*, which may be recognised without detracting from the glory or the originality of the work of Goethe. The *Luise* is written in hexameters, in the practice of which Voss, the translator of Homer, acquired a degree of mastery which had not been reached by Klopstock ; it is an idyll of German life ; it adapts the forms of Greek art to the rendering of a German theme. The household of a pastor, living in the country, forms the centre of Voss's idyllic poem ; the birthday of the pastor's daughter Luise is celebrated in the neighbouring woods, hard by a lake, in a simple, rural fashion ; the visit of her betrothed and the incidents that lead up to the wedded union of happy man and maid are related, not without a certain grace of feeling and of manner. Strength of characterisation, depth of passion, breadth of interest, largeness of conception, the art of composition, are wholly or almost wholly wanting to the poem. The idylls, published separately in 1783 and 1784, were revised and brought together to form the completed poem in 1795. Voss's *Luise* became popular, for it fell in with two streams of tendency—first the return to nature of the pre-Revolutionary period, when Rousseau was a master of men's feelings and imagination, and, secondly, the new sense of the beauty of Greek art, partly developed and largely guided by the writings of Winckelmann.

"I still remember," Goethe wrote to Schiller (28th February 1798), "the genuine enthusiasm which I felt for the pastor of Grünau, when he first appeared in *The Mercury*; I read it aloud so often that I still know the greater part of it by heart; and I gained much good from it, for the delight I had in it became at last productive in me, and tempted me to work in the same *genre*—which resulted in *Hermann*, and who knows what may yet arise out of it?" Recognising the faults and imperfections of Voss's work—its lack of deep passion, its lack of general ideas, its deficiency in concentration and vigorous continuity, its pettiness of detail—Goethe did not scruple to accept from it whatever could serve his own purpose, which, besides the general impulse of the *genre*, some characteristics of diction, and the metrical form, included a few hints for particular passages, and whatever he appropriated was ennobled. Without *Luise*, as he indicates, *Hermann und Dorothea* might never have come into existence; yet the true glory of the parent is derived almost wholly from the more illustrious child.

"I have tried in the epic crucible to separate what

is purely human in the life of a small town from its dross "—so Goethe wrote to Meyer (5th December 1796)—" and to reflect from a little mirror the great movements in progress on the stage of the world." To a superficial gazer nothing could seem more prosaic, nothing more trivial than the life of such a petty German town; and Goethe does not shrink from any realistic details which help to give a body, visible and almost tangible, to the spirit of his poem. The Golden Lion inn, looking out on the market-place, might have been found a century ago in any one of a score of Rhineland towns; the old-fashioned garden of the apothecary, with its quaint figures, and grotto adorned with spars and shell-work, may have been known to Goethe at Ilmenau or elsewhere; nothing in the small dull place is so much to be wondered at and admired as the wealthy neighbour's house, splendid with white stucco and green paint. Is it not a poor scene for an epic poem? and what can be found here to interest the imagination or the feelings?

What, indeed, can be found except the bounty of nature and its beauty, what except the fulness of a rich and beautiful humanity? Here are wedded happiness, a home presided over by womanly tact and sympathy; here are pity for those in need, the heart that plans and the hand that executes good deeds; here are neighbourly good-will and civic virtues, the love of child and of parent, affection for the homestead and the soil, patriotic pride and passion, the wisdom of illuminated manhood, maidenly discretion, maidenly service and heroic strength, and a noble sense of personal dignity; here, above all, is the love of man and maid, swift and final in its happy election, and the sudden unfolding of character under the sunshine of a new and deep affection.

And as a background for the personages and their passions we see not merely the little town, which Goethe views with a feeling of kindly regard that is touched by humour, but a landscape wealthy in summer beauty and wholly humanised. Mere description of external nature, detached from the actors and the action of his poem, is not sought by the poet of *Hermann und Dorothea ;* it is indeed hardly permitted by his conception of a narrative poem ; but the environment of the actors becomes an essential feature or condition of the incidents. The garden, with its apple trees, the honeysuckle bower, the vineyard slopes, where the purple clusters hang heavy and warm in the sun, the field and bending corn crop, are known to us because the mother, now setting right a prop, now brushing away a caterpillar, traverses these as she seeks the distraught Hermann. The pear tree on the summit, which is a landmark for all the neighbourhood, shelters the youth in his lonely perturbation of spirit at noon-day, and in its shadow, while the moonlight shines clear around, he sits with Dorothea's hand in his own. Up the steps of the vineyard path the mother climbs, and it is here in their shadowy descent that Hermann's beloved, stumbling, finds her support upon his breast and shoulder. The linden grove near the neighbouring village, with the well and the sheltered greensward, lives in our imagination because it is here that Hermann awaits the tidings of Dorothea brought by the friendly emissaries, and here that the lovers lean over the water and see, in its mirrored blue of heaven, their own wavering forms as they nod and greet each the other. With little play of what has been termed the "pathetic fallacy," Nature even may be said to cooperate in the action of the poem. The brooding heat of the summer day breaks in the nocturnal thunderstorm. With her wounded sense of virgin dignity Dorothea is about to quit the shelter of the Golden Lion, and go forth, bearing her little bundle, into the night and tempest and downpour of rain; at which moment, while the thunder still growls without, the kindly mother interposes, and there is a clearing at least in the moral atmosphere. The heavens themselves—if there were no stronger powers at work—have made it impossible to permit Dorothea to leave her true home, and thus, as it were, are in league with those who have plotted to render her happiness assured.

There is another and a more formidable thunderstorm—that in the social and political world—which adds largeness and something of terror to the scene, and which at the same time serves to endear to our feelings the tranquil well-being of the little German town. "Who will deny," cries the Judge, "that his heart was uplifted within him when he saw the first beam of the risen sun, and heard of Rights of Man, common to all, of Liberty the inspirer of spirits, and Equality worthy to be praised?" But the sky darkened; and the strife became one not for liberty, but for an evil domination. What, after all, if in this little town and among its quiet citizens there were more of true wisdom—at least for Germany and for the immediate present—than could be derived from the council-chambers of revolutionary Paris? The homely neighbourhood becomes for the moment a centre in which the principles of stability and orderly progress are seen in contention with the principles of the revolutionary reform. Dorothea's first lover, caught by a generous enthusiasm and possessed by the new republican hopes, has abandoned her to the chances of the time, which have driven her forth, a wanderer from her home, and he himself, having effected nothing, has perished amid the strife of ignoble greeds and ambitions. No one can think harshly of the error of his rash gallantry. Hermann is also fired to enthusiasm; the lover rises to the patriot; life has grown good to him, and the homestead and the little town are dearer than ever before. To maintain and to defend what is of so great worth shall be his task; and the future of Dorothea is safe in his steadfast and courageous hands.

The conversations are not, as Edmond Scherer represents them, conducted with "the magniloquence of a Ulysses or a Nestor." They are full of pleasant familiarities, and they are often pleasantly touched with a humour, of which the reader, though not always the speaker, is conscious. Magniloquence is monotonous, but the talk of the host of the Golden Lion and his neighbours rises and falls with a natural variety. And with each speaker it is admirably characteristic. With the Pastor it can rise into the region of general ideas. He is still young in years, but he has received the best gifts of culture both sacred and profane. Faith and hope and charity dwell in his soul, and therefore his heart has been open to the deeper truths of human life. Through his lips Goethe utters some of his own spiritual wisdom, and it is uttered with the simplicity and directness of true insight. His trust in the ways and the wisdom of Nature is large. The *Leichtsinn* of men, which to the Apothecary seems an offence, is seen by the Pastor to be a wise provision of Nature; curiosity seeks for what is new, and through an interest in what is new we pass to a regard for what is useful, and what is useful leads on in turn to what is good. The whole of human existence is viewed by the Pastor as a full and noble harmony. His friend, the Apothecary, has told how in childhood the thought of death was impressed upon him as a thought which might quell or control his youthful impatience. The lines which follow, words of the Pastor presenting life and death as parts of a harmonious and perpetual circuit, are not found in the MS. preserved at Weimar among the Goethe archives; they were a noble after-thought of the poet, and, while wholly in keeping with the young Pastor's spirit, they lie very near to Goethe's own view of life. To the wise man death becomes life, for it urges him to activity; for the pious it strengthens the hopes of futurity; death ought not to be shown to a child as death; let the young learn the worth of a riper age and let the aged look towards youth, so that both may rejoice in the perpetual cycle of existence, and life may be fulfilled in life—

> "dass beide des ewigen Kreises
> Sich erfreuen und so sich Leben im Leben vollende!"

And at this moment the door opens and those who are to bear life onward into the future, with its fulness of good, Hermann and his future bride, "das herrliche Paar," are seen. All is natural here, and all is simple; but never were envoys of a great power more majestically announced than these representatives of life and love by the undersigned appositeness of the Pastor's words.

It is only on this occasion that any one of the speakers attains so clear and rare an altitude. In general the Pastor's wisdom is that of illuminated good sense; he is no dreamer of dreams; and be it remembered to his credit that he can drive a pair of horses round a difficult turning as skilfully as Hermann himself. So also, speaking figuratively, in managing Hermann's love affair, at the moment when Dorothea's outraged sense of dignity threatens a catastrophe, he drives boldly and comes dangerously near an upset; it is only his quick eye and steady hand that avert disaster. The man of ideas, after all, may prove himself an excellent man of affairs.

The Apothecary is a contrasted figure; yet he is not an unserviceable coadjutor in spying out the land in Hermann's interest. He is well advanced in years; his memories go back to the days long since, when all things were better than they are now; grottoes, and shell work, and stone figures have gone out of fashion, and the good old custom of rational wooing by friendly family negotiation has passed away. From first to last Goethe gently smiles, with a not unkindly ironic smile, at the good neighbour, whose cure is that of bodies, not of souls. The timidity of his prudence heightens our sense of the Pastor's more generous prudence, which does not shrink from the ventures of faith. The Apothecary must indulge his grumble against the townsfolk who have hurried after the poor fugitives for sake of the pleasure of an idle excitement; yet he has been one of the curious sightseers himself; he shrinks from a narration of the fugitives' distress, and thereupon proceeds with his tale, omitting no harrowing particular; when his impatience is rising he relates how in childhood he had been cured for ever of impatience. The sight of misery has really disturbed the good man, partly through sympathy with those who have been thrown abroad on the world, to the loss of their easy habitual ways and the loss of not a little property, and partly because he reflects that before long his own case may be like theirs. He sits musing in the inn parlour, and needs the prompting of the Host before he can raise to his lips the glass of eighty-three. One comfort at least he has—if the invaders should force him to fly, his flight will not be embarrassed by wife or child; already he has packed up his valuables, and if person and property can be saved there will be some consolation amid disaster. Life has taught him to proceed in all things cautiously; he would like to regild his sign of the Archangel and Dragon, but the expense has to be considered. In Hermann's affairs of the heart the motto of wise conduct is *Festina lente;* Dorothea looks indeed what a maiden ought to be, but it is not well to rely upon appearances. To trust one's spiritual guidance to the young Pastor may be sensible enough; but is it discreet to trust the safety of one's limbs to such a charioteer? Yet the egoism of the Apothecary leaves him well-disposed and neighbourly; he is prompt to act as plenipotentiary in the great business of wedlock; and, if he does not rashly part with his coin to the unhappy fugitives, he is generous with the contents of his pouch of cherished canaster.

Hermann's father is constrained by the exigencies of the narrative to play a somewhat ungrateful part; he is the chief obstacle which retards young love in its progress, and over which love must find out a way. But Goethe contrives that, notwithstanding his infirmities of temper and a certain deficiency of intellectual and moral delicacy, the host of the Golden Lion shall impress us favourably as an honest and genial householder. We learn to humour him gently, to view his foibles with a smile, and to remain confident that, with a little exercise of tact, he can be brought round to good temper and something like reason in the end. He has toiled since the havoc wrought twenty years ago by the great fire; he has grown well-to-do, and has gained a position of respect among his fellow-townsmen; and now his days of struggle are over, and his personal ambition is appeased; he regards himself with much complacency, and loves—though not ungenerously—his comfort and his ease. Should his temper be ruffled, it is enough if his self-complacency can be restored; a little oil will allay the troubled waters, though he may not be able to deny himself the pleasure of feeling in a measure wronged. The host would not choose to view the misery of the fugitives, but he is willing to give to them of his substance, for "to give is the duty of the rich"; and though he parts from the flowered dressing-gown, with all its associations of repose, as from an old friend, let this go too, for it is no longer in the fashion, and a respected citizen must move with the times. The good host is not, like his neighbour, the Apothecary, oppressed by the fear of French invaders; all anxiety is hateful to him, and he cherishes a comfortable faith in Providence and remembers the sure barrier of the Rhine. His own time for ease has come, but it should be his son's business now to take up his task, and advance in social success from the point to which the father had arrived—for *besser ist besser*. And, with so exemplary a parent, Hermann is an unsatisfactory son; he will not seek a bride from among the daughters of the wealthy neighbour, whose white stucco and green paint glorify the market-place; why should not one of these fashionable young ladies decorate the interior of the Golden Lion and gratify the good father-in-law with fashionable airs on the piano? But Hermann is dull and devoid of ambition; he has been a laggard in his class at school, while others strode ahead; he can content his poor ambition with horses and affairs of the farm; and all this though he has a father who has not only bettered himself but helped to better the town, one who held the office of "Bauherr" six times, and that with general approbation. For certain, Hermann shall never bring across the threshold as bride, bearing in hand her little bundle of belongings, some peasant daughter-in-law—*die Trulle!* And to pardon the host's gross outbreak of speech we must needs bear in mind, as does the wise Mütterchen, that he has quickened his blood with some glasses of the vintage of eighty-three.

Mother and son are joined against him, and the neighbours aid and abet their revolt; they do him wrong, but why should he vex his soul? he will submit and let things take their course. When at length Hermann and Dorothea arrive out of the night, the host has recovered his good humour, and the occasion is one for some harmless banter; but it fares ill with the father's jests; the scene changes to one of indignation and protest, with weeping, demonstrative women. Was ever kind, indulgent father so wronged? Sobs and bewailings, and confusion at the close of the day, when a little good sense might have set all right! For his part he can endure it no longer and will betake himself to his bed. It needs all Dorothea's gracious tact to restore harmony; but the father's heart is in truth sound and warm, and, as he embraces his new daughter, the good man has to hide some happy tears.

The Mütterchen bears a certain resemblance to Goethe's own bright-hearted and sympathetic mother. In reading *Hermann und Dorothea*, though the Pastor with his spiritual wisdom and Hermann with his strong heart and steadfast will vindicate their sex, we have to make some allowances for masculine limitations and infirmities; but the *Ewig-Weibliche* is presented in two exemplars which are wholly admirable. The Mütterchen is in love with happiness and with her own business of creating it for others, and therefore for herself; and to lessen misery is in a way to be a creator of happiness.

She does not sentimentalise over sorrow, but straightway sets herself, as far as in her lies, to chase it away. Being beneficent, she enjoys the sense of power and influence which can be wielded for beneficent ends. And having to deal with a husband whose humours require at times some skilful management, she knows that tact is an auxiliary or a mode of power. Men are wayward and rather irrational creatures, but then they are only men, and it cannot be expected that they should be as intelligent as a woman. Even the Pastor is a little too much given to philosophical reflections on lightness of temper and the virtues of curiosity, and the new, the useful, and the good, when he ought rather to satisfy her curiosity at once with a budget of news; the mother must be pardoned for growing a little restive under his discourse. As for the husband, who twenty years ago wooed her amid the ruins of their homes and bore her in his arms over the smouldering ashes of the conflagration, he is dear to her with all the dearness of happy use and wont; and he is her own to guide and rule, while she will never show that she rules; but her son is wholly her own in even a more delightful way. And, since his happiness is hers, she has no touch of maternal jealousy; through his joy in Dorothea, a daughter after her heart, she will double her own joy. It is true that she had already in imagination chosen for his bride the rich neighbour's daughter, Minchen:

> "Minchen fürwahr ist gut und war dir immer gewogen";

but marriages are made in heaven, and it seems that Minchen is not the bride-elect; therefore Dorothea, though she may bring only a bundle for her dowry, shall be beloved by the mother almost as her own child. We must take our children as heaven sends them; she will not have her Hermann rated for being what God made him ; he has his own gift, and must use it in his own way ; he will prove a model to burgher and countryman, and will not be the last or least in the civic council. And so she departs to seek the good son and comfort his troubled heart.

Never was there more entire sympathy between mother and son. At first Hermann veils his heart, but it is with a veil that is transparent to the loving maternal eyes. What is all this talk about soldiering and drum and trumpet ? Such is not Hermann's true and instinctive form of patriotism ; he is a brave and noble youth, but his vocation is one of tranquil toil and domestic duty. And presently, through her clear divination and womanly courage in sympathy, the veil is wholly dropped and Hermann's naïve confession comes forth—*ich entbehre der Gattin*. It only remains to test a little further the virtues of promptitude and courage ; leading Hermann by the hand, she will confront his father and with the utmost directness will make the situation clear. And happily, just at the moment before the pair enter, the Pastor has been dilating, in words which carry weight however they may appear to be disregarded, on the excellence of such a temper as that of Hermann, calm in its energy, steadfast, bent on acquiring and maintaining what is useful, and unvexed by misleading ambitions. The fumes of the eighty-three have evaporated from the Host's brains, and who can question the result?

Under Hermann's quietude and reserve there lie much sensitiveness, much moral delicacy, and a capacity for genuine passion. It is remarkable that Goethe has succeeded in making us feel at once the solidity of Hermann's character and its natural refinement. This youth is no Werther, incapable of contending effectively with morbid emotion which disturbs the intellect and saps the power of the will. He has attached himself from childhood to what is useful; he is eminently healthful of heart, and, when love takes possession of him, love itself, overmastering in its strength, brings him strength, and is indeed a part of the highest sanity. In the perfect understanding which exists between mother and son we find evidence of Hermann's freedom from the dulness and egoism that are not uncommon with his sex and age. As a schoolboy he was sensitive for his father's honour, and those graceless comrades who mocked at the host's efflorescence of Sunday costume soon found that there was something dangerous in the quiet son, who rarely resented any provocation directed against himself alone. When his father has reproached him unjustly and pronounced in anticipation a sentence against the maiden of his choice, Hermann utters no indignant word, but endures the wound and gently withdraws to unburden his heart in solitude. He is not insensible to the good father's infirmities, but never have his lips opened on this theme to anyone; and when as a hint of guidance to Dorothea he must needs refer to the host's regard for external demonstrations of respect and affection he does so with the finest delicacy; and that he expresses even so much is an indication of his absolute trust in Dorothea, and of the perfect community of feeling already established between them. Hermann hitherto has been the reverse of lethargic; he has diligently attended to the labours of the farm; but half his nature has lain dormant. There was something a little fatuous in his dutiful efforts to cultivate the airs and graces expected by the young ladies of the great house in the market-place; and to poor Hermann-Tamino, when, in an agony of shame, he laid aside his superfine coat and pulled his hair out of curl, the fatuousness was apparent. But now his total self gives authority to a wise passion ; his whole nature is aroused and all its powers are consentaneous. As Hermann, on his return from the errand of mercy, enters the room, the Pastor observes that he is an altered man ; a new animation has taken possession of him ; he, who had been silent or reserved, now can wax eloquent ; he must needs step forth to rebuke the Apothecary for his self-regarding celibate views. And when a little later, under the great pear tree, Hermann pours forth his grief, and announces his patriotic resolve to fight and to die for his country, it is not mere vapouring or the enthusiasm of a dream. The passion of his heart, foiled in its immediate aims, bears him onward to new and generous designs. When once again that passion concentrates itself on Dorothea and the substantial joys of home, it contains within it a better patriotism, founded on a love first for what is near and real, and then for the mother country which presides over and preserves all the blessedness of the hearth and home. Hermann, with his delicacy of feeling, is no confident lover, assured that the son of the well-to-do host must carry all before him ; he has the good sense to trust much to the discretion of his friends ; he is perfectly assured that they can make no discovery about Dorothea which will not enhance her honour ; but, for his own part, he is subject to all a lover's vicissitude of hopes and fears. Whatever she may say cannot but be good and reasonable :—

> "Was sie sagt, das ist gut, es ist vernünftig, das weiss ich"—

but the ring upon the maiden's finger fills him with forebodings ; one so beautiful must surely have been wooed — perhaps won — already ; and Hermann almost to the last fears to put his fate to the touch, " to gain or lose it all."

Yet Hermann's love is that of a heart strong and sane, and it is fixed upon one who is as strong of heart as he, and as good as strong—" so gut wie stark." While he as yet is but half developed, and retains much of the reserve and shy sensitiveness of youth, she has already come into complete possession of her adult powers. Her perceptions are always clear, her judgment always unerroneous, her will always at command and prompt for right action. At the centre of her being is the desire for beneficent service to others ; but she is not careless of her own welfare, or reckless of her future, or insensible of her own rights. In defence of the weak against the outrage of the oppressor she can flame forth with a righteous rage like that of Spenser's Britomart. But she can show her strength as tenderness when aiding the feeble mother with the new-born babe ; and as she turns to depart from the band of fugitives in company with Hermann the cry of children is heard, and they cling to her skirts as to those of a second mother. With wise foresight she inquires of Hermann how she may win the esteem and regard of the master and mistress of the Golden Lion ; and, having been satisfied by his answers, she can inwardly indulge a touch of dawning love and at the same time an outward touch of playfulness in the question :

" Aber wer sagt mir nunmehr : wie soll ich dir selber begegnen,
Dir, dem einzigen Sohn und künftig meinem Gebieter ?"

For Dorothea, if she has none of the modish, ungenerous wit of the young ladies of the great house in the market-place, has a lambent brightness of her own, which is part of her joy in life. We remember her less, however, by any words than by her deeds ;

by what she does and by what she shows herself to be in the unconscious nobility of her attitude, and in every gracious turn both of mind and of person. We think of her, staff in hand, guiding, urging, restraining the great oxen which draw the waggon where the pale mother and the infant rest. We think of her as the armed champion of chastity, an Athene addressed to combat. We think of her under the apple tree, preparing little garments for a child. We think of her, still bent on service to others, at the fountain, bearing the vessels for water in the right hand and the left. We think of her as she sank, in that stumble of good omen, on her lover's shoulder, and, with no awkwardness or embarrassment, at once turned off the significance of the incident and concealed the pain of her wrenched ankle with a jest and a smile. Goethe during his Italian journey and his residence at Rome had aroused and calmed his sense of beauty by the contemplation of classical sculpture. No marble goddess of the Roman galleries has more of dignity than Dorothea, who yet is of warm and breathing humanity, of flesh, not marble, and who withal, in heart and soul, is true German. The circumstances of the time have made her a wanderer, but such upheaval is alien to her nature; she is made to build upon sure foundations the honour and the happiness of the German home. She will not spend herself in aspirations towards the unattainable; but whatever can be attained by dutiful ways, by loyalty, fidelity, steadfastness, disinterested service, will be in the possession of those who are dear to her. The unbounded trust which Hermann reposes in her has no extravagance in its kind or its degree; assuredly all will be fulfilled.

Other poems tell us of the nobility that may exist in suffering; it is well to read a poem which makes us feel the nobility that lives in happiness.

COWPER AND WILLIAM HAYLEY

(From Unpublished Sources)

William Hayley, the warm-hearted friend and the biographer of Cowper, prepared for posthumous publication two manuscripts, each of considerable length, relating to incidents in the life of the poet which were not fully told in his biography. These, which are now in my possession, have never appeared in print, nor in the extended form in which Hayley left them would they perhaps be entitled to publication. One of them tells in detail the efforts of Hayley, at length crowned with success, to obtain a pension for Cowper. The other and the more curious is entitled, *The Second Memorial of Hayley's endeavours to serve his friend Cowper, containing a minute account of Devices employed to restore his dejected spirits.* The first is dated 1794; the second was written in 1809, after Cowper's death, and after the appearance of the *Life of Cowper.*

Fragments of the story which Hayley tells are known; it is known that through his exertions several persons of eminence addressed letters to the dejected poet, which, it was hoped, might bring him cheer; but why it was an urgent matter with Hayley to obtain such letters as these has—so far as I am aware—never been told. Fragments of a well-meant plot, conceived in the service of Cowper, have come to light; but the pivot of the plot has not, if I am right, been ever exhibited, nor has it been shown in what degree Lady Hesketh and Cowper's young kinsman Johnson

(" Johnny of Norfolk ") were amiable accomplices in the plot.

The *Second Memorial* is addressed to Johnson, several of whose letters, as well as letters of Lady Hesketh and of others, are given in transcriptions. The starting-point of Hayley's well-meant efforts was a mournful communication—hitherto, I believe, unpublished—bearing the post-mark of Dereham, but having no signature, which he received at Eartham on 20th June 1797. The contents of the letter and the hand-writing told clearly enough from whom it came; the same fixed wretchedness is expressed in it which appears in the unsigned letter, written a month previously, to Lady Hesketh, and printed by Southey. " Ignorant of everything but my own instant and impending misery," wrote Cowper to Hayley, " I know neither what I do, when I write, nor can do otherwise than write, because I am bidden to do so. Perfect Despair, the most perfect that ever possess'd any mind, has had possession of mine, you know how long, and, knowing that, will not need to be told who writes." The intimation in this letter that Cowper had been " bidden " to write, whether through some compelling force of his own dark mind or through some supernatural injunction, suggested to Hayley that the supernatural might be used as a device to lift Cowper out of his melancholy. His response ran as follows:

" Eartham, *24th June* 1797.

" My very dear dejected Friend,—The few lines in your hand, so often welcome to me, and now so long wished for, affected me thro' my heart and soul, both with joy and grief—joy that you are again able to write to me, and grief that you write under the oppression of melancholy.

"My keen sensations in perusing these heart-piercing lines have been a painful prelude to the following ecstatic Vision: I beheld the throne of God, Whose splendour, though in excess, did not strike me blind, but left me power to discern, on the steps of it, two kneeling angelic forms. A kind seraph seemed to whisper to me that these heavenly petitioners were your lovely mother, and my own; both engaged in fervent supplications for your restoration to mental serenity and comfort. I sprang eagerly forward to inquire your destiny of your mother. Turning towards me with a look of seraphic benignity, she smiled upon me and said: 'Warmest of earthly friends! moderate the anxiety of thy zeal, lest it distract thy declining faculties, and know, as a reward for thy kindness, that my son shall be restored to himself and to friendship. But the All-merciful and Almighty ordains that his restoration shall be gradual, and that his peace with Heaven shall be preceded by the following extraordinary circumstances of signal honour on earth. He shall receive letters from Members of Parliament, from Judges, and from Bishops to thank him for the service he has rendered to the Christian world by his devotional poetry. These shall be followed by a letter from the Prime Minister to the same effect; and this by thanks expressed to him on the same account in the hand of the King himself. Tell him, when these events take place he may confide in his celestial emancipation from despair, granted to the prayer of his mother; and he may rest satisfied with this assurance from her, that his peace is perfectly made with Heaven. Hasten to impart these blessed tidings to your favourite friend,' said the maternal spirit; 'and let your thanksgiving to God be an increase of reciprocal kindness to each other!'

"I obey the Vision, my dear Cowper, with a degree of trembling fear that it may be only the fruitless offspring of my agitated fancy. But if any part of the prophecy shall soon be accomplished, a faint ray of hope will then be turned into strong, luminous, and delightful conviction in my heart, and I trust in yours, my dear delivered sufferer, as completely as in that of your most anxious and affectionate friend,

"W. H.

"Postscript.—If any of the incidents speedily take place, which your angelic mother announced to me in this Vision as certain signs of your recovery, I conjure you in her name, my dear Cowper, to communicate them to me with all the kind despatch that is due to the tender anxiety of sympathetic affection! Heaven grant that I may hear from you again very soon! Adieu!"

Something of comedy mingles with graver matter in the good Hayley's sincere distress and his odd flights of imagination. At the throne of God perhaps members of the British House of Commons, perhaps even judges, ermined and bewigged, perhaps —if one may be so bold as to conjecture—even Anglican bishops, shovel-hatted and aproned, are not set mighty store by as such. As for the Prime Minister and the excellent George III., they, at least on earth, were exalted persons, and difficult of access. The sanguine Hermit of Eartham—Hayley often signed his letters as "Hermit"—never got within hail of prime minister or king for his purpose of raising the poet's dejected spirits, and thus he is responsible for placing the sainted spirit of Cowper's mother in the list of prophetesses who prophesy "a false vision and a thing of nought."

COWPER AND WILLIAM HAYLEY

If Hayley's fancy was somewhat clumsy his heart was generous. With extreme anxiety he waited to learn what impression his letter had produced. On 12th July, Johnny of Norfolk, who was not the most regular of correspondents, wrote to assure him that the perusal of the " marvellous Vision " by Cowper himself, and, ten days later, his listening to the letter read aloud, had a much better effect than could with any confidence have been anticipated. He listened, indeed, in silence; but some movement of repugnance or revolt would not have been surprising. " He never looked better in his life," writes Johnson, " as to healthy complexion than he does now " ; but perhaps this was less owing to the Vision than to Johnson's own prescriptions—" half a pint of ass's milk in a morning, an hour and a half before rising, and the yolk of an egg beat up in a glass of port wine at twelve o'clock."

Hayley's letter he had forwarded by the hand of an acquaintance to Lady Hesketh at Clifton. He ended by entreating Hayley to persuade some one or more who answered the description of the Vision to write to Cowper, from which confirmation of the heavenly announcements he expected the happiest results.

Lady Hesketh at first feared that " dear warm-hearted Hayley's wonderful letter " might only have " sunk the dear soul lower, and made him think it an insult upon his distress. . . . I well remember," she adds, " how *angry* any marks of kindness used to make him formerly." So she writes on 15th July to Johnson; but a fortnight later, in writing to Hayley himself, she has nothing but praise for the " charming Vision," for the " friendly heart which inspired the Idea, and the lively Genius that executed it." She only feared that it would prove impossible to get any part of the prophecy fulfilled, and that should Cowper find none of the promised letters arrive, he might drop lower down in "that cruel gulph of Despair in which he has been so long and so deeply involved." With much feeling she refers to the melancholy letter which she had received from Cowper in May; very warmly she commends Cowper's young kinsman for his unwearied devotion; should Johnson be incapacitated for the service, she would herself, if sufficiently recovered from the illness which had brought her now as a convalescent from Clifton to Cheltenham, "take the charge of this lost creature"; but what could she do at present with her almost total loss of voice?

Hayley, in his reply, is grateful for "the friendly spirit of tender and indulgent enthusiasm" with which Lady Hesketh entered into his purpose and his hope. He evidently wishes it to be thought that the Vision was not wholly a pious fraud, and he explains to some extent his plans for procuring the fulfilment of the "maternal spirit's" prophecy:

"The Vision arose," he writes (6th August), "from my very acute sense of our dear friend's sufferings and my intense desire to relieve them. After reading his most affecting billet of Despair, I fell into deep meditation upon it; and, while my eyes were covered by my hand, I seemed to behold something very like the Vision I described. The images appeared so forcible to my own fancy that I immediately resolved to make a bold, affectionate attempt to render them *instrumental*, if possible (with the blessing of God and good angels), to the restoration of our invaluable friend. I accordingly settled in my own thoughts different projects for producing the series of events announced in the Vision before I ventured to send him the letter, which you so kindly and partially commend. . . . I have reason to believe the dear subject of the Vision has, by this time, received letters from Mr. Wilberforce and Lord Kenyon. Steps are taken that other and more important letters may follow these. . . . Your Ladyship's excellent understanding will show you the propriety, I might say the *necessity*, of keeping the device *as secret as possible* to promote its success. On this principle many persons, engaged to write to the dear sufferer, will not know *exactly why* they are engaged to write to him."

Neither the letter of Wilberforce nor that hoped for from Lord Kenyon had in fact been written, but Hayley was apt to take his anticipations for accomplished facts. Wilberforce was a member of Parliament; Kenyon—the Chief Justice—was a judge; a bishop was still needed to fulfil the first part, and that least difficult of accomplishment, of the celestial prophecy. Five years previously, in June 1792, Hayley on his return from Weston, then full of zeal to procure a pension for Cowper, had breakfasted in London with Lord Thurlow, for whom, in the early days when Thurlow was a law clerk, and the poet spent his hours with his cousins Harriet and Theodora, "giggling and making giggle," Cowper had predicted the lord chancellorship. "You shall provide for me when you are Lord Chancellor," said Cowper; and Thurlow with a smile assented—"I surely will." At the breakfast, to Hayley's surprise, appeared Lord Kenyon; but, undaunted by the two great persons, the Hermit gallantly pleaded the cause of his distressed friend and was listened to with favour. He now ventured, with Cowper's barrister acquaintance, Samuel Rose, as an intermediary—"that friendly little being" is Lady Hesketh's description of Rose—to apply to the Chief Justice for the desired letter.

Why it was needed, beyond the fact that such a letter might cheer the drooping spirits of Cowper, was not explained. To Kenyon it seemed an embarrassing task to address in this way a man of literary eminence who was personally unknown to him. The letter accordingly, to Hayley's great mortification, did not arrive.

Meanwhile Hayley had fixed upon Watson, Bishop of Llandaff, as the mark for his next benevolent attack, while Lady Hesketh of her own initiative, though acknowledging that Hayley was the prime controller of the "complicated machine," hoped, through her companion at Cheltenham, Mrs. Holroyd, a sister of Lord Sheffield, to approach Beilby Porteus, "our good Lord of London"—bishop No. 2—with the like intent. Moreover, in a letter to Johnson (27th August) she added some lines, designed to co-operate with Hayley's letter of the Vision, which Johnson might show to Cowper, if it seemed good to him to do so:

"I dreamt very lately, my dearest cousin," she wrote, "that I saw you quite well and cheerful—restored by a gracious and merciful God to all your comforts and all your religious privileges, and rejoicing in His mercy and kindness, which, you told me, had been exercised towards you in a very wonderful manner. I own I feel strongly impressed that this will prove true, and that I shall once again be enabled to rejoice in the restored health and spirits of a cousin so truly dear as you have always been to your affectionate friend and cousin,

"H. Hesketh."

It was reported to her by Johnson that her postscript had been shown and was well received. Lady Hesketh's innocent "dream" hardly reached the dignity of a pious fraud; it was a genuine hope translated into dream. She had not quite approved of Hayley's audacity in laying the scene of his Vision at the throne of God, and, if only it could be ascertained that Cowper had forgotten the details, she thought that the letter might, to its advantage, be re-copied, with this particular omitted, as a revised and emended Vision. She feared that the audacious Hayley, with all his generous zeal and all his learned acquisitions, might still be a stranger to "the great truths of Christianity"—a fear which Hayley afterwards ascribed to the suggestions of some unfriendly gossip. Whatever his religious opinions might be, his code of morals, in one particular at least, had partaken, as Southey amiably puts it, of patriarchal liberty. His beloved little sculptor, the pupil of Flaxman—a boy of rare promise—though received by Hayley's "dear irritable Eliza" as her own, was a natural son.

Of "those two shining lights of the age," as Lady Hesketh names them, Wilberforce and Lord Kenyon, the former at least was willing to let his beams descend on Cowper. He directed that a copy of his recently published book, *A Practical View*, should be sent to Dereham—it proved to be a book of amazing popularity—and he accompanied the volume with a letter (9th August) conceived in the happiest spirit. Six weeks later came a letter from the Bishop of London, which Lady Hesketh justly described as a "charming performance." Porteus was himself a poet; at least his verses on *Death* had won, nearly forty years previously, the Seatonian prize. In his letter he gracefully applies to Cowper himself, with "'Twere" altered to "'Twas," the lines from *Table Talk*:

> "'Twere new indeed to see a bard all fire,
> Touched with a coal from heaven, assume the lyre,"

and the four verses that immediately follow. Lady Hesketh had playfully reproached the faithful Johnson with his somewhat spasmodic efforts at correspondence. Johnny needed a flapper from the island of Laputa; when he did write he was always in a hurry. He was ordered to choose the calmest and quietest hour he could pick out of the twenty-four, and then he should remember not to "set out with letters *a foot long at least*, and literally with only three words in a line or four at most." But now that a letter from that "wonderful mortal," Mr. Wilberforce, had arrived, and a letter from our good Lord of London, Johnny of Norfolk copied both these documents for Hayley's "infinite gratification," and added a narrative of his own:

"On Thursday (28th September) came a letter from the Bishop of London, and yesterday morning I found the first favourable opportunity of reading it to our beloved Cowper. His remarks were these: 'Never was such a letter written, never was such a letter read to a man so overwhelmed with despair as I am. It was written in *derision;* I know, and I am sure of it.' 'Oh, no! no! no! my cousin! say not so of the good Beilby, Bishop of London!' 'I should say so,' he replied, 'of an Archangel, were it possible for an Archangel to send me such a letter in such circumstances.' This only has passed hitherto, but I suspect that he was gratified notwithstanding, upon the whole. He heard me with the silence of death, and, except at one passage in this amiable Bishop's letter, never opened his lips." A word of Porteus—"That *Love* [of God] you must possess surely in as full extent as any human being ever did" —had drawn from Cowper's lips the exclamation, "Not an atom of it!"

Johnson believed that the sufferer's mind was

occupied very frequently about the letters having come to him, "though I am certain," he adds, "he does not suspect *why* they have come so nearly together." He supposed that Cowper did not connect them in his mind with Hayley's Vision, and he repented a thousand times that he had sent away Hayley's letter to Lady Hesketh. He begged that it might be returned immediately, and resolved to place it, with the letters of Wilberforce and Porteus, on Cowper's desk, where he knew that Cowper would notice it and read it when he was alone. Johnson himself would assume an air of having entirely forgotten the Vision, lest Cowper should in any way "suspect the incomparable contrivance."

To this design Lady Hesketh was strongly opposed. "I think and have always thought it highly necessary," she writes with emphatic underlinings to Johnson (7th November), "that on the arrival of every letter which comes to corroborate the truth of that wonderful Vision you should express (though not violently or in such a way as to alarm him) your surprise and satisfaction at this happy coincidence of circumstances. . . . I could wish you, my dear Johnny, to sift our poor cousin a little, and endeavour to find out what he thinks of the letters he has received, which, you may say, afford to you a full proof that his dear Mother's prophecy is very near its completion." Lady Hesketh greatly desired that letter might follow letter, in order that Cowper's mind might be thoroughly roused and kept in motion with an advancing assurance of hope.

Another letter had, in fact, arrived. Hayley, in September, had expressed his expectation that considerable aid would be derived from "episcopal coadjutors." Lady Hesketh, herself "an angelic coadjutor," had proved her "instantaneous and happy influence over the Lights of our Church " by securing the co-operation of that " angel on earth," Beilby Porteus. A disappointment followed. Dr. Beadon, Bishop of Gloucester, had married a relation of Hayley, Miss Rachel Gooch, " for whom, in her childhood," Hayley writes, " I had felt such affection that during my residence at Cambridge I painted a minute resemblance of the interesting child and had it set in a ring." On Dr. Beadon's marriage the poet had addressed a few friendly verses to the bride and bridegroom; but not many of his friends escaped some kindly effusion of occasional verse. To his surprise and indignation a very ungracious refusal to write to Cowper came to Eartham, not from the bishop direct, but through his father-in-law, Dr. Gooch, whereupon the manuscript before me becomes illegible with its vigorous cancellings which perhaps conceal emphatic words. Do the blurrings and blottings bear witness to one of Hayley's " Triumphs "—or failures—" of Temper "?

More than compensating satisfaction came from a highly-distinguished man, Richard Watson, Bishop of Llandaff, the apologist for the Bible. Lady Hesketh, with a woman's shrewdness, had expected little from Dr. Beadon. " Is he clever? " she asks Hayley, " and will he understand the nature of your request? " But " in regard to the Bishop of Llandaff . . . there can be no doubts of *him*." The result in each instance agreed with Lady Hesketh's anticipations. Watson was now settled at Calgarth Park, Kendal, but he did not fail to visit his diocese three times each year. He was occupied in improving an estate for the benefit of his family, nor did he regard it as his fault that some of the best years of his life had been thus employed. If he had " commenced an agriculturist," he said, " it was because he desired to secure a moderate competence for eight children," and experience had brought him to Lord Bacon's opinion that to cultivate our Mother Earth is the most honourable mode of improving our fortunes.

Hayley, in writing to Watson, mentions the fact that Lord Thurlow had visited the Sussex coast in the autumn of 1797. The summer had been for Hayley a time of anxiety, not only on Cowper's account, but because the dear "juvenile sculptor," his son, had suffered in health from a cold caught from masses of wet clay used in modelling, and all medicines had failed to give him relief. His own favourite panacea, "the salutary sea," was tried with a better result. "We came dripping from it together this morning," he tells Lady Hesketh (6th September), "and saw Lord Thurlow in our way, who has been prevented by the unseasonable rains from passing a morning with us, which he promises to do very soon, and he has, with great good-nature, allowed the young sculptor to prepare a lump of the finest clay to model his grand visage." This, he tells the Bishop of Llandaff, would form "a good prelude for the awful project of modelling your countenance," whenever "the aspiring little artist" could pay his respects at Calgarth Park. From which flattering introduction Hayley passes to his petition for a letter to be addressed to Cowper. The bishop replied in the most genial manner; he would, of course, follow the example of Lord Thurlow, a man of whom he thought highly, "tho' he is not so good a Whig as he might be;" he would sit for the young artist; and as to Cowper, he had obeyed Hayley's commands and dispatched a letter "by this post" (18th October). It was a manly and generous letter, written as if through an impulse of spontaneous gratitude arising from a perusal—not for the first time—of Cowper's poems; it closed with an invitation to the Lakes, and an offer of the hospitality of Calgarth Park.

How Watson's communication was received is told at length in a letter of Johnson to Hayley: "At the very moment of this letter's arrival and delivery into my hands (for the dear soul would not touch a letter himself on any account) we were sitting by the study fire, intent upon that admirable little book of the learned bishop, *An Apology for Christianity*. 'Dear me!' said I, 'here is a letter from the author himself.' You may be sure our poor friend was rather startled at the wonderful coincidence; and so in truth was I, and inwardly thankful to that kind Providence, whose finger I discern so plainly. The dear soul raised his eyes for a moment, but seemed so struck by the suddenness of the affair that I could not profitably read the letter then. I therefore laid it upon his desk, and went on with our book. Before night, however, I broke the seal, and communicated the contents to him. He said nothing while I read; nor yet when I ceased to read; and the matter was left to work upon his mind."

Following Lady Hesketh's advice, Johnson took the first prudent opportunity of connecting the letter from Bishop Watson with Hayley's "inimitable Vision": "One day, after dinner, as we were all using the finger-glasses, 'Miss Perowne,' said I (Miss Perowne was lady-housekeeper to Johnson), 'don't you recollect something about a letter's coming to Mr. Cowper in the summer from Mr. Hayley, containing a wonderful Vision which he had lately had?' 'I certainly do remember it' (said she), 'and have often thought of it since.' 'Sam' (said I), 'take away the water-glasses and set the wine upon the table.' This, as I intended, turned the subject; but in the evening I started up in a great hurry, just as we were sitting down to tea : ‘ By-the-bye, I will go and look for Mr. Hayley's letter.’ Mr. Cowper immediately called out, ‘ No, pray don't.’ *Johnny :* ‘ Because it strikes me there is a kind of accomplishment of what is predicted.’ *Mr. C. :* ‘ Well ! be it so ! I know there is, and I knew there would be ; and I knew what it meant.’ These are the very words that passed, for I slipped out of the room and wrote them down with a pencil on the back of a letter. Since that time I have never mentioned the subject ; but the next letter that comes I will renew the attack. It is some consolation to us in the meantime to know that he has not forgotten the Vision. And now, my dear Sir, let me say that Mr. Cowper is in bodily health much as he was when I wrote last, and much as he was in spirits. But jump for joy when I tell you that he resumed his *Homer* on the 10th of October, and has continued to revise it, and charmingly to correct without missing one day ever since. We go on rapidly, a Book in a week, and sometimes more ; now in the 12th Iliad. Our evenings have been long devoted to Gibbon's marvellous work, *The Decline and Fall of the Roman Empire.* We have delightfully travelled with him to the end of the chapter which he has given entirely to Justinian's laws ; and our poor dear friend interrupts me frequently to remark any striking passage as we go along.”

Still no letter had arrived from Lord Kenyon. It was believed by Hayley that a letter from him, as coming from a stranger, would be more gratifying to Cowper than one from Thurlow, with whom the poet was personally acquainted. Thurlow's interest with the Lord Chief Justice was secured by the indefatigable Hayley. It is stated in Mr. Thomas Wright's biography of Cowper that Lord Kenyon wrote to Cowper. This is perhaps an error. Certainly, as late as 15th March 1798, Lady Hesketh expressed to Hayley some indignation occasioned by his silence: "Lord Kenyon has never written at all, nor will you, I hope, dear Sir, apply to him *any more*. You have done your part sufficiently as regards this luminary of the law; and could the pleadings of friendship have prevailed you would long since have gained your cause; as it is, I hope you will plant your batteries against hearts more penetrable than that of the learned Lord in question."

The diligence of Southey obtained for him two letters addressed by Thurlow to the Chief Justice, which Southey supposed to reveal the whole of the benevolent plot for Cowper's restoration to hope and happiness. In fact they only show that Hayley was the chief conspirator. Lord Thurlow apologetically condenses in his opening sentence the whole situation from his own point of view: "I have been pressed by one mad poet to ask of you, for another, a favour, which savours of the malady of both." The experiment, Thurlow thought, was at least harmless and charitable. Lord Kenyon apparently still demurred, and Thurlow was good enough to draw up for his guidance an outline of the sort of letter which he supposed to be required, or, as Southey puts it, a form of testimonial which was to accredit a man to himself. No word of Thurlow's indicates any acquaintance with Hayley's Vision, nor was this flight of fancy known to Southey. The "mad poet," the Hermit of Eartham, had probably sense enough to be aware that Thurlow was not the man to become a partner in the task of corroborating Visions revealed at the throne of God.

Hayley flattered himself with the thought that his efforts on behalf of Cowper had not been useless. He tried to believe that the resumption of work on

Homer was in some degree due to the encouragement which the Vision and the letters that followed it may have brought to the afflicted translator. In truth Cowper's state of mind while engaged in revising his *Homer* presents a curious problem in mental pathology. His physical health during the year 1797 was but little affected by his malady; he rode out with Johnson, or walked out, every day; his daily half-bottle of wine had been increased to a bottle with excellent results; his cheeks had a certain ruddiness of hue. Nor was he incapable of intellectual exertion. He studied details in his own work with close attention. "What do you think of this?" Johnson writes to Hayley on 5th December, "our blessed Bard *now* said to me in the gentlest of all possible voices, 'Is there such a word as *midmost?*' Johnson's *Dictionary* was in my hand in a moment, and no sooner did I mention Dryden and Pope as having used the very word than he was seated and scratching upon the paper in an instant." Johnson's description in the same letter of how the work went on may be added to somewhat similar records which are already in print: "I know you will excuse a hasty line, because a hasty line is all that I can steal from the importunate demands of *Homer*, who, interleaved and like a mountain, lies before me on the writing-desk, touching my very chin. I am preparing a transcript fairly and for the press of the last alterations of our beloved Cowper: incorporating also certain former variations and notes, which proceeded from his admirable pen before he left Weston, and with which I imagine you acquainted, as I frequently find your handwriting among them. The dear translator is as well as usual, and more than commonly intent upon rendering with *fire* and *faithfulness* a fiery line in the thirteenth Book of the *Iliad*."

Yet while Cowper could thus for a time keep his mind above his misery, the misery lay below, and to make real escape from it was impossible. He was persecuted by both audible and visual illusions.

On the 15th of November 1797, Johnson began to enter in a diary, which was continued during a great part of the next year, the words in which Cowper told, or shadowed forth, his distracted fancies. They are almost too pitiable to put on record, yet taken in connection with the fact that he was revising his *Homer* at the rate of a book each week, they make us feel as if he had, so to speak, a double mind, and that the sane mind and the insane stood independent of each other and apart. The notices of four days, copied by Hayley, probably represent what went on for weeks and months: "November 15—While Mr. Cowper was dressing this morning, and just as the Church clock struck nine, he heard the following words, which seemed to come out of the wall behind his bedstead: 'You shall hear that clock strike many months, in that room, upon that bed.' In the course of the night he had heard several voices of the terrifying sort, but remembered only one, which said, 'Bring him out! bring him out!' 19th November—He heard these words, 'You are welcome to all sorts of misery.' 28th November—Mr. Cowper told me, at two different times in the course of the day, that he had these two notices upon his bed. First he had these words:—'When Mr. Johnson is gone they will pelt you with stones.' This he told me before dinner; and towards evening he said—'I saw a man come to my bedside last night and tear my neck-cloth off; and it will be so, I know it will.' 2nd December—He told me at breakfast he heard this:

"'Sad-win! I leave you with regret,
But you must go to gaol for debt.'

"'Do you know the meaning of Sad-win, my cousin?' (said I). 'Yes, I do, the Winner of Sorrow.'"

Enough of these painful memoranda! Happily no Samuel Teedon was at Dereham to interpret the voices. It is clear, too, that Hayley's device was of small avail; for one in Cowper's state an experiment in the thyroid treatment would have been more likely to bring help than a score of "inimitable Visions."

The death of Mrs. Hayley, the Hermit's "pitiable Eliza," in the late autumn of 1797—not in 1800 as the *Dictionary of National Biography* erroneously states—did not cause Hayley to forget his friend. The Hermit was hardly more a hermit after the event than he had been before it. Hayley and his wife, with kind consideration for their mutual esteem and peace of mind, had lived apart. But the threefold cord which bound together the chief conspirators for Cowper's good seemed for a time to be broken. Johnson, indeed, wrote to Hayley and tried, a little awkwardly, to say "what a owt to 'a said"; but Lady Hesketh found it difficult to write sympathetically in a case so peculiar, and preferred to be silent. The correspondence was reopened by Hayley himself taking the initiative, and inviting Lady Hesketh, with her "good coadjutor of Norfolk" and "the dear Cowper," to Eartham or its neighbourhood. To accept the invitation was impossible, but Lady Hesketh wrote at great length, full of hope for the complete restoration of Cowper's health, expressing her desire that he would devote himself rather to original composition than to the task of a translator, and relieving herself of much indignation against the publisher—another of the tribe of Johnson—who had announced the appearance of Cowper's lines *On the Receipt of my Mother's Picture*, without having obtained permission from either the writer or his friends. Loud also was her complaint against the Treasury, which had neglected to send Cowper his pension. Of twelve quarters due he had received only one, and Lady Hesketh hastily assumed that such neglect was peculiar to Cowper's case. The times bore hardly upon the Treasury, and Cowper was only one of many who suffered.

During 1798 Hayley was overwhelmed with real and deep distress caused by the early stages of the long and fatal illness of his beloved son. There is true feeling and, bearing in mind the facts, real pathos in the words which he wrote, on a closing day of January, to Lady Hesketh: "I have limited the hopes and purposes of my remaining life to these two grand objects—to promote the professional prosperity of my little artist, and to witness and contribute to the recovery of my favourite friend to the utmost of my power." Hayley still believed that his plot had effected some good, and that Cowper was progressing towards sanity, happiness and health. No further efforts, however, were made to obtain letters from members of Parliament, "episcopal coadjutors," or "luminaries of the law." This special experiment to raise the unhappy poet's dejected spirits had come to an end. Lady Hesketh's sense of the Hermit's disinterested zeal on behalf of her cousin found material expression in her gift of "a most elegant standish of cut-glass and silver," gracefullest of ornaments for a poet's table. And never probably in the history of cut-glass did an elegant standish evoke more applause and lyrical enthusiasm on the part of the receiver.

There is a passage in the *Second Memorial* in which Hayley digresses from his immediate narrative and recalls an incident of his visit to Weston in 1792. To extract it will add something to what he, and Southey after him, told of the moment, so dreadful to Cowper, when Mary Unwin was for the second time the victim of a paralytic seizure. His first words to Hayley were, says the *Life*, " wild in the extreme, and Hayley's answer would appear little less so, but it was addressed to the predominant fancy of his unhappy friend." The words actually spoken are recorded in the *Memorial:* " Returning from her apartment to me, with a countenance of absolute distraction, he exclaimed, ' There is a wall of separation between me and my God.' I looked fixedly in his face and answered with equal celerity and vehemence of expression, ' So there is, my friend, but I can inform you I am the most resolute mortal on earth for pulling down old walls, and by the living God I will not leave a stone standing in the wall you speak of.' He examined my features intently for a few moments, and then, taking my hand most cordially, he said, with a sweet appearance of recovered serenity, ' I believe you,' and, as I have said in his *Life* in mentioning that dreadful alarm, from that moment he rested on my friendship with such mild and cheerful confidence that his affectionate spirit regarded me as sent providentially to support him in a season of the severest affliction." When the time came for Hayley to say farewell, and this was not until by his use of medical electricity he had effected a considerable improvement in Mary Unwin's condition, the parting with Cowper was one of affectionate tenderness. Cowper dwelt on the great comfort and support which he had derived from Hayley's visit, pressed the hand of his departing guest, and said with his own peculiar sweetness of voice and manner, " Adieu ! I ne'er shall look upon thy like again."

It may be thought, and not unreasonably, that Hayley's visionary devices for Cowper's restoration were the lost labours of a love which was not wise. This certainly cannot be said or thought of his long and unremitting efforts to secure a pension for his friend; nor should we know how unremitting these efforts were—for Hayley's modesty withheld him from making the facts public either in his *Life of Cowper* or in the *Memoirs* of his own life, prepared for posthumous publication—were it not that he put them on record in a series of unpublished letters, addressed in terms of the tenderest affection to his son, and written almost immediately after the events which they recount. The alarming illness of Mrs. Unwin during Hayley's visit to Weston in 1792 led him to think anxiously of what Cowper's position might be, supported only by contributions from his relations, if he were deprived of her generous care. Hayley's own finances were shrinking. He thought that some sinecure office might be bestowed upon Cowper by the Government, or some office the duties of which could be performed by a deputy. The temper of the time, however, did not favour his project. Cowper was a Whig; a gentleman familiar with the Prime Minister had said in public that, though a man of genius, he was "an absolute Jacobin"; from which accusation, when it was reported to him, Hayley warmly defended the gentle poet. On his way to Weston he had spoken of Cowper to Thurlow, then Lord Chancellor; and the solemn tenderness of Thurlow's voice when he said, "He is a truly good man," lived in his recollection. On his return to London he pleaded with great warmth for Cowper before Thurlow and Kenyon. He even suggested that it might be hinted to the king that to place the afflicted Cowper beyond possible want would be an appropriate act of personal thanksgiving to Heaven for his Majesty's recovery from his own mental malady; but to attempt this, Thurlow declared, would be an affair requiring great delicacy. Though Thurlow's temper was indolent, Hayley believed that his heart was warm. Before the close of June he addressed Thurlow in a letter, made up of verse as well as prose, in which he expressed a hope that his lordship might renew his personal acquaintance with "our dear William of Weston," under Hayley's own roof. He referred to Thurlow's recent retirement from office in flattering terms:

> "Yes! now your hand with decent pride
> Relinquishes that seal unstained,
> Which Bacon, law's less upright guide,
> With many a sordid spot profaned."

But Thurlow's retirement had been virtually enforced; it left him in no mood of amiability; and instead of the gracious reply which Hayley had expected, no answer came at all. "Judge of my surprise and mortification," he exclaims. At length the indignant Hermit relieved his feelings in a series of stanzas which he dispatched to the good cleric Carwardine with a suggestion that, if he had courage enough, he might repeat them to his patron:

> "Why, wrapt in clouds no sun pervades,
> Sullen as Ajax in the shades,
> Why Thurlow art thou mute,
> When courtesy, unstained by art,
> Addresses to thy manly heart,
> An amicable suit?"

Verses—with others that follow—which indignation made.

Hayley, despairing of the ex-Chancellor, now directed his hopes toward Pitt, the Prime Minister, whom he had known as a wonderful boy of fourteen —even a more wonderful boy, he admits, than his own sculptor, Tom—and from whom he had received, at a more recent date, an offer of the Poet-Laureateship, vacant by the death of Thomas Warton. On 11th December 1792 he wrote to Pitt, stating fully the case of Cowper, and mentioning, among other circumstances, that, in her long protection of the invalid, Mary Unwin had expended £1200, "all the ready money she possessed." Mr. Long, of the Treasury, undertook to present the letter in person; "but after detaining my letter many months," writes Hayley, "with continual protestations that he was forever seeking in vain an opportunity to present it in a favourable season, my unfortunate epistle, which had kept me in an agueish fever of expectation and disappointment, returned unopened and unpresented into my hands, in the beginning of June 1793."

Thus more than a year had passed since Hayley's attempt upon Thurlow. He could only, as he puts it, practice the military maxim of drawing courage from despair. The letter to Pitt was now dispatched by post, with some explanatory memoranda, and alas! with the inevitable verses. "The stars," he writes, "did not appear more propitious to my verse than they had proved to my prose; neither the one nor the other obtained for me the honour of a reply." Both "the Jupiter" and "the Pluto of politics"—Pitt and Thurlow—seemed to have scorned his rhymes. Hayley's second visit to Weston in October 1793 quickened his zeal. Although Cowper was able to work with him in revising Hayley's *Life of Milton*, and on his own translation of *Homer*, it became evident that the translator's mind was "sinking under the influence of incipient insanity." Had Thurlow been more active, had Pitt been more generous, Cowper's intellect, Hayley reflected, might have been saved. Wounded as his pride had been by Thurlow's silence, he determined to sacrifice his pride to his friend's service ; he called on "Pluto," the scorner of his verses, and boldly took him—in words only—by the throat.

"My Lord," said Hayley, "you *must* point out to me some method by which I may serve our poor Cowper ; what is it possible to do for him ?" To his suggestion of an appointment for Cowper, with a deputy to undertake the work, Thurlow was adverse. "'No!' replied the gloomy, yet courteous, Pluto, 'an office would only make him mad ; you must get him a pension.' 'I fear, my Lord, these are bad times for a pension.' 'No! they are not bad times for it.' 'I rejoice to hear your Lordship say so, but how can I possibly obtain it for our friend ? I had the pleasure of knowing Mr Pitt when a boy, and, though I have not seen him since that time, I have a great inclination to solicit the favour of a private conference with him, then state the case with all the little eloquence I have, and trust to his heart.' 'I am afraid you would not find he has much feeling ; perhaps you had better write to him.' 'To tell you the truth, my Lord, I have written to him on this most interesting subject already, but not successfully. My letter has not obtained the honour of a reply.' 'Well!' said the softened Pluto (a little touched by this oblique reproof to himself), 'I do not pretend to know much of political affairs at present ; perhaps, as you say you have lately seen Lord Spencer, you know more than I do ; but this I can tell you, that if you could get Lord Spencer to signify to the Minister an earnest desire that Mr. Cowper should have a pension he would soon have it.'"

Gibbon's influence with Lord Spencer was considerable ; he was a friend of Hayley, and was now in London. To Gibbon accordingly he immediately applied. The great historian sympathised deeply with Hayley, desired to be of service, but for political reasons at that time felt that it would not be proper to request Lord Spencer to solicit any favour from the Prime Minister. He urged that Hayley should himself seek an interview with Pitt, and he assured his friend that, conscious of a disinterested motive, he would speak to the Prime Minister with the same ease and spirit with which he was at the present moment speaking to himself. In great uncertainty as to what was best for Cowper's interests, Hayley turned to Lord Egremont for advice. Lord Egremont was not only friendly but eager in his anxiety to be of service. He believed that a letter addressed by Hayley to Lord Spencer as a great patron of literature would give the fairest chance of success ; but Hayley considered that it would be wanting in delicacy, if not in loyalty towards Gibbon, to write to Lord Spencer without his sanction ; and Gibbon still expressing his disapproval of the step, though in the kindest and gentlest way, the design was relinquished.

Driven to bay by repeated disappointments Hayley turned upon Pitt. In a short note he fervently solicited the grace of a few minutes' conversation. An immediate answer came, appointing the place, the day and the hour—Downing Street, on Friday, at eleven o'clock. The early hours of that formidable morning Hayley spent with his friend, the painter Romney. Perceiving his agitation, Romney prescribed a glass of port wine, which medicine succeeded only in producing a stupefying headache. As Hayley stepped into the coach, Romney's petted and coxcombical servant, Joseph, who, it was agreed, should attend Hayley, astonished him by choosing not an outer but an inner seat. Hayley, with the mildest of reproofs, explained that, though on other occasions he might welcome Joseph's company, it was not fitting that master and man should arrive as companions at Mr. Pitt's door; Joseph, with "an obliging alacrity," mounted behind, and the Hermit arrived in a fit of laughter at the appointed place in Downing Street. Pitt received his visitor, not with the solemn condescension of the Atlas of the State, but with the endearing gaiety of a friend; he listened with the kindest attention, and every appearance of sympathy. When Hayley rose to leave, he promised to consider the various possibilities and choose that one which seemed most for Cowper's advantage; he begged, however, that for the present no communication as to the favourable turn the interview had taken should be made to Cowper; "wait a little," he added; "you are going immediately, you say, into Sussex; I will see what can be done, and write to you very soon on the subject." Tears came to Hayley's eyes and he kissed the hand of Pitt "in a transport of sensibility."

Pitt's promise was made on 29th November 1793. During December Hayley waited daily for the post with eager anxiety, but no letter came. The year closed with disappointment and mortification. The new year opened with the mournful tidings of the death of Gibbon. One dear friend was gone, but one remained whom still it might be in Hayley's power to serve. In writing a letter of sympathy and condolence to Lord Spencer, he took the opportunity of urging once again the claims of Cowper, and explained the circumstances which had withheld Gibbon from being himself the advocate of Hayley's surviving friend. He recited the story of his conference with Pitt, and begged Lord Spencer to recall to the Prime Minister's mind—if a favourable occasion should arise—the promise which had not been fulfilled. The answer of Lord Spencer was sincere, frank and gracious. The state of politics did not lead to frequent communication with Pitt; but should chance bring them together at the house of some common friend, he would not fail to recall the subject to his remembrance. The good Hayley was again sanguine of success. But now came from Rose (11th February) a report of Cowper's melancholy state—despondency so deep that it might seem as if no advantage in point of fortune could send any ray of sunshine through the gloom. Moved to indignation with Pitt, yet finding for him such excuses as had been suggested by Lord Spencer, Hayley determined to put his fate, as regards the effort to obtain any advantage for Cowper, to the touch, and gain or lose it all. The following courageous letter to Pitt deserves to be placed on record:

"It is not often that a Hermit can be deceived by a Prime Minister; yet I am an example that such an extraordinary incident may happen; for in truth, my dear Sir, I most credulously confided in your kind promise of writing to me soon concerning your liberal intentions in favour of my admirable friend Cowper. Alas! instead of hearing from you such tidings as I hoped would make him happy, I have just heard from another quarter that he is recently sunk into that gloomy wretchedness and half-frantic despondency from which I was sanguine enough to expect that your just esteem and beneficence might preserve him.

"Now, perhaps even your kindness may hardly give him a gleam of satisfaction. Your enemies (a great man cannot live without enemies) affirm that you have little feeling ; this opinion I have long rejected, from my disposition to cherish an enthusiastic regard for you ; but the rejected opinion I am now unwillingly putting to the test. You must have little feeling indeed if this intelligence does not make you lament, as I do most cordially, that an unfortunate delay in providing for a man of marvellous genius may have conduced to plunge him in the worst of human calamities.

"How far it is probable that your favour might have preserved him from this evil, or may be likely to restore him from it, perhaps my Lord Spencer may be able from fuller information to judge better than I can at present. He is a neighbour and a friend to the great afflicted poet, yet, if I remember right, not personally acquainted with him ; and his Lordship has kindly promised me (should opportunity arise) to recall to your remembrance what I said to you in Cowper's behalf. Lord Spencer enters (as you kindly did when you allowed me the honour of conversing with you) into the cruel singularity of Cowper's situation, and I am confident you both sympathise in thinking that our Sovereign's munificence could not be more worthily exerted than towards this wonderful man, whether it shall please Heaven to bless him with a restoration of his rare mental endowments, or still to afflict him with a melancholy alienation of mind.

"I will not utterly relinquish the hope that you may yet be able to serve him ; afflicting as the delay has proved, I am inclined to impute it to such difficulties as men, even of excellent hearts and high stations, too frequently find in their endeavours to befriend the unfortunate.

"I write in the frank and proud sorrow of a

wounded spirit, but with a cordial and affectionate wish that Heaven may bless you with unthwarted power to do good, and with virtue sufficient to exert it.

"I retain a lasting sense of the very engaging kindness with which you allowed me to pour forth my heart to you on this interesting subject, and I am most sincerely, my dear Sir, your very grateful though afflicted servant, W. HAYLEY.

"EARTHAM, *27th Feb.* 1794."

"The Minister," writes Hayley, "did not condescend to answer this letter."

The rest of the story is well known—how Hayley was summoned to Weston by Mr. Greatheed, in the hope that his presence might be of some service to Cowper, how the little sculptor followed his father and was kindly received by the invalid; and how a letter (19th April 1794) from Lord Spencer arrived announcing that a pension of £300 a year had at last been granted. Hayley's delight was great; his labours of two years had not been unavailing. But the delight was tempered by the circumstance that Cowper himself was in no condition at that time to be disturbed even by tidings of good cheer.

AN EIGHTEENTH-CENTURY MYSTIC

A curious document in the history of eighteenth-century religious life lies before me—a manuscript written by a careful hand on rough paper in ink now somewhat faded by the passage of the years. It is an English version of the manuscript autobiography of a Protestant pietist, born in France, but a resident in Germany—Charles Hector, Marquis St. George de Marsay. A transcript of the original by a friend of the author is preserved, I believe, in the Provenzial-Kirchenarchiv at Coblenz. A portion of a text, in all essentials identical with that of Coblenz, was printed in De Valenti's *System der höhern Heilkunde*, 1826; but I am not aware that any account has been given to English readers of Marsay's strange history, except a brief sketch which forms part of a note in the second volume of Vaughan's *Hours with the Mystics*. The young writer of that interesting, but slender study of a great subject tells us that he had been lent by Mr. Tindal Harris a manuscript copy of the English *Life of De Marsay*. Whether the copy used by him was the identical volume now in my possession I am unable to say. More than one copy may have been made of a book supposed to tend to edification. Certain works, even in comparatively recent times, have enjoyed a life of considerable, though circumscribed, activity in the ambush of manuscript circulation. So it was in the earlier part of the eighteenth century with the *Vie de Spinoza* attributed to the physician Lucas. Marsay was no heresiarch like Spinoza, but his confessions are of so intimate a nature that disciples may have felt that they were hardly suited for the crowd of ordinary readers. As they come to us now they have more than a private and personal interest; they furnish materials for the study of the psychology of a people and a period.

German pietism of the seventeenth and eighteenth centuries was a great affair in the life of the nation. It was an escape from the tyranny of dogma that had stiffened into mere intellectual tradition. It was a restoration of moral life after the wreck and ruin wrought by the Thirty Years' War. It was, at a later date, a recoil of the emotions from the rationalism of the deists. Pietism satisfied after a fashion a real need of the time, a need felt not in Germany alone, but throughout every country of Europe. Molinos in Spain, Fénélon, Madame Guyon and Antoinette Bourignon in France, Spener and Francke and Zinzendorf in Germany, William Law and John Byrom in England, differing, as they did, in many respects, were agreed in demanding for the soul a warmer emotional life than that approved by the religious orthodoxy of their day. We perceive from the "Confessions of a Beautiful Soul" in Goethe's *Wilhelm Meister* that the influence of the pietistic movement was not exhausted in the second half of the eighteenth century. But its sources had been to a great extent diverted to feed the literary movement of the time. Freytag has justly observed that the sentimentality of the Werther period was the step-daughter of the emotional excitement of the elder pietism. In each there is a like habit of self-observation and endless self-confession, in each a like tender sensibility of spirit. And indeed the extravagances, irregularities and licentiousness of the sentimental period can be paralleled, and more than paralleled, by the sensual orgies of perverted pietism, when, in its ambition to transcend the limitations of the flesh, it overleaped itself and fell on the other side.

Charles Hector de Marsay was born in Paris in the year 1688. His parents at the time of the persecution of the Reformed Church had left their estate near La Rochelle, and hidden themselves in the capital. The infant was baptised "in a Roman Church." It would seem that the family had fled soon after this from France to Germany. We know little of Marsay's boyhood except that he was carefully educated in the reformed faith of his mother, and that he was attracted by the Scriptures and the books of devotion—writings of Jurieu and La Placette—which she had placed in his hands exhorting him to read them three times a day. At an early age he became an ensign in the British-Hanoverian Regiment, which fought under Marlborough during the war of the Spanish Succession. Amid the distractions of the camp he strove hard to give himself up to contemplation and prayer, but being "entirely ignorant in the Inner Ways" he found that it put a severe and constant strain upon him to bring into some degree of harmony his duties as a soldier and his secret life of devotion.

"When the feast of Easter approached I doubled my exercises of contemplation, prayer, and self-examination, in order to prepare myself worthily for the Communion. I withdrew from all society of the officers, and spent the days, as far as my calling would permit, in a quiet retirement. God gave me at that time much grace, and such a zeal and taste of his love, that I prayed three or four days without intermission, if not with the mouth yet always within myself; and although during this time our regiment was on a march and in a post where we were obliged to be under arms day and night, yet this troublesome circumstance did not hinder me to continue in prayer. It seemed to me I was already in Paradise, and was so simple as to believe this state would continue during life."

Such ecstatic happiness could not long endure, and with the trouble of mental distraction there came also bodily illness. Believing that death was near Marsay lay sick for three months at Lille, and, though calm in mind, it now seemed to him that his past joys of the soul were nothing but baseless fancies. He might have learnt, as he tells us, from the *De Imitatione*, which was by his side, that the substance of true devotion does not reside in " felt sensibilities " and " sweetnesses," but in " love of the cross, self-denial, and the resigned will to receive all from the hand of God with equanimity, the sweetnesses as the bitternesses, the attention as the dissipation, the courtings of the divine bridegroom as his absence, the banishment of the heart as the love;" but he understood not what he read, and grasped with a spiritual greediness only at what might satisfy his zeal. Failing in his desires after perpetual luxury of the soul, he had almost resolved to " let God enjoy his happiness in Heaven, and to make himself merry on earth " in the common ways of the world, when a letter reached him from his comrade, Lieutenant Cordier, dated from the camp at Bethune, in which the writer assured him that the devotion they had hitherto practised was nothing, exhorted him to make acquaintance with the writings of Antoinette Bourignon, and informed him that he, Cordier, had resolved for his own part to quit the military service, to forsake the world, to withdraw to some desert, and there to lead a poor retired life. The letter added that the chaplain of the Hanoverian Regiment, M. Baratier, had taken the same resolution, and it closed with an invitation to Marsay to join them in their retreat.

Bayle, in his *Dictionary*, having described Antoinette Bourignon's extreme uncomeliness of person, goes on in his mocking way to assert that she possessed not merely *immanent* but *transitive* chastity, the rare gift of "penetrative virginity," or infrigidation, which not only preserves its possessor's heart from temptation, but freezes up the passions of all persons who may approach her. The most virtuous of *religieuses*, he adds, have in general been content with the more common gift of immanent chastity. Eagerly Marsay bought up the writings of this illuminated lady in whose birthplace—Lille—he happened to be, and as he recovered strength read them diligently, though not without some fear lest he might fall into heresy. When restored to health he rejoined his regiment, now engaged at the siege of St. Venant, but it became clear to him that he must follow the example of his companions, abandon the career of a soldier, and lead henceforth a poor evangelical life in retirement. A regard for honour kept him from seeking his discharge until the campaign was ended; he faced the dangers of the trenches and received no hurt, but it was a joy when at length in garrison at Brussels he could invite his soul and yield himself up to such writings as *The Obscure Night* of St. John of the Cross and the *Life* of St. Teresa. After considerable difficulty and delay the discharge from military service was obtained, and late in the autumn of 1711, at the age of twenty-three, Marsay joined his two companions at Schwartzenau, where they had been permitted to settle on the property of the Countess of Wittgenstein, a devout lady who had already drawn into her neighbourhood many pious souls.

Marsay shall himself record for us the doings and the trials of this period of his life. Let those persons who smile at the religious distress caused by his hearty craving for food remember that he is not singular in such sensibility of conscience. It was a light of the Oxford movement, Richard Hurrell Froude, who made the pathetic entries in his diary: "Looked with greediness to see if there was goose on the table for dinner"; "Meant to have kept a fast, and did abstain from dinner, but at tea ate buttered toast." There was something to warrant repentance, at least from an epicure's point of view, in Marsay's choice of a cold potato as his criminal *bonne-bouche*.

"We three then began our community as Eremits, and lived very retired and solitary. Our outward order which we observed was thus regulated: we rose at four in the morning, and laboured each in his work with great stillness, after we had heard some chapters of the Holy Scriptures read by one of us. Mr. Baratier took care of the economy of the kitchen. Mr. Cordier and I went from four in the morning till seven o'clock, this spring 1711 [-12], out in the field to work and till the ground, to sow some fruit that we might have our bread. At seven we returned home and ate our breakfast of dry bread which we had baked ourselves. From that time till noon everyone had his work. Mr. Cordier's work was to spin wool, and mine to card wool and knit. It was also his part to go on errands, when it was needful to fetch something for us, and it was my part to gather leaves of trees, instead of straw, to lie upon, and to cleanse the stable. At noon we dined. Baratier boiled for us all the seven days of the week the same food. During one week we had a dish of peas and nothing else, neither before nor after, except a piece of bread to eat with the peas; the following week we had barley; the next buckwheat groats; the next oatmeal pap, and so on by changes. After dinner somebody of us read some part out of A. Bourignon's writings, then everyone went to his work until four o'clock. Then Cordier and I went again into the field to work till seven o'clock, which was the hour of supper. This consisted in a dish of pulse or salad, groats, turnips, yellow turnips, or something else, as the season of the year did furnish. After supper we remained in our chamber at work till nine o'clock, when we retired to rest.

"So we spent the day, and kept silence in our employments. Our exercise was to be in a constant recollection, to be turned inward and remain in the presence of God. We spoke or asked nothing but what was necessary. Our drink was clear water, and when it pleased Mr. Baratier to give us a special treat, he boiled groats in milk for us. I can say that this was so delicate food that I could not master my appetite in it as I would. I tried it and sometimes took wormwood to overcome my taste, but all in vain, and I had constantly to fight against my desire of eating what was a grievance to me. For I had so warm a desire for the hour of meals and longed so much for it, that it put me in a continual conflict and caused me much suffering. For I had a great appetite to eat, and yet dared not satisfy the same without fear and doubt. I would during the meal keep my thoughts to the presence of God, but was much interrupted in it by my desire of eating, which many a year has exercised me. Among other things I remember that once I ate a potato between meals, for which I was severely reproved in my conscience. I would excuse the matter within myself and not confess my fault to God; but I fell into inward darkness, which was so terrible that it seemed to me as if I was plunged into the deepest abyss. I went out into the wood, and sat comfortless down on the stump of a tree. It appeared to me as if God had rejected me, and would have nothing to do with me, having given me up to myself, which gave me a deep and inexpressible pain. But this did not last long, and when I confessed my fault it pleased his goodness soon to dissipate this dark cloud and to restore me to my former calmness of mind."

It will be noticed that in this record of a day's doings no regular hours are mentioned as being set apart for prayer. The members of the little community, says Marsay, endeavoured, in accordance with Antoinette Bourignon's directions, to make all they did a prayer, by doing it in God's presence and to please and serve Him. He himself ceased from his laborious efforts at contemplation, and his prayer became a childlike babbling of the heart to the invisible Friend: "this was the reason that I read but little, and what Brother Lawrence of the Resurrection mentions of this exercise of the presence of God which he practised in his kitchen work and when he made dumplings, that was also my business that I performed all my poor work in His love and presence."

Suffering much, however, for a time from spiritual aridity, he thought it well to consult and beg for the prayers of a pious shoemaker at Schwartzenau, one Maximilian Daut, who had written a prophetical book of some repute. On his way home from this visit, Marsay heard the words of Scripture pronounced in his inward senses: "Is there no God in Israel that thou goest to Baal-zebub?" whereupon with a loud voice he took up the words, and repeated them again and again, while light and joy arose in his heart. Still he looked to Daut for help of a humbler kind. For having a frequent combat with his laziness, he would have learnt the shoemaking business from the prophetical cobbler, but his whole body had grown lean and his fingers cracked and sore, which hindered him from his desire. It may indeed have been well for him that it was so, for he had always to strive against his inclinations, which would violently enter into whatever he undertook, and would dwell in this with pleasure, and the fascination of the awl and last might have won his affections from higher things. Even his knitting had a strange charm as he sat with his tackle before him: "and as I in this constantly received an inward reproach, I was often under a necessity to leave off from working, and to follow the attraction of God, who drew me softly and yet strongly into his holy presence." On one of these occasions, when he was drawn away from his work, it was suddenly disclosed to him that the activity of his intellect and the multiplicity of his desires in prayer were a hindrance to true communion. The voice spoke to him: *Thou art only a babbler! Be silent!* "This word stunned me, and made me immediately to do it, in that it gave me to perceive the intimatest unction, and a much more substantial presence of God than I had ever had in all my babbling, which I forsook from that time." The meaning of the prayer of silence had been disclosed to him. But now the body, that despised companion of the soul, began to take its revenge. Physically lowered as he was by Mr. Baratier's culinary economy it is no wonder that Marsay's desire of eating and laziness troubled him sorely; no wonder that the three members of the little community, not recognising the cause, and attributing their state to Satan, became hysterical and light-headed. "Instead of silence and being turned inward, which hitherto we had observed, we began from morning till night to prate. My two companions were in the same situation with me. Finally we were no longer masters of ourselves. It seemed we were three merry brethren, which did nothing together the whole day but laughing, sporting, and playing the fools. This gave me great pain and sorrow. I thought, 'My God, what state is this and how will it end?' When I would reflect upon my lamentable state and endeavoured to restrain myself, a laughing so violently seized me that I thought I should burst, just as if I was possessed by a spirit who mocked my reflection and care." He was under the feet of the evil spirits, who seemed to be given power to deal with him as they pleased.

Deliverance from this lamentable condition came not through active resistance, but through entire resignation to the will of God, through yielding, without terms, at discretion, to the Father who had sent this trial as a rebuke to his self-righteousness and self-will. Were it God's will, writes Marsay, that his fall and utter ruin should be brought about, he was prepared to consent even to this; at which the transcriber, taking alarm, appends a note: "Some reader might think that the author had here pushed the resignation too far. But such souls as are destined for so high a union with God are led through these abysses." The hysterical extravagances into which the three cenobites had found themselves falling must have led them to question the wisdom of their austerities, and it was easy for them to regard these as mere works of the law—" our severe and exactly limited manner of living received a mighty shock; it was no longer possible to stick to the rules to which we had bound ourselves." The writings of Antoinette Bourignon lost their power over Marsay; he had learnt to renounce his own will, and the thoughts which invited him back to his past way of severity seemed a temptation of Satan. He had before him as a warning the example of his companion, Cordier, who, unwilling to enter upon the gentler way of grace, withdrew for a time into complete solitude. "But Satan seduced him through pride, and when he had found a woman that on the outside had a great appearance of spirituality, in regard to her poor and severe life, in which she as a hermit lived all alone in a little hut in a distant place, he suffered himself to be seduced by this creature, that was a bad spirit, to marry her," and so, declining from bad to worse, became in no long time an Epicurean addicted to the world and the lusts of the flesh and under the power of Satan.

Happier was Marsay's lot when, being brought gradually into the path of humility, discretion, sobriety and modesty, he was called to enter into the state of holy matrimony, in order that he and his wife might live together in entire abstinence, yet in entire spiritual union. "One day," he writes, "when in great calmness of mind I was sitting under a tree with my knitting tackle, it was shown to me, if it was true that I was willing to be the property of

God without exception, it was his will that I should give Him the first proof thereof in marrying the Lady Clara de Callenberg that then lived with the Dowager Castell." The Lady Clara was thirteen years older than her husband. She had grown up under the care of elder sisters, for at her birth her mother had become deranged and did not ever recover sanity. A deep impression had been made on the minds of the Ladies Callenberg, when Clara was about twenty-five years of age, by the conversation of certain Swiss and German pietists. As long as these spiritual teachers were persons of rank the ladies' brother endured their presence, but when two men of low descent took their place it was otherwise; the pious culprits were brought before the master of the house, who bade his servants cudgel them soundly, and then ordered them to prison. Fearing that the curse of God would descend upon their father's house, the five ladies resolved to remain in it no longer, and one Sunday, while their brother was at church, they packed up their things, dressed themselves meanly as daughters of common people, and accompanied by two maids, set forth—the seven virgins—on foot for Cassel. It was their purpose to push on to Erfurt, where living was cheap, and there support themselves by fine needlework. "While they were upon their way they saw that their brother came on horseback just meeting them, but, as he was shortsighted, they hid themselves behind a thicket of bushes on the side of the highway; so he rode past them very near without observing them." Before they could leave Cassel they were cited to appear before a commission appointed by the Landgrave to inquire into matters of religion in connection with the movement of pietism. It seemed to them that the examination was meant only to delay and harass them, and so, asking no leave, they departed on foot for Allendorf.

At this point the story of the Ladies Callenberg brings them into connection with the celebrated Eva von Buttlar, whose Philadelphian Society, founded somewhat on the model of the English associations of Pordage and Jane Leade, became infamous as a centre of the wildest extravagances of opinion, the maddest aberrations of the religious imagination, and the most reckless moral disorder. Eva had not yet risen to her highest eminence as the Door of Paradise, the New Jerusalem, the Second Eve, the Mother of us all, the Wisdom from Heaven. The little Mother (*Mama'chen*), with her companion Winter, the little Father (*Papa'chen*), and her young follower, Appenfeller, had not yet been elevated by their disciples into the Earthly Trinity, Father, Son and Holy Ghost. But when Clara de Callenberg and her sisters (among them the unhappy Sidonie, whose spiritual wedlock bore fruit in an illegitimate child), were admitted to the community of Mother Eve, there was already enough loose familiarity visible among its members to give Marsay's future wife a great disinclination to their companionship. She could not join them in their salutations and embracings, and thought that if this was the way which led to God, she could never hope to enter into his presence. Inheriting possibly some tendency to insanity from her mother, she fell into a profound melancholy, and "often designed to throw herself into some deep pit where no one could draw her out; but the good hand of God constantly preserved her in a hidden manner." Even after she had quitted the Philadelphian Society her mental distress continued: "When she looked out of the window and anyone passed by, she drew herself back, because she believed that all that cast their eyes upon her were bewitched by that looking on her, as she firmly had persuaded herself that she was a witch, and had founded that opinion upon the thoughts that were suggested to her, viz., that when God would not help her, Satan must." Her brother kindly received her back, and she, hopeless of salvation, pleased him by returning for a time to worldly ways, though with a deep sadness in her secret heart. At length deliverance came. One day walking in the garden as she listened to the joyous songs of the birds, a sudden desire possessed her to sing a spiritual song; she entered into her chamber, sought for her Halle hymn-book, and opening it came upon the hymn, "Immanuel, whose goodness is past numbering"; she lifted up her voice and sang amid a flood of happy tears. A passage from Jacob Boehme's writings gave her courage to seek and choose the higher way; she left her brother's house, ceased from lifeless church-goings and sacraments, and lived in holy freedom with certain godly friends at Cassel. Not indeed without trials, for she had to sustain the shock of an attack from evil spirits and the magic of certain persons (Eva's people) with whom she was before combined; at night she heard mournful voices and the hissing of serpents; but the consolations of angels would follow while she sang divine songs in a voice so much above her usual voice that it seemed to be that of some holy spirit who had joined her. The trial was ended by the vision of a Lamb with a pearl on its neck, and a book shut and beautifully bound with three silver laces—the book of her Inner State which the Lamb opened; as the evil spirit withdrew she could not refrain from calling after him, "*Be ashamed, Satan! be ashamed!*"

To draw her again into connection with Mother Eva's community, the Lady Clara's sisters sent to her, with letters of commendation proposing marriage, one Jacob Sander, the son of an apothecary of Wannefried, who, under a repute for piety, concealed a life that was grossly vicious. Clara would have avoided him, but the arts of magic had been practised; she found it impossible to rise up, and before Sander departed her troth had been plighted. Happily, through the influence of her brother, the licence of marriage with a person so much beneath her in rank was refused, and Sander, perceiving that he would in no case receive a dowry from the Lord de Callenberg, was content to let the matter drop.

The fact that the proposal of marriage had been made and accepted was sufficiently humiliating and did not serve Clara's reputation. For her comfort and guidance she saw one day when praying a cross let down from a clear sky, and supported on each side by a hand. At the foot of the cross was a finger-ring, and the words sounded in her ears, "Espouse thyself to the Cross." With only one dollar in her pocket she withdrew to Schwartzenau, took up her abode with a pious gunsmith, and as he, his wife and new-born infant had but a single room, she would climb at night to a loft where she roosted till morning "like a hen." At a later time she was received by the Lady de Dahlwig, but still lived in poverty and self-denial. "She was a diligent spinner, went herself to the next park to fetch wood for her fuel, and was very subservient to a countrywoman with whom she kept her economy; which woman was also a good instrument used by God to exercise her in denial and subjection." Clara was thirty-eight years of age when she was joined in wedlock by the late army chaplain Baratier to Marsay.

The joint fortune of the newly-wedded pair amounted to fifteenpence; but they possessed the "capital of faith," and were under no care at all for earthly things. Clara had not married below her condition, and was accordingly entitled to a dower of two hundred florins from a public foundation in Hesse. This her husband had the prudence to secure. Cordier, the former companion of Marsay, was about to undertake with his wife a journey to Jerusalem, and offered the bride and bridegroom the use of his little cottage perched on the declivity of a mountain amid a forest on the side of the Gersbach Valley. This clay hut, with earthen floor and one small window, enclosed a space about eight feet by eight. The nearest human habitation was a quarter of a league away; Schwartzenau was twice that distance from them. But when their furniture had been removed to the cottage in a wheelbarrow, they needed nothing for their happiness: "We thought we were in Paradise, such a delight and inward peace it pleased God to give us."

The news of his marriage did not please Marsay's mother, nor had she entire confidence in the wisdom of setting up house on the capital of faith. To quiet her apprehensions, and if possible to effect her conversion, Marsay left his wife in the year 1713 and set off on foot for Geneva. The French were besieging Landau, which obliged him to make a detour; he was warned of dangers from robbers, but encountered none of the marauding gangs which infested the disturbed country. He walked swiftly by roads that were unknown to him, yet only once strayed from the way. When in doubt as to his path it was his custom to shut his eyes, turn in faith to God, and proceed without reflection. But though he reached Geneva in safety the object of his journey was not at once attained. His mother was loyal to the Reformed religion; her Separatist son set all its defects before her ; " we spent our time," he writes, " chiefly in disputing." After ten days he turned his face towards Schwartzenau, and was once again in his hut upon the hillside after an absence of seven weeks.

Perhaps it was the heat aroused within him by the contention with his mother which now transformed itself into a desire to go forth and preach to all nations ; in doing so he would fain follow the example and assume the contemptible attire of the apostles. His wife had been always sickly, but she announced her intention despite every weakness to follow him throughout the world. By the wise counsel of Baratier he was led to distrust his own missionary fervour, and after a time came to look upon the design which had so strongly attracted him as a device of Satan to bring him to destruction through spiritual pride and ambition.

The household economy in the cottage was of the simplest kind : " We were quite filled with sensual sweetness [in devotion], and strongly attracted to the prayer of rest, so that we grudged the time to be spent in boiling our soup, and would therefore try to eat nothing but bread and butter and drink clear water." This diet did not suit Clara's weak health, and it was an advantage in some respects when they joined the poor widow Gruber in a somewhat larger house, a quarter of a league distant from the hut. From her they learnt housekeeping ; her garden was large, and two goats supplied them with milk. But the active duties enforced by the widow, though wholesome for the body, were a hard chastisement. The sweetnesses of prayer had to give way before the necessity of carrying dung up the hillside, of cutting wood or fetching grass and leaves for the goats. " It was shown to us that this honest widow was given to us to break our own will and to afford us exercise. This indeed she did in a masterly manner, and gave us daily opportunity of self-denial." After their open-air labours an occasional treat was permitted them of little rye-meal cakes mixed with pounded yellow turnips. Flesh meat was a luxury unknown to the cottagers. They gathered wood-herbs for their food in spring, and in summer the mountain slopes provided abundance of wild strawberries.

At this time Cordier, with his wife, returned from Damascus, where they had stopped short, being unable to pay the sums demanded by the Turks for admission to the Holy Land. They settled in the unoccupied clay hut, and wore an appearance of pious self-denial; but their true principles soon appeared in an attempt to effect a separation between Marsay and his wife, whom Madame Cordier regarded with hostility. Enraged by her failure to effect this object she induced her husband to accuse Marsay, his wife and the widow Gruber of abominable living. They were summoned to appear before the authorities, but when the accusers were required to bring their charges home, Anna Maria Cordier could say no more than that her Heavenly Father had manifested it to her. This evidence was not held to prove the defendants' guilt; Madame Cordier was told that she had her information from the devil, and so the matter ended.

The widow Gruber, though innocent of the accusations brought against her, was a tyrannous presence to her contemplative companions, with her overwhelming energy and masterful ways. "She did as much as possible according to her own will and disregarded our will; this tempted me to an averseness to her and occasioned a good deal of suffering." An amicable separation was effected, and Marsay and his wife were once more in solitary possession of the cottage.

About this time, one day in mid-winter, a woman of the Palatinate came to visit their nearest neighbour, Mr. Gross, formerly a minister, at present a devout Separatist, the husband of Mrs. Gruber's daughter. The visitor, Sophia, had formerly known Mr. Gross, and now sought his spiritual consolation; she was in extreme distress of mind and "had enfeebled her body to a great degree by fasting, watching, laying herself in the snow and water, suffering frost, to do penance as she said." Her visit was almost at an end, for she had announced her intention to return home next day to the husband with whom she had led an unhappy life. At midnight she opened the door and slipped out into the darkness. Apprehensive lest she might hurt herself, Mr. Gross and his wife followed her, roused Marsay and his wife, and accompanied by them searched through the wood, calling loudly on Sophia as they advanced. After some hours' search they heard a lamenting voice and found the poor woman lying quite naked upon the ice. They wrapped her in her clothes which lay scattered about, and bore her back to Mr. Gross's chamber, where, after some hours, she expired. A coffin was procured, and it was intended to bury her in Mr. Gross's garden. On the night before the burial the coffin was placed outside Mr. Gross's cottage door; but, in doing this, he and his wife were seized with an inward anguish, which was also experienced by Marsay's wife. They felt themselves constrained by their dead sister to bring back the coffin into the little chamber; then the anguish ceased, and the four companions sat up that night and waked the corpse, being very joyful in the Lord and calm in mind, while they lifted up their voices in spiritual songs. They had an assurance that poor Sophia had been received into the grace of God, but because she had been self-willed in her severities against herself and deficient in meek resignation, it was needful that she should submit after death to a brief period of painful yet blessed purification, which she might have sustained in this life by patient suffering, but would not. As she yet entirely lived in the inner senses, and had not attained to the higher life in the spirit, "she had after death," writes Marsay, "a power to communicate herself to our inner senses, because we were not come farther than to the state of the senses within. For the souls that live in the same ground and principle have a mutual communication."

What follows may be commended to the consideration of the Psychical Society:

"We buried her the next day in our garden. The following night, when we were gone to rest, we heard that the door of our little house was opened. I thought I had not rightly locked it, got up to shut it, and reflected no further. The night after that door, though locked with a good lock, was again opened. I went again to fasten it, and neither I nor my wife thought then that there was anything extraordinary in it. The same opening of the door happened the third night. Then we had the next day a strong impression that Sophia did thus, in visiting us, to draw comfort in her suffering condition.

"This impression seized us entirely; at night we lay down in a persuasion she would come again, and when we had extinguished our lamp our room door, which we knew was very well shut, was opened. 'This is Sophia,' whispered we to each other. I began courageously and without any terror to say to her, 'She was welcome; if she would go with us to Jesus, there we would meet one another, there alone would we be found.' I exhorted her to take her refuge to Him; if this was her resolution, as it was ours, her visit would be there pleasing to me. My wife was in fear because she had often suffered from such spirits, and pushed me to be silent. When I had done speaking, the door, which I had shut after the entry of Sophia, was opened again, and I told my wife, 'Now the soul of Sophia departs.' My wife was full of joy and called these words after her: 'Ah! my dearest Jesus, make to thyself a pure dwelling in my heart, that I may never forget Thee! May it be so with thee, poor soul; go hence into the rest of the Lord!'

"I rose again and locked our room door. After that time she never came again to visit us, but we had a strong impression that her soul was again entered into the order of the Lord, and consequently into rest also, which is always in his will and order. We have seen nothing with our corporal eyes, but the impression of her soul on ours was very calm and soft. When she opened our door it was done gently and quietly, without boisterous noise, as a token of the state in which she found herself, not in rebellion or opposition to God, but in a restful, humble suffering."

From this time onwards Marsay's life, though it underwent no violent alteration, turned outwards; ecstasies and visions are rarer, and he moves onward in closer communion with his fellowmen, and, on the whole, with a wiser and a calmer mind. Perhaps the sufferings of poor Sophia had opened his heart in sympathy with sorrow. The change first showed itself by his employing himself in useful works on behalf of his neighbours, watching by the sick, or working with his hands for those who needed a labourer in the woods and fields. A timely gift of thirty dollars from his mother re-awakened his affection for her and his desire to see her converted. Accompanied by his wife he set off (1715) once more on foot for Switzerland. They walked from six to nine leagues a day: "My wife was often as half dead with weariness. She then threw herself on the ground in the presence of God, and when thus she had rested a little while, God gave her new strength to continue her way." Clara remained at Neufchatel while her husband pushed forward to Geneva. But the meeting with his mother brought little happiness; she strongly desired that her son should find some worldly employment, and the situation of book-keeper to a great merchant in Paris was offered for his acceptance, but he could not entangle himself in the cares of business. Devout ladies welcomed Marsay and his wife to Berne. There they spent the winter of 1715-16, preserved from overmuch society by the great snow of that year. It was not till the autumn of 1716 that, having voyaged down the Rhine, they once more found themselves in their retreat at Schwartzenau.

They looked back with a sense of shame at the faults into which intercourse even with godly persons had betrayed them, and determined to live henceforth in greater self-denial. They divided among the poor their store of victuals and such linen and other goods as they possessed; they sold their house for thirty-five dollars, distributed twenty to those who had greater need of the money than themselves, and with the remaining fifteen dollars bought a little room on the impoverished ground of Christianseck, a solitary place on a height, where stood a few scattered houses inhabited by pious people, about a league from Schwartzenau. But light and joy did not attend this self-denial: "I went and spent half-days in the wood in the hope of recovering spiritual sweetnesses in that solitude, but all in vain. How much soever I endeavoured to enjoy the presence of God, in a manner that conveys delight to the inner senses, it was all without effect, and I perceived my gradual falling into dryness and aridity."

During these days Marsay willingly accepted the alms volunteered to him by godly persons. But he now questioned whether this could be rightly done since he might claim from his brother a portion of the family property, and his wife was entitled to a share of her brother's wealth. Husband and wife, though not possessed of twopence, determined to start on their several journeys, the one to Paris on his way to the home of the Marsays near La Rochelle, the other to the lands of the house of Callenberg near Cassel. A friend furnished them with a few dollars, and they bade each other farewell. "On my way, as I travelled alone," Marsay writes, "I had a strong impression that God had assigned me an angel for a companion, whereof I was so sure, as if I had seen him with my corporal eyes; this made me to travel with a joyful mind through an unknown land." On reaching the French frontier he feared that he might be arrested if he were known to be a Frenchman entering from foreign territory. "The means I used to prevent this was to clean my shoes, and to fit myself up as if I was no traveller. Thus the sentry permitted me freely to pass at the gate of Verdun, which was the first city I passed. I had no pack nor baggage, and but a shirt in my pocket. After the guard had let me pass I was called back again and asked, 'Sir, from whence do you come?' to which a sergeant that was there replied, 'Let him pass, he is a man of Sirk' (Sirk is a little city two hours from Verdun, and belongs to the Elector of Trier). I said, 'I come from Sirk;' thus they took me for a German, and suffered me to pass without further examination." On 18th October 1717 he entered Paris.

It was the time of Law's financial schemes, when Marsay, occupied with the private financial affairs, reached the capital. To his surprise he learnt that his brother had been appointed British envoy at Geneva, and was no longer in France. A kind letter assured the penniless wanderer of his brother's warm goodwill, and enabled him to procure an ample supply of money. His wife had been less fortunate, but now they were placed above want, and it was arranged that she should proceed to Berne, where her husband would rejoin her after he had visited his kinsfolk at Geneva. The change was great from their previous state of poverty, and Marsay feared lest it might fare ill with his soul amid this worldly prosperity. But Providence, as he felt, was leading him, even by such gentle means, to humility and a surrender of his own will. "God pulled all my pillars away which I had secretly built up in my manner of living formerly practised, and He removed me besides out of that lightsome faith full of assurance and certainty, in which hitherto we had stood, and made me enter into that mere or bare and dark faith which is divested of all those certainties, and in which you must be led as a child without light by the hand of the parent." His brother was surprised and pleased to find him so little of the austere ascetic; in a few days they became very good friends, and went together to sermons and holy communion, a concession which had not been expected from the recluse. A yearly allowance was assigned to Marsay, and when a little later he departed for Berne he took with him his brother's best wishes.

For a considerable time he remained in Switzerland, finding both at Berne and Vevey persons of his own way of thinking. Although his outward self-denials were fewer than before, he felt more strongly than ever "the attraction to the Centre," which draws the will into harmony with the Divine will. "This attraction and impulse is so spiritual, and so far above all what is in the sphere of the senses or reason, that they cannot reach to it;" of such inconceivable subtlety that when you desire clearly to know and consider it, the attraction disappears and is gone. A new and strange anxiety, however, troubled him; he feared that his annual income might not suffice for his expenditure, and, moved by this and other causes, he decided to return to his little room at Christianseck. On the journey, about half a league from Bâle, his wife became seriously ill; it was evening, no house was near, and the passers-by were hastening to enter the city before the gates should close. "I confess that among all the trials that had befallen us this was one of the most sensible—to be near the gates of a large city without the least assistance. I fancied no one in the world was so unhappy as we, that could stay in no place but were fugitives like Cain." Night drew on, his wife's death seemed imminent, and he could not bear to leave her alone while he sought for help. "At last, after some hours' suffering, my wife found a little ease. I went softly along with her, and we arrived in the city, going through a great part of it till we came to the Baroness de Planta, who received us kindly and procured us a lodging."

Once more in a house of his own at Christianseck, Marsay felt the need of some regular occupation, without which he could not keep his "ground," knew not where he was, and even feared that he might fall into libertinism. His mother would have been pleased to see him return to the military profession, and he was ready to submit even to this, but his brother wisely opposed a project so little suited to his temper of mind. A better way was opened for him when Divine Providence brought a good soul to lodge with him, one Godfrey Koch, "a watchmaker and an Israelite in whom was no guile." Together the two men studied the mysteries of wheels and pinions and escapements: together they pored over the deeper mysteries of the soul as explained in the spiritual writings of Madame Guyon. In the course of a year Marsay had acquired much skill and knowledge in his craft as watchmaker. A great circuit had been traversed from the ambitious days when he dreamed of playing the part of an apostle through all lands : " Now I saw myself as one cast to the ground, and reduced to that abject state as to work from morning till night upon a watch and to be busy about earthly things. This was a great abasement in the eyes of my self-loving spirit, but my ground rejoiced and whispered to me, ' See ! thy pride is stung at eating grass like an ox with Nebuchadnezzar, but really such material things are at this time better and less dangerous for the sensual and rational part of the soul, or for her inferior part, than the spiritual matters, when the soul will take them into her own comprehension and capacity, and this is that death which is absolutely necessary ; by it God will bring thee to the life of the spirit, that the Centre may be discovered and disentangled.' " Seven years were thus spent in quietness and patient work, without any remarkable external events.

In 1724 his wife's declining health, which suffered from the cold air of Christianseck, induced Marsay to move to Heidelberg. Here he continued his work as watchmaker under a more skilful master than Koch, but all the deftness of his fingers seemed to be lost. He was as awkward as if he had never handled a file. " I observed," he tells us, " that God would restrain me from being entangled and captivated by this mechanical spirit, and not permit that I should become so ingenious and accomplished a watchmaker. This made me tired of the subtile working." The more delicate craft expected by his Heidelberg master, no doubt, was unattainable by the elderly pupil of a journeyman like Koch.

The illness of his mother brought Marsay again to Switzerland. He was saddened to find that many of his former friends had turned back to the world. Among these was the Abbé de Watteville, a correspondent of Madame Guyon; he was now married, and declared that all that had passed within him in the days of his fervid faith was like a dream; "in short, everywhere was misery and dissipation to be seen among our old friends, with a mortal deadness, and we ourselves knew not where we were." An invitation from the Countess of Wittgenstein-Berleburg determined Marsay and his wife to fix their abode in her neighbourhood. They were warmly received at Berleburg by high and low; so much time indeed now began to be spent in useless conversations that Marsay decided to entertain his visitors by reading aloud a sermon for them; but somehow this edifying species of good-fellowship did not entirely succeed. He longed for solitude, and yet in solitude he suffered much misery. It was a comfort to him when he learnt, first from books and then in his own experience, that involuntary dissipations of the imagination do not necessarily hinder the prayer of rest. Three times a day he placed himself without trouble or commotion of mind in the mental attitude of prayer, and accepted whatever degree of the spirit of devotion might be granted to him. And now, through the persuasions of "the famous Dr. Carl," he was induced to take a part in certain assemblies where everyone had liberty to propose a divine matter, to speak concerning the same, or to pray. For some weeks all went well, and everyone pressed to these meetings of the devout; but the concord and communion of saints were of short duration. "Spiritual pride, love of mastership, spiritual voluptuousness, and all other abominations of this sort, a desire of new things, curiosity, envy, hatred, sensual adherence followed one another successively, and all these poisonous animals entered our meeting. It is true they came not barefaced but masked." Many high-flying spirits would consent to no way but their own. Marsay began to perceive that congregations or societies of this kind cannot subsist without human laws ordained to restrain the spirits within the limits of reason, decency and regularity. The overflowing pleasure which he had felt at first in his own extempore prayers seemed to him before long to be rather a carnal than a spiritual delight.

Soon after his arrival at Berleburg letters had come from America, describing Pennsylvania as an earthly Paradise. With two or three hundred dollars one might purchase a considerable parcel of land ; the soil was fruitful ; there was full liberty of conscience to live as a good Christian in solitude ; there was employment for all, and especially good employment for one skilled in watchmaking. A large number of persons, nearly one hundred, resolved to emigrate, and Marsay, with his wife, had a mind to join the party. His mother and brother, however, strongly opposed the project, and for a time it was dropped. When it was revived in 1726, Marsay contrasted in his fancy the charm of solitude in the earthly Paradise in Pennsylvania with the bickering and backbiting of the religious meetings at Berleburg. He was ready to depart, and had taken leave of his friends, when letters arrived, giving a lamentable description of the misery endured by the emigrants ; many had died from the hardships of the voyage, among them the good old widow Gruber and her daughter. At first it seemed to Marsay as if these tidings were a call to him to endure hardness, and that the prospect of suffering and death made it more than ever desirable that he should commit himself to God and embark. He saw, as in a vision, his wife dying in great misery and her body thrown into the sea. His heart was touched to the quick, yet he could not desist from his resolution. But a way of escape was opened : " One evening when I was preparing for rest, and in my prayers placed myself and my wife before God as two animals of sacrifice, that with full consent and surrender would expect nothing else but to be offered up, there rose at once from my inner ground a soft and placid conviction in my understanding, which showed me, ' It was enough ; the sacrifice was made, we had now offered our Isaac, God did not require any more from us ; ' and this offering of Abraham was in a quite peculiar manner represented to me, with an addition of signifying that we should no longer think of the voyage, but keep ourselves quiet." This sufficed for the occasion ; but it was afterwards shown to Marsay that the desire he had for outward solitude in the Transatlantic world was an impure passion, having selfishness for its chief ingredient.

In September 1730 the Count von Zinzendorf arrived at Schwartzenau, whither Marsay still resorted in the summer. Zinzendorf was by many years the younger man, but he was already famous for his talents as well as his piety, and had already established his common order of worship for the brethren at Herrnhut. Marsay and his wife dined with him at the house of the Countess Dowager de Wittgenstein : " but notwithstanding all the good opinion the public had of him, it appeared to my wife as if he had such a physiognomy, more internally than outwardly, which was quite contrary to her, and made her to have an aversion against him." From Schwartzenau the Count proceeded to Berleburg, and there every day held spiritual assemblies, where by his fine appearance and humble yet eloquent words he drew many souls captive. Among these, notwithstanding their dislike on first acquaintance, were the Marsays, and it may perhaps have been that the magic of evil spirits, against which Marsay afterwards wrote, contributed to the fascination. An attempt was made to establish at Berleburg another community like that of Herrnhut. On three successive Sundays Marsay supplied the place of a brother who had fallen sick, and preached with such unction and power that he himself wondered at it, for he had never before delivered a public discourse. It almost seemed as if it were in his choice to become another Zinzendorf. He stood, as it were, at the parting of the ways. Should the watchmaker rise into the apostle ? His answer was given without hesitation : "When I was in my prayer the choice was given me inwardly, whether I would be enriched with the like gifts to edify my neighbour, and by being endued with extraordinary talents, that bear a great appearance, be esteemed as a saint among the godly . . . whether I would be in a state of a clear light and tasting faith, which enables us to apply these talents with a great perception in the senses, and with a zeal that conquers them ; or whether I would choose to be stripped of all these things and to die off from them in the way of a dark faith and terrible desert that had no end but to die off from all. The inclination of my ground did then without any hesitation immediately choose the latter state and rejected the first." And from that moment all his gifts of unction and eloquence departed from him. He withdrew from the public assemblies of the saints, and would enter into no dispute with this one or that —" It is best to be silent and keep your mystery to yourself." His wife, with some uncertainty as to whether she was right, followed his example. When any person would persuade her that her conduct was erroneous she defended it with energy, but as soon as the person was gone her former doubts returned.

The some time Separatist, Marsay, now desired to frequent again the Reformed Church, after he had "got rid of all the little divided sects that had occasioned us so much suffering and with which we would have no further connection." Not that he would allow church-going to be a slavery; he still claimed the liberty to attend public worship or to stay away as he was moved by his inward "ground." He had through much pain and shuddering awe been given "a propensity to that pure intuition, which is the continual office and privilege of the seraphim," but he no longer undervalued the outward ordinances of religion. He had seen at Schwartzenau the miserable results of the Separatist movement on young people, who had been brought up without attendance at the services of the Church, who had not inherited the internal godliness of their parents, and who had given themselves up in many instances to the spirit of libertinism. Still for his own part he was happiest alone with his Bible or his *De Imitatione —in angello cum libello.* And a way of usefulness to others was discovered to him when in 1734 he found that he could employ his pen with good effect in the cause of religion. It seemed to him that he was like a man "that for many years on a long voyage had been carried through many unknown countries with tied-up eyes; when the band that blindfolded him is removed all is a wonder to him when he reviews all the ways through which he has been led." In September of that year he felt as though the pure fire of the Divine love possessed him wholly: "one night especially, which I shall never forget, God alone knows what then passed; it is beyond description; I must not speak of it, but be silent and adore. Only this I will mention, that from that period of time all my troubles, anxieties, and griefs are vanished, there is now no care nor sorrow for anything whatever remaining." We shall not pry with conjecture into that mystery of joy.

On 21st February 1742, after twenty-nine years of spiritual union, for in this sense only was it marriage, Marsay lost his wife. Two letters which he wrote on that occasion are preserved. The closing weeks of her life were darkened by a terrible despair of her salvation. "She experienced," writes her husband, "the descension to hell with Christ," nor was there any lightening of her anguish before the end. It was happy that before this sorrow Marsay had gained a dear friend in Mr. de Fleischbein, who had first sought his services as a watchmaker, and afterwards had come to love him with a brotherly affection. Other friends were found in some young kinsfolk of his own, children of his second sister, the Lady de Carlot. His elder years were calm and happy. The substance of his faith in its final form is thus expressed in his own words:

"I have lost all thoughts of a mystical state, and rest humbly and simply on the grace in Jesus Christ. . . . Not that I reject or disbelieve the truth and substance of all the mystical states whereof I have wrote. No! but the thoughts, the form and the image of them is taken away from me by the aforementioned state of humiliation." To the last, however, his devout habit of discovering special providences in the incidents of his life remains. He had found that the use of a prayer-book was necessary to him for purposes of private devotion and had chosen

Gottfried Arnold's *Prayers of the Spirit.* He had presented his own copy to a certain nobleman, and tried to procure another copy, but all in vain: " this made me believe it was not the will of God I should any longer offer my prayers to Him in that fashion. And really from that time it pleased Him in His infinite goodness to restore to me gradually the attraction to the simple internal prayer, whether in silence in His presence, or in words expressed by love, or in simple thoughts and love-affections, quite unrestrained and free as it pleased Him to give."

At Ambleben, on 3rd February 1753, Marsay died, aged sixty-five. Mr. de Botticher, his sister's son-in-law, and the Pastor Gerhard were with him during his illness. He looked forward to his death with cheerfulness. " I swim and bathe in joy," he said a few days before his death, " that I shall now soon obtain what, through the grace of our Saviour, I have so long ardently wished and hoped for." Only one harsh gesture was observed before he drew his last breath.

I have ended my task as recorder of this fragment in the history of Eighteenth-Century Pietism. If there be morals to be drawn and practical applications, I must leave these to the reader.[1]

[1] A translation of some of Marsay's writings appeared (1749) in Edinburgh, under the title, *Discourses on Subjects relating to the Spiritual Life.*

SOME OLD SHAKESPEARIANS

(*From Reed's MS. Note-Books*)

In that common fosse where are buried so many respectable bones of eighteenth-century men of letters, Nichols's *Literary Anecdotes*, may be found a notice of Isaac Reed, editor of the *Variorum Shakespeare*, 1803, of Dodsley's *Old Plays*, and many other volumes, a notice dictated by Nichols from what he described as " a bed of pain and anguish," being his " last tribute of respect to so exemplary a character." He speaks of the pleasant gatherings of eighteenth-century Shakespearians in the autumn of several successive years at Cambridge, where the author of the *Essay on the Learning of Shakespeare*, Dr. Farmer, the Master of Emmanuel College, made the parlour a centre of hospitality. " At that period," says Nichols, " the Theatricals of Stirbitch Fair had powerful patronage in the Combination Room of Emmanuel, where the routine of performance was regularly settled, and where the charms of the bottle were early deserted for the pleasures of the sock and buskin. In the boxes of this little theatre Dr. Farmer was the *Arbiter Elegantiarum*, and presided with as much dignity and unaffected ease as within the walls of his own College. He was regularly surrounded by a large party of congenial friends and able critics ; among whom Mr. Reed and Mr. Steevens were constantly to be found." Steevens, though as quarrelous as a weasel, had, the biographer goes on to say, an inviolable attachment to Reed. Two other persons stood within the same charmed circle, safe from his capriciousness of temper—the Master of Emmanuel and Tyrwhitt, the editor of the *Canterbury Tales*.

If we could join the party in the Combination Room and the parlour we might happen to hear some interesting talk before the charms of the bottle had been superseded by those more classical ones of sock and buskin. Well, in a poor, imperfect way we can be eavesdroppers. At the sale of Isaac Reed's great library in 1807 his old friend, James Bindley, was the successful bidder for a miscellaneous lot, which included certain manuscript note-books, memoranda, adversaria. Bindley was himself a mighty hunter after books and engravings, with which and with the reading of the proof-sheets of Nichols's *Literary Anecdotes* he beguiled the leisure remaining to him after the performance of his duties as Commissioner of the Stamp Office. His broad face smiles in an engraving by Basire from opposite the title-page of the fourth volume of the *Literary Illustrations*, and to him the entire collection of *Anecdotes* is dedicated. Thirty-one of these note-books in the handwriting of Isaac Reed are now in my possession, and I am not aware that any use has been made of them since they passed into James Bindley's hands in December 1807. One series is devoted to diaries of the visits to Cambridge in successive years from 1782 to 1795, from which we can ascertain in a general way how the days went by. Two years after the latter date Dr. Farmer died.

According to the *Dictionary of National Biography*, Isaac Reed was born on 1st January 1741-42. He himself enters under the date 12th January

1801: "My birthday, æt. 59." The earliest of the note-books before me is of the date 1762, when Reed had just passed his twentieth birthday. He seems not to have kept a regular diary, but rather to have recorded whatever marked a day as in some degree illustrious. And among the red-letter days of all his life, those on which he visited the theatre, the Sundays on which he listened to some eminent preacher, and, as he became known to other distinguished men, those days on which he met contemporary scholars and artists and actors were, in the word of Dickens, the "reddest-lettered." But there were now and again other things to be recorded. The entry for 10th July 1762 is the following: "This whole day I was at Guildhall. Heard the Tryal of the Cock Lane Ghost, which began at 9 in the morning and continued to ½ past 9 in the evening, when the Revd. Mr. Moore, Mr. James Parsons, his wife, and Frazier were found guilty." He goes of course to see the lions at the Tower, and pays a visit to "Bethlem"; when May arrives he is punctual in securing an early view of the Artistic Exhibition in Spring Gardens and that in Pall Mall; he hears the famous and often-repeated "Lecture on Heads"; sees Astley's equestrian performances and Lunardi's ascent in the air balloon; witnesses at Sadler's Wells the dancing of Grimaldi; attends the trial of Mr. Warren Hastings in Westminster Hall; is present in the Abbey at the Handel Jubilee; takes part in thanksgiving services and public rejoicings for the King's recovery; listens to debates in the House of Lords and the House of Commons (Can anyone tell me offhand what was "Mr. Glyn's motion" and what became of it?); listens to other debates at the Robin Hood Society on such grave questions as "Whether Human Reason alone is capable of conducting us through all the Moral Duties of Life?" and "Is Good Friday a Day of Joy or Sorrow?" He gazes at the procession of convicted criminals on their way from Newgate to execution; and on one quite crimson-lettered day—it was the 1st August 1770—he writes at night:—"Went with Bailey to see the execution of Jno. Stretton at Tyburn. After, to Westm^{r} Abbey. Even^{g} at H. M. (Haymarket). Saw the *Lame Lover and Midas*."

On Sunday mornings, afternoons and evenings Isaac Reed was still on pleasure bent—or pleasure, let us say, united with profit. He was liberal in his ecclesiastical sympathies. Dr. Porteus, Dr. Newton, Bishop of Bristol, Bishop Warburton, but more frequently than any of these Archbishop Secker found in him an attentive listener. Perhaps Dr. Dodd, forger and divine, with whom Reed had some personal relations, was his favourite Anglican preacher. But the Rev. Dr. Fordyce, an acquaintance of Johnson, a poet as well as an eloquent preacher, often drew him to a Presbyterian church; at a Methodist Meeting House he heard a fervent Anglican divine, Mr. Romaine, discourse; once at least he attended a silent meeting of Friends; and once he dared to enter what he terms "a Popish Chappel."

Six days as against one, however, gave the stage heavy odds against the pulpit, and, indeed, "exemplary character" as Nichols calls him, and as in fact Reed was, with his advancing years theatrical performances and the round of dining-out with distinguished friends leave scanty space for his record of Sunday services and sermons. The names of every distinguished actor and actress, and those of many who never rose above subordinate parts, appear upon his manuscript pages. Garrick, Sheridan, Barry, Woodward, Foote, Weston, Shuter, Young, Kemble, Henderson, Macklin, Wilkinson, Bannister, Palmer, Cibber, Pritchard, Bellamy, Pope, Abington, Baddeley, Siddons, and among vocalists—Catley, Linley, the " Messiah Singers," the " Spirituale Singers," and many others appear and reappear. Among Reed's " first nights " of the performance of pieces which are still a part of literature were 29th January 1768, when *The Good-natured Man* was given at Covent Garden, and Goldsmith wept and swore that he would never write again, for the success was not quite unqualified ; and 15th March five years later, when Johnson, Burke and Reynolds were present to applaud *She Stoops to Conquer*. That year, the last complete year of Goldsmith's life—" that absurd creature, Goldsmith," he is styled by Reed—was one of triumph ; his new play was presented at the Haymarket as well as at Covent Garden, and at the latter theatre *The Good-natured Man* soon followed upon *She Stoop's to Conquer*.[1] Again, on 8th May 1777, Reed was a spectator when, on a first night, *The School for Scandal* had its dazzling victory. With Garrick in all his leading parts Reed was well acquainted, and on 10th June 1776 he saw the great actor, as Don Felix, take his farewell of the stage. Somewhat later he breakfasts and dines with Mr. Garrick. The *Biographia Dramatica* of 1762, founded on Baker's *Companion to the Playhouse*, had evidently an editor qualified by theatrical tastes and experience in Isaac Reed ; he collected materials for an enlarged edition, but that which appeared in 1812, some years after his death, was the work of Stephen Jones.

The early hours of the eighteenth century gave

[1] I assume that Reed's entries as to plays and theatres may be trusted.

ample time for after-dinner talk before the playhouse opened. Through the booksellers and publishers, Newbery and Nichols, Dodsley and Dilly, through the actors Macklin and Henderson, and at Enfield through Richard Gough, the antiquary, Reed made his entry into society. That was a pleasant gathering on 23rd March 1788, at Mr. Malone's, when he dined with Johnson's friend, Bennet Langton, Dr. Farmer, Sir Joshua Reynolds, Mr. Boswell, and Mr. Kemble; and that again, on Shakespeare's birthday, two years later, when Alderman Boydell was the host. In that year, 1790, the artistic alderman was elected Lord Mayor, and his Shakespeare Gallery was receiving many additions; among the guests at dinner were West, and Sandby and Sir Joshua. Again two years, and Reed was one of the mourners at Sir Joshua's funeral at St. Paul's. With George Steevens he seems to have become intimate about 1777; the first mention of Farmer in the manuscript jottings occurs, I think, in the spring of 1782. When the Master of Emmanuel College came up to town he would often dine with Reed and accompany him to the theatre. Their passion for old books was a bond of friendship, not a ground for rivalry. On 18th March 1791 they went together to see "Madame D'Eon's library"—Madame D'Eon being the famous epicene Chevalier.[1] Both were welcome guests at Steevens' house, the "Upper Flask," at Hampstead. On 17th August 1790 occurs an entry of interest: "Went with Mr. Steevens to St. Giles's, Cripplegate, to search for the body of Milton. Found what was supposed to [be] him."[2] On 22nd January 1800 Steevens died.

[1] Mlle. D'Éon, in the catalogue of the library, is *Chevalière*, and a preface gives a narrative of her "very extraordinary case," as the title calls it.

[2] For an account of the exhumation see *N. and Q.*, 7th series, ix. 361-364.

Reed attended the funeral of his friend at Poplar Chapel. The clergyman of Poplar, the clergyman of Hampstead, an apothecary, a Mr. Nettleship, and "Little Meen," as Steevens used to call him, a poet, a prebendary, and classical scholar, together with Reed himself, were present. In his note of the event Reed adds the aspiration "*requiescat in pace*," which had a special propriety in the case of one who while he lived could not easily keep the peace. Six months later he went (12th June) "to Poplar Chapel with Mr. Flaxman, the Statuary, Mr. Long and Mr. Braithwaite, to fix on a place for Mr. Steeven's monument." The monument—a bas-relief portrait—was the work of Flaxman. The entry for 20th September of that year indicates for Reed the beginning of the end: "From this day to Christmas Day confined with a paralytick affection, which during the greater part of the time incapacitated me from assisting myself even in the slightest manner." He recovered, however, resumed his dinings-out, and before the end arrived did much work, as is evidenced by the *Variorum Shakespeare* of 1803.

In summer and early autumn Reed sometimes went for short excursions abroad—now to St. Omer and Dunkirk, now to Ghent and Bruges and Brussels, and once to Holland. More frequently his holiday was spent in his own country. He was an early follower of the poet Gray—the interval was only three years—in visiting the English lakes. Sometimes Tunbridge Wells or Bath contented him. In 1796, on his way to Bath, he stopped at Reading, and records that he bought some books from Mrs. Smart, widow of the unhappy poet whose "Song to David" has been so enthusiastically praised by Robert Browning and Dante Rossetti. In the biography of Sheridan by Mr. Fraser Rae, it is stated that Sheridan's verses entitled "Clio's Protest, or the Picture Varnished," were written as an answer to "The Bath Picture," by Mr. Miles Peter Andrews, a minor dramatist to whom Gifford deals hard measure in "The Baviad." Mr. Fraser Rae has probably excellent evidence for his statement, but it may be worth putting on record the gossip heard at Bath by Reed. "Palmer and Oliver talking of a Captain Rice, who had been a poet and insane, Palmer mentioned a poetical piece by him called 'The Picture,' which was followed by another by Mr. Sheridan called 'The Picture Varnished.' Query, Where is the last to be found?" In answer to the query it may be said that Sheridan's verses, which include the well-known lines:

> "You write with ease to show your breeding,
> But easy writing's damned hard reading,"

may be found in the first volume of *The New Foundling Hospital for Wit.*

With Bath in the eighteenth century we are all familiar. We are not so intimately acquainted with the health resorts of Derbyshire. In the autumn of 1766 Isaac Reed stayed at Matlock and Buxton, and he gives a detailed account of all the wonders of the Peak. He speaks with an eighteenth-century townsman's feeling of the awful mountains among which Matlock is lodged: "The Prospect, though confined, is the most romantick imaginable, the Mountains on all sides being so extreamly lofty that they at once strike the Imagination with horror and delight." The residence and bath-house is carefully described. "This Place," he goes on, "is conducted in a different manner from any other place of Publick Entertainment, it belonging to Eight Gentlemen in the County, who about the year 1746 took a Lease of it, and have ever since managed it by their Servants. The Expenses are small, no more than 8d. being paid for breakfast, 1s. for Dinner, 6d. for Supper, and nothing being demanded on account of Lodging, and the Attendance and Accommodation [being] both good this may be considered as the cheapest Place of Publick Resort as well as that at which you may reside with the most Ease and Satisfaction." In the Long Room, at dinner and supper, "all the Company compose one Family, the Gentlemen sitting at one side of the Table, and the Ladies opposite to them on the other." Half-way up the ascent, on the other side of the Derwent, across which a ferry conveyed parties of twelve or sixteen, was a resting-place where they might "drink Tea," and if "attended by Musick," enjoy a more composite pleasure. "The Sound of Musick among these Rocks," says Reed, "is beyond Expression charming."

The description of Buxton is less attractive: "From the miserable appearance of Buxton it could hardly be supposed that it would [be] chosen as a place of Residence by any Persons except those who are drawn thither by Motives of Health. Yet in the Summer Season I am informed it is much frequented as a Place of Entertainment. It is situate in the midst of a very barren desart Country, the buildings (except the Inns) are despicably mean, and there appears nothing to recommend it as a Place of Diversion."

Reed's autumnal visits to Emmanuel College seem to have begun in the year 1782. The first of the diaries appropriated to a memorial of these visits is named by the writer "A Specimen of a History of a Man's importance to Himself;" later note-books are headed "More Proofs of a Man's Importance to Himself," and "Self-Importance." On the evening before starting for Cambridge Reed ordinarily made his way by coach or on foot from his rooms in Staple Inn to the house of George Steevens at Hampstead. "I left Staple Inn," he writes (13th September 1790) "at eleven o'clock, and at Middle Row met with Boswell, who told me Malone would finish his edition of Shakespeare in a fortnight. Then went to the Shakespeare Gallery"—he means that of Alderman Boydell—"to meet Mr. Steevens, with whom and with Mr. Dodsley I remained some time in conversation. Walked with Mr. Steevens to Hampstead. Dined and Slept there." The sheets of Boydell's Shakespeare, which Steevens revised, followed Reed to Cambridge, and had the benefit of his proof-reading. A scholar's wardrobe, conveyed to the "Upper Flask" and meant for display at the university, was not extensive; the most important items in Reed's list of 1793 are "1 suit of Black Cloaths, 7 Ruffled Shirts, 6 Socks, 1 Wig," with his shaving box and razors. On one occasion, however, an addition had to be made at Cambridge of "black buckles for the mourning for the Duke of Cumberland." Next morning the friends would start early, either in a chaise or the Cambridge Fly, and on the way would breakfast at Epping, or Ware, or Wade's Mill. They were usually in the rooms at Emmanuel College, assigned to each of them, by the afternoon. Reed, unlike his learned and lazy host, the Master, was an early riser. About six o'clock he was commonly out of bed, and, before breakfast in his rooms, walked, if the morning was fine, in the Fellows' Garden. A second breakfast about ten o'clock with Dr. Farmer was not infrequent. Then followed visits to colleges, hours in the libraries, calls at Deighton's shop or at those of other booksellers, with the inevitable purchase of books or pamphlets.

Dinner, unless invitations took Mr. Reed and Mr. Steevens elsewhere, was in Hall or at the Master's table. And by-and-by they drank tea and played cards, at which last Reed seems to have been highly favoured by fortune, for he records his winnings on one occasion of five shillings, and on another of four. "Concluded in the parlour," commonly brings to an end the record of each day.

Sturbridge Fair, or, as one finds it both in print and manuscript, Stirbitch Fair enlivened Cambridge and its neighbourhood in September. Reed was seldom absent when each year the civic and university authorities on the 18th of that month proclaimed the fair. On the completion of the ceremony he and the Master would dine in the proctor's booth, or, entering some other hospitable booth, would mix with London tradesmen in eating oysters. Nor was the Puritanic casuistry of "Zeal-of-the-land Busy" needed, as in Jonson's play of *Bartholomew Fair*, to justify the eating of pig in the tents of the wicked. Here is the record of Tuesday, 1st October 1782. It may, however, be observed first that Homer, who is mentioned and who consorted much with Reed, was not the author of the *Iliad*—though the place was classic ground—but another gentleman of the same name, a friend of Dr. Parr, and a Fellow of Emmanuel who edited the *Heroides* of Ovid and many other Latin works. "Breakfast at Jude's, and then went to the Fair with Wilcox, Homer and Steevens. We were met by the Master and Mr. Nichols there," Mr. Nichols, of the *Anecdotes*, had come down from town, "and adjourned to a Booth to eat Pork. Dined in the College Hall, and in the afternoon went with the Master and Mr. Nichols to the Theatre. Saw *As You Like It* and *Tom Thumb*. Supped in the

Parlour. This day has been a more than ordinary pleasant one."

Exactly a week after the fair had been proclaimed came the great day, the 25th, being Horse Fair day. Steevens and Reed, like the author of *Venus and Adonis*, on whom they commented, were not without an eye for the points of a horse. In 1789 Reed, in company with Grosvenor Bedford, visited Ely, and called on the historian of the cathedral, James Bentham, then over eighty years of age, whom they found a "very hearty and lively" old gentleman. He showed them over the cathedral "with great intelligence and good nature," and Reed climbed "almost as high as the Lanthorn." But perhaps his enjoyment was as great when Mr. Page drove him in his chaise to Tattersall's "to see the famous horse, Highflier, for which the Duke of Bedford had offered 10,000 guineas. Great as this sum is, the wonder diminishes," Reed goes on, "when I heard that he had actually produced 4700 guineas to his owner last year, and would more the next. He is 15 years old, a stately beast, playful, who suffered himself to be led about, biting a stick in the servant's hand, and handled by us all." Twice on one of the Sturbridge Horse Fair days Reed was drawn to inspect the show, and in 1793 he and Steevens were companions in paying a visit to the wild beasts of a travelling menagerie. Somewhat later in the day they would attend a drum, and finally, "conclude in the Parlour."

There were other important days besides 25th September. Reed seems to have regarded it as a pleasure or a duty to be present in St. Mary's at the Concio ad Clerum delivered by Dr. Kipling, of St. John's. It was a pleasure which many persons found it possible to deny themselves. Dr. Kipling's voice had not the vast resonance of that of a younger namesake. But he gave its origin to a word. I learn from the *Dictionary of National Biography* that the errors of his edition of the *Codex Bezæ* and the bad Latinity of the preface were so conspicuous that in the slang of the university a " Kiplingism " came to be synonymous with a grammatical blunder. Yet he delivered successive *Conciones* and became Dean of Peterborough. In 1787 exactly nine persons listened to his *Concio*, but among the nine were Farmer, Reed, and Tyrwhitt, with another person soon to become illustrious, or at least notorious, William Frend, whose prosecution for publishing his pamphlet, " Peace and Union recommended to the Associated Bodies of Republicans and Anti-Republicans," was promoted by Kipling, while on Frend's side stood the whole body of undergraduates, and among them one was dangerously prominent, Samuel Taylor Coleridge. In 1793, the year of Frend's prosecution, Dr. Kipling's Latin discourse was attended only by the Vice-Chancellor and the beadles.

In the following autumn, that of 1794, this same undergraduate, S. T. Coleridge, was the subject of conversation among the dons who dined on 8th October with Mr. Masters at Landbeech. One of the company was the head of his College—Jesus College—Dr. Pearce, who, Coleridge told his brother, behaved " with great asperity," when, on 12th April of that year, he was admonished before the Fellows. In fact, Pearce seems to have made every effort to reclaim Coleridge from what he regarded as the error of his ways. It was the time of the early alliance between Southey and Coleridge—the days of golden dreams of the Susquehanna and Aspheterism. Coleridge had cut short a discussion with his friendly monitor by assuring him that he quite misconceived the position, " he was neither Jacobin nor Democrat, but a Pantisocrat." Isaac Reed's report of the talk at Mr. Masters's is as follows ; and no correction of its errors in a few details need here be made : " In the afternoon Dr. Pearce gave us the following account of Mr. Coleridge, who had just published a drama called *The Fall of Robespierre*. He is one of three sons of a Devonshire clergyman ; his brother, an usher at Newcome's school, Hackney. He has imbibed the wild democratic opinions floating about at present concerning religion and politicks. He is a disciple of Godwin, the author of two quarto volumes on the foundations of religion and politicks, and like him has entertained a foolish notion that the life of man might be protracted to any length. He is an enemy to all establishments of religion, and conceives there should be no publick worship. He is also of opinion that everyone should learn some mechanic art, and has accordingly put himself an apprentice to a carpenter. He is going to America. Dr. P. said that he (C.) was in town lately, and having no money to carry him to Cambridge, he wrote a poem, an elegy, he thought, and sent it to Perry, the Editor of *The Morning Chronicle*, offering his correspondence to the paper, and desiring the return of a guinea, which he received.[1] He asserts that his play was written in 8 hours. Dr. P. speaks of him as a very ingenious young man, bating these extravagant and foolish notions which he entertains." *The Fall of Robespierre*, it will be remembered, was partly the work of Southey ; the first act alone was written by Coleridge, and it runs to no more than 274 lines. Southey's two acts were written,

[1] *See* J. Dykes Campbell's note on the "Elegy, imitated from Akenside," which first appeared in the *Morning Chronicle*, 23rd September 1794.

he says, "as fast as newspapers could be put into blank verse."

Four days after the opening of the Sturbridge Horse Fair came a day of collegiate importance—that in commemoration of the founder. The attendance at the service and sermon in the Chapel was always considerably smaller than that of the diners at a later function in the Hall. In the year of the talk respecting Coleridge, the congregation, as Reed notes, was "larger than usual, being at least 14 persons." Even on that distinguished day the dinner did not necessarily forbid a visit to the theatre. Although Sturbridge Fair had begun to decline, dramatic companies of merit arrived from London or from Norwich. In 1789 a new theatre, as large, according to a newspaper of that date, as the Haymarket, was opened, and on 28th September Reed had the pleasure of seeing, as Miss Hardcastle in *She Stoops to Conquer*, Miss Elizabeth Brunton, whom in Coleridge's early verses Thalia, the Muse of Comedy, claims as *her* Brunton, leaving her sister Ann, afterwards Mrs. Merry, to the Tragic Muse. The newspaper from which I have quoted goes on to inform the public that "three of the great Shakespearians, Dr. Farmer, Mr. Steevens and Mr. Reed, are here, and seldom miss a night; and to the honour of the actors let it be recorded that these gentlemen are liberal in their commendation." The fourth great Shakespearian, Mr. Malone, came and went, but was not a regular visitor at Emmanuel in Sturbridge Fair time. Steevens had on slight grounds found a grievance against him. The Master, however, was dear to Malone, and is described by Reed as "sitting," in 1788, "for his picture," which was to be the possession of Malone. In 1790 Steevens was suddenly summoned away from Emmanuel

College by the death of an old lady, which involved him in business; but he did not forget his friends at Cambridge, and a haunch of venison, in good time for the feast of the Founder's Day, arrived from the absentee. On Reed's earliest visit one of his first proceedings was to view the old apartments of his friend Steevens at King's College. From one of the windows he transcribed four lines which show Steevens, who, like Reed himself, was wedded only to his library, in the unexpected character of a lover—

> "'Tis hard, my Betsy, but the gods are kind,
> And for the just have future joys designed,
> That lovers when they part may ease their pain
> With pleasing hopes of meeting once again."

If these are his own verses they are more amiable than some others that came from his satirical pen.

On a morning of early October during several successive years the Master's fishpond was dragged for a pike, and Reed duly records the weight of each year's take—eight pounds, ten pounds, and, in 1792, "twelve and a half pounds." The diversion of the eminent scholars on a morning of 1795 was that of determining bets as to "the possibility of a person going to several parts of the College blindfold." On the afternoon of the same day Mr. Masters produced a pint bottle of malt liquor brewed in the year 1688, "on the occasion of the birth of a Mr. Simpson, formerly [*i.e.* before Reed's time] one of the beadles. It had little taste of malt liquor, rather of wine. It had not lost its strength." Such incidents as these formed interludes in the almost unceasing round of examining old books, copying manuscripts, and adding new acquisitions to the overflowing library gathered in the rooms at Staple Inn.

During Reed's visit to Emmanuel of the year 1786, at a dinner given by the Master of Christ's

College, Dr. Watson, Bishop of Llandaff, was among the guests. He had held from 1764 to 1771 the Professorship of Chemistry at Cambridge. Early in 1765 Dr. Johnson, with his friend Topham Beauclerk, visited the university. Boswell's account of this visit is chiefly drawn from a letter of Dr. John Sharp quoted in *The Gentleman's Magazine*, a letter reprinted in full by that indefatigable Johnsonian, Dr. Birkbeck Hill, in his annotated edition of Boswell. I have not looked into Watson's *Anecdotes* to ascertain whether he there notices the proceedings of Johnson on this occasion, and shall be content to quote a passage from Reed's manuscript: "Dr. Watson mentioned Dr. Johnson's visit to Cambridge and his behaviour to himself. On his coming to the Laboratory of the Chymistry Professor, Dr. Watson asked him if he should show some experiments of curiosity as for Ladies or such as were more calculated for Philosophers. A rough answer ensued, and a process was exhibited with which the Dr. expressed himself both satisfied and surprised, and wondered he had not been able to do it himself. In the evening Dr. Farmer, whose guest he was, had invited Dr. Watson, Dr. Lort and some others to spend the evening with him. Dr. Johnson after supper took up a Candle and left the company for two hours to themselves, and went into the Library. On his return the Company were about to depart. Dr. Watson observed, however, that he uttered one sentence for which he excused all his rudeness, as it was strong and forcible, and deserved to be remembered as well as his other *Bon Mots*. Speaking of the addiction of Country Squires to Rural Sports and Diversions in preference to other pursuits, he said—'Sir, I have found out the reason of it, and the reason is that they feel the vacuity which is within them less when they are in motion than when they are at rest.' "[1] It may be added that during two hours of the evening on which this conversation took place Mr. Isaac Reed and the Bishop of Clonfert endeavoured to forget the vacuity that was in them over a game of cards. In 1783, some time after Johnson's stroke of palsy, he was visited by Murphy, who found the Doctor engaged in reading Watson's *Chymistry*: "Articulating with difficulty, he said, 'From this book he who knows nothing may learn a great deal, and he who knows will be pleased to find his knowledge recalled to his mind in a manner highly pleasing.' "

The evidence for a gruesome story about the body of Laurence Sterne has been questioned. Mr. Percy Fitzgerald has exhibited that evidence, and though the following, from Reed's diary of 12th October 1787, adds nothing to what has been related, it is perhaps worth quoting as a piece of testimony: "After breakfast went with the Master, Professor Harwood [Professor of Anatomy] and Malone to see the Anatomy Schools. . . . Concluded the day with the family [of] Dr. Harwood. Present Dr. Farmer, Mr. Masters, Mr. Barnes, Mr. Wilcox, Mr. Malone, Dr. Harwood and myself. In the course of the evening Dr. Farmer said that he was informed by Dr. Collignon, deceased, that the body of Mr. Sterne had been sent down to Cambridge and was anatomised. It was stolen from the burying-ground beyond Tyburn, where it was interred, and was recognised by several persons who knew him. I remember Becket the Bookseller once told me that he and, I think, another were the only persons who attended the Funeral. Mr. Stevenson Hall [*i.e.* John Hall-

[1] Croker, in his edition of *Boswell*, records this utterance in nearly the same words. He says that Johnson was "tired by his previous exertions, and would not talk."

Stevenson], the Author of *Crazy Tales,* was applyed to, but refused to attend or give himself the least concern about his deceased friend's body." When this story was related by Dr. Farmer, twenty years and upwards had passed since the publication of *Tristram Shandy*. Farmer had been guilty of what George Eliot called the most gratuitous form of folly —a prophecy. "However much it may be talked about at present," said he, speaking of Sterne's great piece of fantasy and humour, "in the course of twenty years, should anyone wish to refer to it, he will be obliged to go to an antiquary."

A yet more gruesome story is related of a contemporary of Sterne, and to this incident that invaluable treasury the *Dictionary of National Biography*, which devotes a couple of columns to Robert Butts, Bishop successively of Norwich and Ely, makes no allusion. Before transcribing my citation from Reed, it may be worth while to note that the date of Farmer's birth as given in the *Dictionary*, and the date given by Farmer himself, as recorded by Reed, are not in agreement. The *Dictionary*, following Nichols's *Anecdotes*, gives the date, 28th August 1735. On Tuesday, 5th October 1790, Reed enters in his diary: "Dr. Farmer said this evening he was born 4th May 1735." "Dined in the Hall," the diarist writes on 11th October 1790. "The conversation turning on Bishop Butts, Mr. Cory said he had heard from Mr. Masters that that Prelate had been buried before he was dead, and Mr. Hardy had been told to the same effect by Mrs. Owen, the Bishop's daughter. The fact seems to have been as follows: The bishop had the Gout, and was in the habit of taking laudanum. By a mistake a greater quantity was administered than was intended, and he to appearance died. The body was delivered to the undertaker, put into the Coffin, and closed up. On the night preceding the funeral a person who slept in the adjoining Room thought she heard a noise and persisted in her assertion; the coffin was opened, the body found turned on its face and the elbows bruised." A pompous inscription glorified the bishop's monument in Ely Cathedral, but, according to Cole, his chief merit was that of "hallooing at elections." [1]

Another note-book of Reed's contains *Anecdotes of Celebrated Persons*, including an account of Horace Walpole's relations with the poet Chatterton, as communicated by Walpole to Reed in a conversation of February 1777; Glover's reminiscences of the author of *The Spleen;* Lord Mansfield's anecdotes of Pope, and various odds and ends of which the greater part have in some form found their way into print. From one of these records it is pleasant to learn that Steevens—Johnson had called him "mischievous," but would not allow that he was "malignant"—was admitted to see the Doctor while he was still suffering from the stroke of palsy of June 1783, and that Johnson confided to him the same details of his composing in Latin verse a prayer that his understanding might be spared which appear in the well-known letter to Mrs. Thrale. Possibly it may add something to what is known to mention that Dodsley told Reed that Sterne received the sum of £250 for the first two volumes of *Tristram Shandy*, for which Dodsley himself, before they were printed at York, had—as is known—refused to give fifty pounds. In the copy of the poem, "The Sick Monkey," in the Bodleian Library is a manuscript note by Reed stating that he

[1] The *Dictionary of National Biography* makes the bishop over sixty years old when he married his second wife, whose age was twenty-three. His age was in fact fifty-one.

had learnt from Garrick that he was the author of this attack upon himself. But perhaps the following —with which I shall end—may give somewhat fuller information than the Bodleian note: "26 Febry, 1777. I received from Mr. Garrick a Poem I had lent him entitled, 'The Sick Monkey, A Fable,' Quarto, 1765, and which he informed me he was the Author of himself. The occasion of writing it was this. Being at Paris studying la Fontaine he wrote this imitation of that author and sent it to Mr. Colman in order to be ready to publish as soon as he arrived. The imposition succeeded, and his friends were very angry at this supposed attack upon him, which they spoke of to him as equally cruel and indecent. The Design to it was by Gravelot."

The sale catalogue of Reed's library, in which his portrait appears, in an "advertisement," speaks of the number, the accuracy, and the interest of the notes which he prefixed to many of his books. It adds a character of the collector of the books which is written without extravagant eulogy. It speaks of his generous communication of his knowledge to his fellow-scholars. "He was, indeed," says the writer, "a most friendly man; endeared to all who knew him by his unassuming manners, his instructive conversation, and his honest heart. He was stern, and justly stern, only when he detected in others the violation of truth, and observed sophistry assuming the place of argument. With an independent spirit he displayed also a truly modest and retired disposition; surrounded with books and content with a very moderate income, to him, as Prospero says, 'his library was dukedom large enough.'" The sale of his library kept collectors on the watch during thirty-nine days.

A NOBLE AUTHORESS

(From Unpublished Sources)

In 1903, among the decennial publications of the University of Chicago, appeared a large volume, edited by Myra Reynolds, which aimed at presenting a collection, as nearly as possible complete, of the poems of Anne, Countess of Winchilsea. The Introduction, of upwards of a hundred and thirty pages, is admirable in the evidence it gives of research, sound judgment and good taste. To the writings of the Countess already known through her *Miscellany Poems* of 1713 and other sources in print the editor added a large body of verse from manuscript volumes placed at her disposal by the Earl of Winchilsea and Mr. Edmund Gosse. She was not unaware of the possibility that other manuscript collections might somewhere lurk in ambush. The Countess was born in 1661 and died in 1720. The later in date of the two manuscript volumes is supposed to be of the year 1702. No poems belonging to the closing period of the life of the Countess seem to have been accessible to the diligent and well-informed editor of the Chicago volume. I wish that some swift intelligence had sped through the air from Dublin to Chicago and informed the editor where another manuscript lay, which would probably have rendered her collection complete. Its contents would gladly have been offered for her use.

Wordsworth was the first of nineteenth-century writers to do honour to the poems of Lady Winchilsea. In the album—lately edited by Professor Littledale—of transcribed passages of verse, which Wordsworth selected for presentation to Lady Mary Lowther in 1819, thirty-two pages are occupied with pieces chosen from the volume of 1713, which he knew so intimately. More than ten years later he wrote to Dyce of her "style in rhyme" as "often admirable, chaste, tender and vigorous." It was left for Mr. Edmund Gosse to become her champion in our own day. "The singular merit of this lady" came through him, he tells us in *Gossip in a Library*, as a "revelation" to Matthew Arnold. I have no claim to be Ardelia's champion. It seems to me to be possible to praise her poems injudiciously and over much. And, notwithstanding the revelation that came to Matthew Arnold, I think the praise has erred on the side of excess. Mr. Gosse thanks the divine Ardelia for her ghostly generosity in conveying to his hands the folio manuscript volume which had been sold among effects of the Creake family. It was indeed well and wisely done. But Ardelia was indiscreetly generous when she transferred to my less worthy hands that vellum-bound folio on which she wrote "For transcribing my poems," and in which out of a hundred pages, containing her latest verse-makings, some four-and-twenty are, as I take it, in the autograph of the Countess. She was not so gracious to Mr. Gosse, I think, as to present him with her own transcriptions; she put him off with the clerkly penmanship of a hired scribe. She added in my manuscript two of her letters, which include pieces of verse, to show what a pretty hand she had in "epistolary correspondence." A great lady is capricious in her favours, and knows how to make arbitrary distinctions.

I cannot describe the later poems of the Countess

of Winchilsea as a treasure trove of great importance, but in their general level they are not inferior to her earlier poems, and what would have interested Wordsworth and Matthew Arnold, what would interest her champion, Mr. Gosse, may not be without interest for other readers. They fall into the two main groups of verses secular and verses sacred. Anne Finch was always a serious-minded person, but she always knew that a serious person may be also gay. In 1715 she suffered from "a violent and dangerous fit of sicknesse," and on her recovery she made her pious vows in verse:

> "Let everything extol Him that has breath,
> Who here adjourns, hereafter conquers, Death."

But in the poem of which this is the closing couplet she anticipates that she may need relaxation and "sink to trifle for a little space." And in fact after that date she trifled when she pleased, for with hei sincere and sometimes enthusiastic piety she was by no means an ascetic.

Let me, without regard to the dates of the poems which cannot always be determined, first present Ardelia in her lighter mood. She has anticipated Burns in a dialogue between dogs—a "Dutch mastiff" of Cleaveland Row (where the Countess resided) and his sage counsellor, the elder "pugg" of Leicester Fields. And why should not pugs discourse as well as gallants, whom they so closely resemble?

> "For, tho' they neither read nor write,
> If they make love, can play and fight,
> Are comb'd, and powder'd, and appear
> At either Park, and called 'My dear,'
> If they know how to push their fortune,
> And the best giver can importune,
> So supple they've their masters lick'd
> The very moment they've been kick'd,

Have all fidelity maintain'd
Until by larger proffers gain'd,
Who can pretend to go beyond 'em ?"

The inconstant affection of their mistresses is the sorrow of both the elder and the younger pug. He of Leicester Fields, once "called handsome fellow, stroked and patted," has been disregarded by his lady's eyes since by chance they fell on Yanica :

"Tho' Yanica is small and jetty,
Sleek as a mole and wondrous pretty,
Her beauty in its youthful splendour,
Such embonpoint, so soft, so tender,
Minion ev'n when she's most untoward,
Genteelly coy and chastely froward,
A bitch that any heart could soften,
And no wise dog would see her often,
Yet had you heard my dame commend her
You would have wish'd a rope might end her."

Ardelia's interest in Dutch mastiffs called forth a letter from Sir A. F., the bearer of which was one of the breed—"an impertinent young Dutch woman," as Sir A. F. writes, coming "with a design to thank Ardelia for the honour she has done her relations by her poetry, and to beg her instructions about dressing her head (for she has been told that lady not only writes but dresses better than any of her sex) ; she thinks her mourning deep enough for the drawing-room, but the ends of her pinners are out of fashion." The thanks of the Countess for Sir A. F.'s gift of the "agreeable brunette" takes the form of a poem in which she criticises unsparingly every pretended mark of good-breeding possessed by the young Dutchwoman, yet admits that she has the nameless charm that triumphs over all :

"Which, beyond rules and shapes and places,
Scatters innumerable graces,

Yet often from some trifle rises,
And in a patch or curl surprises,
An esclavage, a knot, a feather,
A thousand je ne scay quois together."

An "esclavage," it will be remembered, was a necklace, coiling in several rows of gold or jewels, and I may add that this example of the word is some thirty years earlier than any found for the New English Dictionary of Sir J. Murray. The fashion of such splendid fetters must date from before 1720.

That nameless charm which the Countess found in her pug, a charm that is independent of beauty, she finds also in Valeria (would that we could identify the lady), and makes it the subject of some verses that bear a certain resemblance in idea to the well-known lines of Hartley Coleridge beginning "She is not fair to outward view." The opening words of Ardelia's poem are identical with those which open that of Hartley Coleridge:

"She is not fair, you critics of the town
That court her smiles and tremble at her frown,
She is not fair, and, though I burn like you,
I to my better judgment will be true;
Nor could a painter borrow from her face
One line that might his fancied Venus grace;
No feature that might countenance the rest
Is perfect or superlative confest;
Whence then without a charm that we can tell
Does all that's charming in Valeria dwell,
That whensoe'er she speaks, or looks, or moves,
The observer listens, sighs, admires, and loves,
And wonders at the unexpected smart,
Who sees no quiver though he feels the dart?

These are vigorous verses (for some omissions I offer an apology to Ardelia), and the last line has in it the epigrammatic point of Pope, who sang Ardelia's praises.

The recreations of the Countess were sometimes

of the town, as when she went to Count Volira's ball and saw Lady Carteret—daughter of her friend, Lady Worsley—" drest like a shepherdess." Strephon and other swains, straying through the ballrooms and touching the tapestry sheep, despair of making any impression on this beautiful shepherdess, and resolve to return to their valley, there for ever to devote themselves to the praises of the cruel nymph. Lord Carteret—the friend afterwards of Swift—in 1719 was appointed minister plenipotentiary to the Queen of Sweden. From Stockholm he sent to Ardelia a miniature of the hero of her imagination, Charles XII. Her transports in prose and verse occupy two folio pages. She had already written verses to be placed under the King of Sweden's picture, and now thanks to " Cartret," who alone " genteelly gives and trafficks for the mind," she could bear her hero on her breast :

" Charles, lord of peace and thunderbolt of war,
The Christian hero, terror of the field,
The Church's banner, and the kingdom's shield,
The early theme of my aspiring muse,
The star which now in heaven my verse pursues."

Her news in prose is that " your amiable Lady continues in perfect health and beauty, and the fortitude and soft concern with which she and my Lady Greenville support your stay are exemplary qualifications of which you never can be a witness, since only to be exercised in your absence. Your two sons, our future plenipotentiaries, are the delight of all that see them. And your daughters grow and improve so fast that description cannot reach their tender but ingaging airs. Whilst your numerous friends cry out with our pathetick Cowley :

" 'Great is thy charge, oh ! North, be wise and just,
England commits her CARTRET to thy trust.' "

The grateful compliments were at least not painted in miniature. The Chicago editor considers whether the "Salisbury" praised in Ardelia's "Nocturnal Reverie" was, as Leigh Hunt maintained, Frances Bennett, wife of the fourth Earl, or Ann Tufton, who became Countess at fifteen or sixteen years of age in 1708-9. She supports the claim of the latter. It is certainly this Countess who in her maiden days was the "Lamira" of a petition in verse addressed to her by a white mouse. The mouse prays that he may be the beautiful girl's first captive and the earliest to wear her fetters:

"I sue to wear Lamira's fetters,
And live the envy of my betters,
When I receive her soft caresses,
And creeping near her lovely tresses,
Their glossy brown from my reflection
Shall gain more lustre and perfection;
And to her bosom, if admitted,
My colour there will be so fitted
That no distinction could discover
My station to a jealous lover."

This happy mouse—for such a petition could not be refused—has a tragic companion of dusky hue, who struck terror into the hearts of the Ladies Hatton and Temple, and who perished for his crime:

"These ladies dreaming of no ill,
Who fragrant tea did drink and fill,
And but for laughing had sat still,

Were aim'd at in a treacherous sort,
Low as their feet—as some report—
And petticoats, you know, are short.

The solemn foe was cloathed in black,
To hide him in the sly attack,
And gone too far e'er to draw back.

When Temple, who th' assailant spies,
(For who can 'scape from Temple's eyes ?)
Into a chair for safety flies.

Hatton, who stirr'd not from her place,
Confest her terror by the grace
Of the vermilion in her face."

When calm returned, and pulses were temperate, and tea again began to flow, it was supposed that the enemy had ignobly fled, but in fact he had chosen to die by "the honourablest foot," and had found a monument of lace.

Lady Winchilsea's intimacy with great people laid her open to the attack of petitioners who sought her mediation on their behalf. Among these was a Rev. Mr. Bedford, who may possibly have been the Rev. Arthur Bedford, devout collector of seven thousand immoral sentiments from the British dramatists, or possibly his non-juring namesake, Hilkiah, who suffered three years' imprisonment as the writer of a book which he had not written. Whatever Mr. Bedford's cause may have been the Countess was eager to make it her own. She flies—as her verse relates—to her coach, her gown unpinned, her hood awry, Mrs. Mary at her heels, here giving a twitch, there aiming a pin, and at the door flinging her ladyship's ruffles into the carriage. Her toilet completed while Jehu scours along the streets, she enters his Lordship's ante-rooms :

"He spies me thro' a suite of rooms,
And forward moves with courtly grace,
Till, noting my requesting face,
He puts on a refusing air,
And bids his footman call a chair ;
Then draws his watch—' 'Tis two and past,
You find me in prodigious haste,'
He cries as he on tip-toe stands.
' Yet, madame, what are your commands ?

I'll serve you to my utmost power ;
The Houses have been met this hour ;
Shall I conduct you to my wife ?
I have no interest, on my life !' "

Mr. Bedford's special pleader closes with a promise of renewed and never-ceasing importunity.

Sometimes the Countess left London for the little town of Wye, near Canterbury, where was a college founded in the fifteenth century by Cardinal Kempe, which in the time of Charles I. had passed into the possession of her husband's family, the Finches ; sometimes when her ladyship suffered from that malady which she has celebrated in one of her best-known poems, "The Spleen," she sought assuagement for her griefs at Tunbridge Wells. In March 1702 "the firing of my chimney at Wye College" occasioned a display of "fearful temper," for which she must needs apologise in verse. She confesses that she is one—

"Who all things fear whilst day is shining,
And my own shadow, light declining,
And from the spleen's prolifick fountain
Can of a mole-hill make a mountain."

But she is of the sex that charms by timorous graces. Did not Cleopatra fly at Actium and did not "Tony" follow? Why might not Ardelia, when at midnight her chimney blazed, fly half-clothed from room to room, and entreat the ladies in their nightly attire instantly to quit the house? How insensible were they not to perceive the beauty of her soft alarms ! At Tunbridge her troubles were of a different kind ; it was charged against her that she herself had set the Baths on fire with a lampoon. She does not believe that satire—from that of Juvenal to that of Donne—ever reformed an age :

"The errors of the times have still prevailed,
The laughing and the weeping sages failed."

Her part has ever been praise rather than censure. Whereupon follows a celebration of the beauties—Effingham and Hern, Warner and Hornby—who at this moment made Tunbridge glorious. Perhaps it was at the Wells that the wicked rumour went abroad that Ardelia was indifferent to the spells of music. To repel an accusation so unjust a poetic advertisement is needed in the *Gazette*, the *Flying Post* and the *Weekly Journal.* All the musical instruments of a St. Cecilia's Day or an Ode on the Passions are duly honoured in her verse. And is it not enough to say that she has friends of the Fleming family?

"Be 't known the Flemings I have heard
With such attention, such regard,
Such transports, when their notes they raised,
When soften'd, so becalm'd and pleased,
As if the hand that ruled the art
Had missed the string and touched the heart."

A poem of 1718 addressed to Mrs. Catherine Fleming tells of the charms of music and of intellectual converse, which flows brightly but gently:

"Nor ever noise for wit on me could pass,
When thro' the braying I discern'd the ass."

Not loud laughter but a brightening eye announces the flash of wit, "as fire precedes the sound from opening heaven."

Ardelia, though she could enjoy the diversions of the town or of Tunbridge Wells, was, as readers of the *Nocturnal Reverie* and *The Nightingale* are aware, a true lover of the countryside. This, indeed, is one of her chief distinctions as a poet of the so-called Augustan age. I wish I could give at length "A

Ballad to Mrs. Catherine Fleming in London from Malshanger Farm in Hampshire." Perhaps there is a little of the Marie Antoinette manner of playing shepherdess in it, but this renders it only the more piquant. These four verses may suffice to represent a piece of three times that number :

"From me, who whilom sung the town,
  This second ballad comes,
To let you know we are got down
  From hurry, smoke, and drums,
And every visitor that rowls
In restless coach from Mall to Paul's,
  With a fa-la-la-la-la-la.

For jarring sounds in London streets,
  Which still are passing by ;
Where 'Cowcumbers !' with 'Sand, ho !' meets,
  And for loud mast'ry vie.
The driver whistling to his team
Here wakes us from some rural dream,
  With a fa-la, etc.

From rising hills, thro' distant views,
  We see the sun decline ;
Whilst everywhere the eye pursues
  The grazing flocks and kine ;
Which home at night the farmer brings,
And not the post's but sheep's bell rings,
  With a fa-la, etc.

Beneath our feet the partridge springs
  As to the woods we go,
Where birds scarce stretch their painted wings,
  So little fear they show ;
But when our outspread hoops they spy,
They look when we like them should fly,
  With a fa-la, etc."

Why should Ardelia ever forsake the solitude she loves? Emperors have "greatly chose to be forgot," and why not a countess? How ever quit Malshanger

Farm, unless indeed Mrs. Catherine, like old Orpheus, should draw the Countess and all the woods along? But as it might surprise the town to see her travel so, she must submit to fate, and too soon return in open chaise—" with a fa-la-la-la-la-la."

The Chicago editor justly observes that no object in inanimate nature attracted Lady Winchilsea more strongly than trees. The beautiful poem, "The Tree," was one of Wordsworth's selections for the album of Lady Mary Lowther, and Mr. Gosse, with his fine instinct for what is excellent, could not fail to include it among the pieces chosen for Ward's "English Poets." Laurence Eusden is now best remembered by the fact that Pope conferred on his name an unenviable immortality. But on Christmas Eve of the year 1718 Eusden succeeded the dramatist Rowe as Poet-Laureate of England. Frances, Countess of Hertford, a friend of Lady Winchilsea—afterwards a patroness of the author of *The Seasons*—in her pride of rank and caprice of youth, imposed a poetic task on Eusden, like that of the Israelites who were compelled to make bricks without straw: he was to write upon a wood, but to mention no tree except the aspen nor any flower except the king-cup. A long remonstrance in verse against her cruelty to a poet was addressed by Ardelia to the Countess, and in it all her lore and love of trees are left on record. She imagines what the incomparable Eusden might have done had he been free to delight in "the soothing sweetness of the natural Muse." The lines which describe the grove seen from a little distance, and the flowery paths that lead towards it, remind us of some of the landscape paintings of later years of the century, in which a genuine feeling for Nature is harmonised with something of a conventional mannerism :

"Had Eusden been at liberty to rove
Wild and promiscuous he had form'd your grove,
Of all the sons of Earth that ever grew,
From lightsome beech down to the sable yew;
To which a walk of limes should have convey'd
From the throng'd palace to the lonely shade,
Stretch'd thro' a meadow, bordering either side,
Which from the next a river should divide.
The swans in view, the birds upon the spray,
Should cheer the sight and hearing in the way;
Nor king-cups only in the grass should rise
(Tho' all but king-cups your command denies),
But Flora's gifts should amply there be seen,
And every beauteous dye emblaze the green;
Cowslips and daisies over all should run,
And the broad ox-eye stare against the sun."

The poem goes on, in a later passage, to describe the grove seen by moonlight:

"Doubtful the moon each varying object brings,
Whence goblin stories rise and fairy rings,
Misshapen bushes look like midnight elves,
And scarce we know our shadows from ourselves."

Here wanders Eusden's ghost, haunting all other trees, while he avoids the hated aspen—that paralytic among the rest—and here his shrunken quill seems to impress such characters upon the air as are the ghosts of syllables.

In her maiden days the Countess of Winchilsea, then Anne Kingsmill, had been one of the maids-of-honour of the Duchess of York, Mary of Modena, afterwards Queen of King James II. Colonel Heneage Finch was groom of the bed-chamber to the Duke of York. In her marriage licence (1684), as Miss Myra Reynolds notices with a smile, she is described as "a spinster aged about eighteen years, at her own disposal"; in fact her age was twenty-three. In two of the manuscript poems she recalls the happy days of early womanhood. The slighter of these was occasioned by the death of Colonel Baggot, who had held the same position with Colonel Finch and Captain Lloyd in the service of King James. Baggot was the first member of "the triple league" to be called away by death, and his two old comrades seem to have been by his bedside at the end. The vigour and restraint of the verses were evidently inspired by a genuine passion of sorrow. The second and more important poem must belong to the year 1718, for it is suggested by the death of the Queen. Mary of Modena was an ardent member of the Roman communion; the Countess of Winchilsea was a loyal daughter of the Church of England. Religious differences, however, put no check upon the enthusiastic reverence with which the Countess regarded her former mistress. She summons back the happy season of her own youth:

> "Recall'd be days when ebon locks o'erspread
> My youthful neck, my cheeks a bashful red;
> When early joys my glowing bosom warm'd,
> When trifles pleased, and every pleasure charm'd;
> Then eager from the rural seat I came
> Of long-traced ancestors of worthy name,
> To seek the court."

She goes on to picture the Queen in her time of prosperity receiving the ambassadors of the various states of Europe, and replying to each in his own speech:

> "The Roman accent, which such grace affords
> To Tuscan language, harmonised her words;
> All eyes, all listening sense, upon her hung,
> When from her lovely mouth th' enchantment sprung."

And by-and-by the eulogy passes on to represent the Queen in her adversity, an exile from the land of her adoption, and a widow. Ardelia was not a disloyal subject under the Hanoverian monarchy, but her heart remained faithful to her own youth and to the Stuarts.

The Countess did not, like some great ladies, make politics her trade ; but she had no tolerance for the mere time-server, who is all things to all men. Such is the Sir Plausible of her epigram :

> "Sir Plausible, as 'tis well known,
> Has no opinions of his own ;
> But closes with each stander by,
> Now in a truth, now in a lie,
> Fast as chameleons change their dye ;
> Has still some applicable story
> To gratify a Whig or Tory,
> And even a Jacobite in tatters
> If met alone he smoothly flatters ;
> Greets friend and foe with wishes fervent,
> And lives and dies your humble servant."

She herself could reserve her deeper feelings, but could not falsify them.

The religious poems in the folio volume form a considerable proportion of the whole but do not very well lend themselves to quotation. A paraphrase of the last chapter of Ecclesiastics is inscribed to Mrs. Catherine Fleming, who perhaps was the "Flavia" who suggested the task, and whose thanks in verse are prefixed to the poem. Two pieces are in dialogue form. In one of these a poor man stays a rich man with his entreaty for alms at the door of a cathedral ; the good Samaritan is full of charity, and by his kind delaying fails to be present when the Gospel for the day is read aloud. But the Gospel is that passage which tells how Christ's followers who have done a service to the least of his brethren have done it to the Master himself ; the absentee from church becomes assured that he has indeed been in the presence of the Lord. Had she been born at a somewhat later date the Countess might have been a writer of religious verse, in which her real warmth of feeling might have found lyrical expression, delivered from that didactic and moralising tendency which was characteristic of her time. As it was, her more ardent utterances sometimes seem like music played upon an instrument that had not been properly tuned. A few lines from a fragment on Mary Magdalen at the Tomb will show that she could now and again write with both passion and harmony :

> " 'Twas scarce the dawn, nor yet the distant east
> Of night's dark shades was dispossess'd,
> Scarce to the verge approach'd the rising day,
> When weeping Mary to the tomb
> Where her dear Redeemer lay
> Brings her second rich perfume,
> Does new floods of tears prepare,
> Once more dedicates her hair,
> Which His feet had bathed and dried,
> Now to bind His hands and side ;
> Cruel spear ! to close that wound
> Where thy steel a passage found,
> When thy senseless bearer ran
> On the seeming vanquish'd man."

Here this notice of my Winchilsea folio must close. America has done more honour than England to this eighteenth-century poet, and the fragments here given may be regarded as an imperfect supplement to the excellent Chicago volume.

IS SHAKESPEARE SELF-REVEALED?

"The English Association" issued to its members in July of the year 1909 a paper by Dr. Sidney Lee, entitled "The Impersonal Aspect of Shakespeare's Art." It deals with an interesting question: "Can the man Shakespeare be discovered through the work of the dramatist?" and, subject to certain qualifications, the writer returns a negative answer to the question. Dr. Lee will not be satisfied with vague generalities, indicating "everyday virtues and repugnances which most men of repute share alike"; he seeks for a "tangible personality," and his conclusion is that it cannot—so baffling is the aloofness of the dramatist's art—be found.

Professor Raleigh had said that the impersonal view of Shakespeare's art "would never be entertained by an artist, and would have had short shrift from any of the company that assembled at the 'Mermaid' Tavern." A haunter of the "Mermaid," Ben Jonson might have been cited by Professor Raleigh in confirmation of what he said:

"Look how the father's face
Lives in his issue, even so the race
Of Shakespeare's mind and manners brightly shines
In his well-turned and true filèd lines."

What Ben declares we all feel to be true; we could hardly think of any play of Shakespeare's as the work of Jonson or Fletcher; we could hardly think of any work by Jonson or Fletcher as coming from Shakespeare; the children of Shakespeare's mind resemble in some quite distinctive way one another, and are unlike the children of any other Elizabethan dramatist; and this family likeness is derived from their father. We can separate a portion of *Pericles* from the rest of the play, and assign it to Shakespeare because it bears the impress of his mind; we can refuse without hesitation to attribute to him certain scenes. Why? Because, as we say (summing up many particulars in a phrase), they are "un-Shakespearian." We are familiar, in a word, with the family likeness.

Giving "short shrift" to Professor Raleigh's statement, Dr. Lee cites as a witness against him a true artist, Robert Browning, and a poem which most appositely bears the title "At the Mermaid." Shakespeare in the poem assures the company assembled at the tavern that his work—the "scroll"—is theirs, but his soul and his life are not given with his work, these remaining inaccessibly his own. Browning had been pestered and irritated by the critics when he wrote certain poems of the *Pacchiarotto* volume, and the Shakespeare who speaks here proceeds somewhat aggressively, under the inspiration of the "sherris," to tell much about his soul, his views of life and immortality, of joy and sorrow, of men and women; whereupon this "Shakespeare" goes on to contrast his own feeling for life and art with that of his immediate poetical predecessor—Byron! The nineteenth-century "Shakespeare" is Browning himself, and the truest comment that could be made on the poem would be that hardly any English poet more clearly betrays himself—his aspirations, his hopes, his passions, his beliefs, his likes and dislikes—in his verse than our professedly inscrutable Robert Browning. We can collate now his life with his art, and in all that is most inward they are of a piece. But had you met Browning in a club or at a dinner the external man would not have betrayed the inward man, who is far better known through his art than through the drossier part of his so-called life; nor is this strange, for an artist's "works" constitute that portion of his life which most truly and most intensely lives. "We must come back to real life," said Balzac, after expressing his regret for the illness of Jules Sandeau's sister, "consider Eugénie Grandet!" In the poem which immediately follows "At the Mermaid"—that named "House"—Browning returns to the same theme. Prying eyes may inspect the house-front, may even peep through the window, but no inquisitive foot shall cross his threshold. The poet thrusts his head out of the window and cries aloud that on no terms is he to be seen. It is here that he again touches on the objectivity of Shakespeare's art in the often-quoted words concerning the Sonnets:

> "'*With this same key*
> *Shakespeare unlocked his heart,*' once more!
> Did Shakespeare? If so, the less Shakespeare he!"

But it should be remembered that Browning admits the possibility of discovering the interior of the house, even though the door be shut and the walls unshaken:

> "Outside shall suffice for evidence:
> And who so desires to penetrate
> Deeper, must dive by the spirit-sense."

And it is precisely by this "spirit-sense," with all the aids and checks of scholarly "evidence," that such critics as Mr. Raleigh attempt to dive and pluck out the mystery—the open secret—of Shakespeare's personality.

Dr. Lee sets over in contrast with what he calls

Browning's conception of Shakespeare that of Emerson. "Shakespeare," wrote Emerson in *Representative Men*, "is the only biographer of Shakespeare. . . . We have his recorded convictions on those questions which knock for answer at every heart. . . . What trait of his private mind has he hidden in his dramas? So far from Shakespeare's being the least known, he is the one person in all modern history known to us." Something must be allowed for Emerson's desire to startle the hearers of his lecture into the sudden perception of what seemed to him a truth. He certainly did not mean that we can gather from the plays and poems such facts as Dr. Lee has brought together, with a zeal and industry for which we are all grateful, in his *Life of Shakespeare*. Emerson did not think scorn of any knowledge which we can obtain respecting Shakespeare's outward and material history. He was glad to learn that "about the time when Shakespeare was writing *Macbeth* he sues Philip Rogers in the borough court of Stratford for thirty-five shillings, ten pence, for corn delivered to him at different times." Information like this, he says, was well worth the pains that have been taken to procure it. But another man than Shakespeare might have been competent to sue a Philip Rogers. Dr. Lee asks whether we can discover the idiosyncrasies of Shakespeare through the plays? Emerson thinks that his chief idiosyncrasy, that which specially distinguishes him from other men, is that he could write such plays; and believing that all Shakespeare's highest powers, in their conjoined and fullest energy, passed into this imaginative work, he holds that in the works we possess the man. No other writer poured so great and abounding a mass of his and our nature into his works—the great acts of his life—and therefore, in Emerson's way of putting it, "he is the one person in all modern history known to us." But what is most distinctive of Shakespeare is not his private opinions or any casual experiences peculiar to himself and unrelated to that greater life lived in and through his imaginative creation. Shakespeare can speak only to the Shakespeare in us. His distinction is that he felt and expressed more profoundly than any other man what is common to us all: "An omnipresent humanity co-ordinates all his faculties; . . . he has no peculiarity, no importunate topic; but all is duly given." It might be interesting to know that Shakespeare was fond of cold mutton, which does not perhaps excite a general enthusiasm; but a more interesting point of distinction is that he could turn the food he ate, whether mutton or beef, into such poetry as no other human being has created, and poetry at the same time which gives a new life for each of us, not to what is peculiar in each, but to what we possess in common with all men who think and all who feel.

Thus Browning, who admits that the interior of the "house" may perhaps be penetrated "by the spirit-sense," can hardly be reckoned among the supporters of Dr. Lee's view; while Emerson, if understood aright, can hardly be reckoned among Dr. Lee's opponents, though, indeed, he puts things in a different way, and draws out the meaning, in his own fashion and with characteristic vivacities of phrase, of a commonplace until the commonplace seems to be full of a novel sense.

"An author," Dr. Lee admits, "gives in the written page an expression of what is in him. He can have nothing else to give." But the chief inward possession of the tragic poet is, according to the critic, a faculty which releases him from the necessity of experiencing the passions which he expresses, and enables him to " summon out of nothingness all manner of emotion "—the faculty of imagination. Forgetting his own thesis that the *dramatis personæ* of Shakespeare are not to be quoted as delivering the poet's own opinions, Dr. Lee cites as Shakespeare's testimony on his behalf the well-known words of Theseus, the great man of action, who lightly classes together the lover, the lunatic and the poet as creators of the unreal, phantasts who give to airy nothing a local habitation and a name. He confirms the words of Theseus with those of Touchstone—" the truest poetry is the most feigning "—and discovers by the inner light that Touchstone is communicating to Audrey Shakespeare's views on art. Dr. Lee might just as well have cited, as Shakespeare's own belief, the words of Hamlet which tells us that the end of dramatic representation " was, and is, to hold, as 'twere, the mirror up to nature," and the quotation would have served the purpose, for a mirror should simply reflect the object. The tragic poet, according to Dr. Lee, need not, and should not, feel passions vividly; for " the power of alert observation of life and literature, the power of analysing with calmness what is seen or read, is the main instrument with which the imaginative faculty does its work in dramatic poetry." Shakespeare could portray the murder of Duncan and the death of Desdemona, yet we need not suppose that he had any personal murderous propensity. When Walter Scott was asked how, amid his private anxieties and concerns, he could write *Waverley* and *Guy Mannering*, he replied that his fancy " ran its ain rigs in some other world." " As soon as I get the paper before me," he went on, " it commonly runs off pretty easily."

Dr. Lee confines these remarks to tragedy, probably because if the persons of a play are witty or humorous it certainly does occur to us that the inventor of their speeches was not himself devoid of wit or humour. But the most inspired revelation of the passion of lovers, according to this theory, does not imply that the poet had himself ever known real love; his imagination summoned the passion "out of nothingness," or he observed in it life and literature and analysed with calmness what he had seen or read. And yet we are forced to ask: Would not the signs and demonstrations of love—seen or read upon the printed page—have been mere hieroglyphics in an unknown tongue, unless the poet possessed the key to the hieroglyphics, by virtue of some veritable feeling? Walter Bagehot long ago suggested that people do not keep a tame steam-engine to write their books. Even if the tame steam-engine be named "imagination" it will not write the books unless the coals have been supplied and kindled. Dr. Lee's psychology of poets is somewhat too simple. Their faculties are not constructed in water-tight compartments; imagination is one mode of energy belonging to a living, complex creature. Out of nothingness it can summon nothing. But it can separate, combine, enlarge, diminish, transmute, create new compositions of feeling, and colour them with variously-mingled hues. Schiller, when in "The Diver" he described the turmoil and terror of mighty waters, had never seen a whirlpool; but he had carefully observed a mill-stream, and his imagination expanded the motions and forces of the slender stream into the vast tumult of his roaring Charybdis. When he wrote "William Tell" he had not visited Switzerland; but he knew the Swabian hills, and from this knowledge, with suggestions for the transmutation furnished by the eyes and pen of Goethe, grew the scenery of his Alps.

Next in rank to Goethe and Schiller among the classical dramatists who have written in the German language stands Grillparzar. He was a close student of Shakespeare and of Lope de Vega. His plays, ideal like the *Hero and Leander* and the *Medea*, or historical like *King Ottokar* and *The True Servant*, are, as are Shakespeare's plays, of an objective kind, although, it may be noticed in passing, one pretty incident from a love-passage of his own is transported bodily into the *Hero and Leander*, and the heroine of that play and the formidable heroine of the *Medea* were studied from persons whom he loved. It is of some interest to compare the view of an eminent dramatist concerning a craftsman in his own trade with the view of an eminent critic like Dr. Sidney Lee. Grillparzer censures Schiller for "speaking too often himself without allowing his characters to speak." He does not find Shakespeare guilty of this offence; but he does not suppose that Shakespeare evoked his world out of nothing or out of mere observation of men and books.

"Much has been said," writes Grillparzer, "about the gift of great poets to depict the most diverse passions and characters foreign to their own nature, and there has been much talk about observing and studying man, and of how Shakespeare gathered material for his Macbeths and Othellos in taverns and among sailors and cart-drivers, and how, when he had a bushelful of such impressions, he sat down and made a play of it. O the wiseacres! Genius, in my opinion, can give nothing but what it finds within itself, and will never depict any passion or conviction that it does not harbour within its own bosom. Hence it happens that some young man will look with searching eyes deep into the human heart, while one who has long been familiar with the world and its ways, sharp observer though he may be, will give you nothing but a patchwork of phrases that have been used a hundred times over and over again. Would you say, then, that Shakespeare must have been a murderer, thief, liar, traitor, ingrate, madman, because he has depicted all these in so masterly a manner? Yes! That is to say, there must have been a tendency to all this within him, although the predominance of reason and the moral sense did not allow it to come to the surface. Only a man with colossal passions can, in my opinion, become a dramatic poet, but these must be under the sway of reason, and in ordinary life must not show themselves."[1]

Elsewhere Grillparzer expresses his assurance that in *Le Misanthrope* Molière portrayed himself. He speaks of the many intimate little touches, only to be obtained by actual experience, and refers to the influence of Molière's unhappy marriage on the tone and temper of his dramatic work. Coleridge's account of Shakespeare's method nearly coincides with that of Grillparzer. "He describes," said Coleridge, "feelings which no observation could teach. Shakespeare made himself all characters—he left out parts of himself, and supplied what might have been in himself."

The lives, as far as we are acquainted with them, of some of Shakespeare's early dramatic contemporaries do not suggest to us that they knew passion only through the imagination. They drank, they quarrelled, they fought, they had their irregular loves. Marlowe perished in a tavern brawl. Greene confessed the misery to which the errors of his heart and will had brought him. Jonson killed his man and suffered in fortune through his violent outbreaks of temper. The distinction of Shakespeare was that, after a hasty marriage, and after loving not wisely but too well Sir Thomas Lucy's deer, he learnt the lesson of good sense, and closed his days in a position of dignified prosperity. He was never in prison for an indiscretion or a crime, as were other dramatists

[1] Gustav Pollak's translation, *Franz Grillparzer*, pp. 403, 404.

of the time. He never, as far as we know, had to go begging to a theatrical manager, as did some of his fellows, for a handful of pence. And yet if he deposited in the *Sonnets* any genuine emotion he could still be hurried hither and thither by passion, and could at times suffer conscious defeat in the struggle between " blood " and " judgment." Some readers of the *Sonnets*, even among those who regard them as poetical exercises, will recognise the personal accent in those lines which, with a touch of bitterness, describe as the right inheritors of the graces of heaven the men

> " Who moving others, are themselves as stone,
> Unmoved, cold, and to temptation slow."

It is true, as Dr. Lee maintains, that passion in its native crudity is never expressed by art. This holds good even of lyrical poetry. The crude passion of a Burns has its outbreak in the way of a man with a maid. When he writes a song, the emotion is recollected, if not " in tranquillity," as Wordsworth has it, at least in combination with an artistic instinct and effort, which effect a Katharsis and give the passion a higher and more enduring form. Who could name a more distinguished exponent of Dr. Lee's doctrine of the impassibility of the artist than the author of *Madame Bovary* ? " We arrive at producing beautiful things," Flaubert wrote, " by dint of patience and protracted effort; control the violent workings of your mind . . .; fever destroys the intellect, anger has no overpowering force; it is a Colossus, whose knees totter, and which wounds itself more than others." But Flaubert was much the reverse of a man " unmoved, cold, and to temptation slow." " If having sensitive nerves were enough to make a poet," he tells Madame Colet, " I should be a greater poet than Shakespeare, than Homer . . . I, whose viscera have been seen through my skin leaping and bounding." Let us hope that no spectacle so disagreeable was inflicted by Shakespeare's viscera on his private friends. But Flaubert, the impassive artist, had behind him Flaubert the singularly excitable man. And, indeed, the supposed impassibility is only a transmuted, and often, as with Wordsworth in his earlier years, a most exhausting kind of excitement. The wheel spins so rapidly that it seems motionless.

When Scott's fancy " ran its ain rigs in some other world " than that which immediately surrounded him, none the less the total man was supporting his fancy, was supplying his fancy with materials, and was determining the mode in which his fancy presented those materials. Had Lockhart never written the *Life of Scott* we should have a less intimate but still a very considerable acquaintance with the author of *Waverley*. Indeed, long before the *Life* was written a young graduate of Oxford, J. Leycester Adolphus, had published those ingenious *Letters to Richard Heber*, in which he demonstrated, by evidence chiefly internal, that the author of *Waverley* was identical with the author of *Marmion* and *The Lady of the Lake*. He showed—to notice only some points in one or two out of the eight letters—that the tastes, studies and habits of life of the novelist were also those of the poet ; that both were Scotchmen and habitual residents in Edinburgh ; that both were antiquaries ; both German and Spanish scholars ; both equal in classical attainments ; both deeply read in British history ; both lawyers ; both fond of field sports ; and both (though not soldiers) lovers of military subjects. Adolphus found the same good sense and good morals in the novelist and the poet; the same familiarity with the manners of good society; the same love of romantic story, yet romantic story which was not repugnant to common sense. He selected for special commendation the character of Colonel Mannering—"one of the most striking representations I am acquainted with, of a gentleman in feelings and in manners . . . a gentleman even in prejudices, passions and caprices." Lockhart tells us that when *Guy Mannering* was first published, "the Ettrick shepherd said to Professor Wilson, 'I have done wi' doubts now. Colonel Mannering is just Walter Scott, painted by himself.'" When this was told to Scott, adds Lockhart, he smiled in approbation of the shepherd's shrewdness, and often, in speaking to Ballantyne, referred to himself under the name of Colonel Mannering.

If a study of the Waverley novels gives us an assurance that the action of such an imagination as Scott's, when working at its highest, may veil but does not really conceal the personality of the inventor, it also indicates some of the difficulties and dangers which beset the critic, who, as in the case of Shakespeare, works under the disadvantage of knowledge so incomplete that his conjectures or divinations can in many instances neither be confirmed nor controlled by ascertained facts. I must ask the reader's permission to offer him, as if something new, one paragraph from a buried and forgotten page of my own of more than ten years ago; if it is not new, perhaps it may have the merit of falling in aptly with the course of the present argument:

"Let us suppose that the facts of Sir Walter Scott's life were unknown; we should find his character, his moral temper, his likings and aversions, his intellectual culture, and some of the habits of his life written at large throughout his novels; and the equable temper of many of these would lead us to infer that his spiritual progress was rather on a high table-land than through any Inferno to a Purgatory and a Paradise. We should find it extremely difficult to determine the chronology of the Waverley novels; we might perceive a failing hand in a few; we might place these in a period of decline, and might be encountered by critics who would place them in a period of apprenticeship. If we succeeded in dating *Waverley* correctly by its second title, should we discover that it actually belongs in its origin to some ten years earlier, or that the event which led to its resumption was neither the visit of the allied sovereigns nor the failure of the Catholic Relief Bill, but simply that Scott searched an old desk to find some fishing-tackle for a guest? We might, perhaps, discover the first conception which gave its origin to *Guy Mannering;* but should we not be tempted to invent some superfine reason for its being laid aside, while the real cause was that Scott ceased to believe that it would interest his public? *The Heart of Midlothian* was written because an anonymous correspondent communicated the story to Scott, and he thought it would please his readers. He turned to *Ivanhoe* because he feared that he might weary his readers with Scottish themes. In the year at the close of which *Ivanhoe* appeared, Sir Manasseh Lopes, whose mother was named Rebecca, was convicted and sentenced. How irresistible such a coincidence would be for literary conjecture. But Scott's interest in the Jews was unconnected with Lopes; his friend Skene had, in his youth, observed the Jews in Germany and tried to amuse Scott, in the intervals of acute bodily suffering, with reminiscences of the past. The tale of Jeanie Deans is connected only by contrast with the tale of the *Master of Ravenswood*, which lies so near it in order of time; but the trial of Jeanie, an unconventional heroine, suggested some years later the possible success of an unconventional hero in *The Fortunes of Nigel*. *The Pirate*, of 1821, had its biographical source in its author's voyage, seven years earlier, with the Commissioners for the Northern Lighthouse service. The subject of *St Ronan's Well* was chosen through a mere desire for novelty. Thus we learn from a study of Scott the importance of considering the relation of an author to his public; . . . we learn also that the treatment of one theme may compel a writer into an opposite direction, or, as in the case of *The Abbot* and *Kenilworth*, may push him forward in the same direction."[1]

[1] From a Review in *The Bookman* of "William Shakespeare," by Brandes.

Assuredly the progress and development of Scott's art as a novelist was not determined wholly from within by some sequence of spiritual states, each of which demanded artistic expression. Shakespeare could touch heights and depths of the inner life unknown to Scott, but doubtless he, too, had an eye to pleasing the public. He may have turned about 1600 from comedy to tragedy not because some recent experiences had saddened or darkened his view of life, not because he needed the aid of art to overmaster a private grief or mood of trouble, but because he had for the time exhausted his comic vein, or because, as Dr. Lee suggests, he now aspired to the highest form of dramatic poetry, or because tragedy had become the fashion of the day. All we can be sure of is that he tried to write comedy, but the joyous temper of *Twelfth Night*, for some cause or other, had departed; comedy now became in his hands serious, ironical, bitter—more or less an indictment of society or of life. He devoted himself to tragedy, and whatever in thought, in feeling, and in his gathered experience accorded with the view of human nature and human existence proper to tragedy now for the first time found complete expression.

Among modern novelists, not of the lyrical order like George Sand, but of what may be termed the dramatic or objective order, the nearest parallel to Shakespeare as a creator is assuredly Balzac. In prefaces or occasional digressions Balzac may designedly show us something of himself or put forth opinions of his own, but in the main he creates and maintains a population of men and women among whom he does not himself intend to move. With him experience, in the grosser meaning of that word, bore an unusually small proportion to invention. It needed all his strength of artistic feeling to dominate his imagination; his visions threatened to possess him rather than submissively offered themselves to be his possessions; he worked in a rage of creation. In Emerson's sense of the words he is fully known to us through his writings. Of those shreds and patches which help to make up part of what is styled a "tangible personality," but which of themselves could only make up a scarecrow, we can, by prudent interrogation of the *Human Comedy*, secure several. We might guess that Balzac had some peculiar and vivid intimacy with the city of Tours, where, like a less happy cathedral jackdaw, the Abbé Birotteau nestles, even though we were not aware that Tours was Balzac's native city. All the provinces are known to him, but how specially he loved what Mr. Wedmore speaks of as the large gentleness of the landscape of Touraine! The record of Balzac's schooldays, of what he thought and felt at his college, is given in the history of *Louis Lambert*. For three years Balzac was a student of law, and his sister assures us that a notary of her acquaintance kept among his law-books a copy of *César Birotteau*, for in truth it was an unerring text-book on questions of bankruptcy. It may be, however, as Brunetière suggests, that Balzac learnt more of law from his combats with creditors than from the instruction of a notary. Somewhat later, when just starting on his great career, the novelist tried his luck as type-founder and printer, an experiment which ended in disaster. Who but an actual printer could have told so exactly and with such a mastery of detail the gallant struggles of the printer, David Séchard, and his faithful Eve at Angoulême. Who, again, but a collector of art objects like Balzac could have collected in a dream the treasures of Cousin Pons? The question of money was a great affair in Balzac's life, and it is a great affair in his novels. He loved Madame de Bernay, and his feeling for her inspires the portrait of Madame de Mortsauf in the *Lys dans la Vallée*, and from another point of view that perhaps of Marguerite Claës in *La Recherche de l'Absolu*. "In no one of his characters, nor anywhere in his work, not even in the numerous letters of his *Correspondence*"—so writes Brunetière—"has Balzac better expressed than in Balthasar Claës the nature of his affection for this great friend of his youth—always ready to sacrifice everything to him, and he, like Balthasar in his quest for the philosopher's stone, always ready to strip her of her possessions and drive her to despair, even while he idolised her." He loved Madame Hanska, who in the end became Balzac's wife; she stimulated that kind of crude mysticism which lay in Balzac's nature, and connected the great naturalist with the romantic art of his time; the influence was not all to his advantage, and to Madame Hanska and this vein of crude mysticism we owe *Séraphita*.

Thus some of the features and details of a "tangible personality" can be discovered in work even as objective as that of Balzac; but these scraps of knowledge are insignificant in comparison with the involuntary presentation of his total mind, a turbulent ocean, through his art. We are tempted to accept as true the paradox that a lyrical writer is known to us only at an angle, only at a point, through a cry, through a passion, whereas the writer who loses himself in his art is known to us on every side, in the round, in his totality of intellectual and moral power.

It would serve this discussion little to confront Dr. Lee's theory of art with the case of a great writer who was rather an idealist than a realist. Manifest as are Milton's personal passions and beliefs in his epic poetry, in the story of the warfare between heaven and hell, with earth for its centre, and in the story of the great duel between Satan and the young Jewish hero, he is thrust forward more prominently in drama. The spirit of "the lady of his college" is transferred, whole and unflawed, to the lady of *Comus*; the blind champion of Israel fallen on evil days is no other than the blind champion of the English Republic. But a gulf of difference divides Milton from Shakespeare. We may, with hope of a better result, put Dr. Lee's theory once more to the test by applying it to the writings of a great poet whose work, during at least one period of his long career, aimed at an escape from mere self-expression to a marmoreal and classical self-detachment.

Did Goethe in drama and novel make us acquainted with himself? Was it out of nothingness that his imagination summoned the passion which it embodies? Is Goethe's art intimately related to his life? To ask these questions is to meet an instant and inevitable answer leaping forth to the lips of every student of Goethe's life and works. Whatever he wrote is part of a great confession; through drama and novel he is intimately known; the passion of art is constantly used by him to overmaster, to relieve and to clarify the crude passion of the actual day and hour.

To exhibit the truth of these statements in detail would be to write a history of Goethe's mind and art. A few glances across his work must here suffice. In Leipsic, he tells us in his Autobiography (and the Leipsic years closed when Goethe was nineteen), "began that inclination to transform everything which pleased, annoyed, or otherwise occupied me, into a picture or a poem, and thus to put the matter aside, at the same time correcting my ideas of external things and restoring my peace of mind." The little pastoral play, *Die Laune des Verliebten*, is rightly described by Düntzer as a poetic atonement to Käthchen Schönkopf for the fits of jealous rudeness of which the writer was guilty; Eridon is Goethe himself; Amine is Käthchen; it is not unlikely that in the pair of happy, trustful lovers we have sketches of Horn and Constanze Breitkopf. The play is a trifle, but already Goethe's method as an artist is in existence. With *Götz von Berlichingen* and *Werther* he took the world by storm. He thought in *Götz* to give a dramatised history of one of the noblest Germans, to rescue from forgetfulness "the memory of an honest man." But the play became much more than a dramatised history; it is the cry for liberty and for nature of Goethe in his period of Storm-and-Stress; we see here the heavings of his breast in those days of aspiring and turbulent youth. We look a little closer, and we see things more intimate. Goethe sets to work his invention; he adds to the Götz drama the characters of Weislingen, Adelheid, Marie and Franz. The idyll of Sesenheim and Friederike had been marred by a bitter close, but Goethe could not forget the pastor's daughter. "She wrote me a letter that lacerated my heart," he says in the autumn of 1771. It was the time when he first took up *Götz*, Goethe's biographer, Bielschowsky, tells us: "His soul was burning with the consciousness of a great wrong. The attempt to atone for it was partly responsible for the existence of the Weislingen-drama, and thus of the whole chronicle-history of Götz. . . . 'Poor Friederike will feel to some extent consoled when the faithless man is poisoned.' Thus Goethe wrote to Salzmann when he sent him a copy of *Götz* for Friederike." Poor Pastor's daughter! It was hardly a satisfying consolation.

It is surely unnecessary to collate the story told in *Werther* with the story of the author's residence in Wetzlar and his passionate attachment to Lotte Buff. Everyone is aware that Goethe fashioned his hero from the half of himself, which afterwards reappeared as a Tasso and as the Edward of *Elective Affinities*. But it is not always remembered that Goethe had thought of throwing the imaginative version of his recent passionate experiences into the form of a drama. Goethe, of course, was no Werther; it was Jerusalem, not Goethe, who committed suicide; yet thoughts of suicide had often passed through Goethe's mind in those moods of profound dissatisfaction resulting from the contrast between the world as it is—this pinfold here—and the world desired by the heart, a contrast which is a leading motive in the novel. A mill-stream, turbulent but well embanked, has grown, as in Schiller's poem, into a whirlpool. Lotte is an idealised portrait; Albert does a certain wrong to Kestner, but the likeness is still apparent through an altered expression required by the artistic composition. For the latter part of the novel colouring had been found in the troubled course of the marriage of Frau von Laroche's beautiful daughter, Maxe, with the Frankfort merchant, Brentano. At the centre of the web which he had spun sat Goethe. He had contended with a real, though not an overmastering, passion. Through the *Katharsis* of art he had delivered himself from the Werther mood.

These were works of Goethe's early manhood, and of a time when sentiment and romance opened the flood-gates for lyrical effusion in art which was not lyrical. When trained to self-restraint by his manifold public duties at Weimar, when impressed deeply by the generalising and impersonal character of classical sculpture as seen in Rome, did Goethe detach his art from his individual life and his private experiences? The answer is "Yes and No." We observe in *Iphigenie* and *Tasso* a more deliberate and complete mastery in dealing with personal emotions for imaginative purposes; but Goethe still finds the inspiring spirit of his creations in his own heart. He, like Orestes, had been pursued by the Furies: "Perhaps the invisible scourge of the Eumenides," he wrote in 1775, "will before long lash me again out of my fatherland." And he had found in Charlotte von Stein one who could wave the Furies back, an Iphigeneia, who could hold in check his passions, calm his tumult, and assuage his griefs. The purest of ideal dramas is a hymn in honour of the woman whom he loved and who had given him a new and higher life. From the outset *Tasso* was recognised as a fragment of transmuted autobiography. On reading the first scene Herder exclaimed to his wife: "Goethe cannot do otherwise than idealise himself and write everything out of his own experience." Late in life Goethe described the play to Eckermann as "bone of my bone and flesh of my flesh." The Court of Ferrara is the Court of Weimar; the princess is Charlotte von Stein; neither Tasso nor Antonio is the complete Goethe, but he distributes between the two the poet and the man of affairs contained within him, and he adds to his Antonio features taken from one or two unattractive Weimar contemporaries. "Anyone who is familiar with the history of Weimar during the decade from 1776 to 1786," writes Bielschowsky, "feels, in reading the drama, as though he were listening to real conversations of that period." Yet we can set all that is personal aside, and enjoy the play with the highest satisfaction merely as a piece of dramatic art.

Such an examination of Goethe's imaginative work in prose and verse might be pursued to the close, through *Wilhelm Meister's Apprenticeship* and *Elective Affinities* to the *Second Part of Faust* with like results. In *Elective Affinities* he again distributes his total personality between the more self-indulgent Edward and the stronger and more self-controlled Captain. We know that Goethe at this time had himself contended with the feelings awakened by the charm of Minna Herzlieb, and that again he turned to art as a means for wrestling down passion to which he would not yield. The strict views of the sanctity of marriage expressed in the book were his nailing the colours to the mast in the fight which he had undertaken against himself. As to *Faust* it is enough to say that from the first scene, where the weary and disillusioned scholar utters a measureless sigh for nature and freedom, for youth and joy, to the scene in which the old man finds his happiness in limited and useful toil, it is an idealised re-creation in art of the entire course of the writer's life. Layer upon layer, stratum upon stratum, of that great process of development during the course of upwards of half a century are here exhibited. The age of Rousseau is left behind and we touch the age of Comte. Through all moves the spirit of Goethe, gathering experience of love and grief, lore of statecraft, of finance, of science, of art, of war, until the close is reached with humanitarian effort and the hopes and aspiration which lead to the highest attainments of the soul. The life and the art are essentially one.

From our general survey, which might easily be

extended, we return to Shakespeare with two assurances—first, that a writer may be truly dramatic and yet may betray much that is personal; secondly, that a dramatist does not always "summon out of nothingness" the emotions which he expresses in his art, but, on the contrary, often recurs to the person who is nearest to him—himself of the past or the present—and from the inner experience of that person obtains the material, which he re-handles, modifies, varies, or transmutes. These are encouraging assurances. Evidently there would be nothing strange or singular if, as a fact, Shakespeare deposited in his art much that was immediately derived from his own heart and brain, much of the emotional experience, joyous or bitter, of his actual life. But some of his experiences might be so mingled with foreign elements or so altered by the processes of the imagination as to be of little or no avail for the purposes of the critical detective. Our comparative ignorance also of Shakespeare's life, apart from his acts and all that he did as a poet, forbids our passing to and fro between the life and the works, as we pass in the case of Goethe, and with confidence reading the one into the other. We should often be reduced to conjectures incapable of being verified or tested, and the value of such conjectures is small. A critic, for instance, might conjecture that some woman, attracted by the genius and the free and open nature of Shakespeare, played towards him the part which Madame de Bernay played towards the young man of twenty-three from Tours, or the more discreet part which, with far less disparity of years, Frau von Stein played towards the author of *Werther*; that under her influence his powers rapidly matured; that by her he was in a great measure formed, refined, instructed in knowledge of the world and in the secrets of a woman's heart; and that his gratitude and homage to her were uttered in passages of his plays, the meaning of which was well understood between them, such as that ardent speech of Biron:

> "From women's eyes this doctrine I derive;
> They sparkle still the right Promethean fire;
> They are the books, the arts, the academes,
> That show, contain and nourish all the world."

Stranger things than this have happened; our critic might contend that his theory would illuminate much that is obscure in Shakespeare's life and writings. But the theory could not be advanced towards certainty; and in our scientific days an acre of barren fact—"long heath, brown furze, anything"—is worth more than a thousand furlongs of unverified conjecture.

Yet without the advantage of very detailed knowledge of Shakespeare's life, a number of persons who were not, and are not, in general given to the pursuit of will-o'-the-wisps, among them Masson, Ingram, Bagehot, Leslie Stephen, Goldwin Smith, Bradley, Raleigh (not to speak of foreign critics), have sought to discover the man Shakespeare in the works which proceeded from his heart and brain; they adopted various methods; not one of them supposed that his inquiry resulted in failure; and it is a curious and striking fact that the Shakespeare of each portrait-painter resembles the Shakespeares of the rest with quite as close a resemblance as portraits commonly possess which are drawn from a real face at various points of view by artists "indifferent honest." The features of similarity are important and numerous; the details of difference are hardly appreciable.

Nor are these likenesses vague and general. Dr.

Lee asks for " distinguishing idiosyncrasies, individual characteristics, peculiar experiences of mind or heart." The combination of size, gait, manner of gesture, and all that we sum up as the bearing of a figure and the expression of a face, constitute an idiosyncrasy, and identify for us a friend even at a distance which does not permit us to see whether he possesses a certain well-known wart, with three hairs growing from it, under his left ear. Dr. Lee wants " frequent pronouncements " in Shakespeare's writings on " religion, ethics, political economy, and the like, qualifying or questioning accepted beliefs " ; and he finds instead quite opposite statements on one and the same matter uttered by the several *dramatis personæ* of Shakespeare's art. Now among the portrait-painters there is a substantial agreement as to Shakepeare's opinions on some of the topics named by Dr. Lee ; they represent him, if not as " a Tory and a gentleman," at least as leaning, like Scott and the mature Goethe, towards a conservative view in social and political affairs ; not as a revolutionary spirit, governed by doctrinaire abstractions, yet as one who sympathised with the trials and sorrows of the poor ; a man who disliked mobs, and distrusted the politics of the citizen class as self-interested and narrow ; one who perceived the value of what Ulysses terms " degree." They say that he was not a religious enthusiast nor a theological dogmatist ; that he did not, like Shelley, set himself against existing beliefs ; that he was no Puritan ; that he had a spirit of reverence and a deep sense of the mystery of things. But really a man's opinions, though an important part of the contents of his mind, are often not a distinguishing part of his personality. The way he holds his opinions is more important than the opinions themselves. In the matter of opinions, " le style c'est l'homme." That Shakespeare could see two sides of a question and could put opposite views of truth into the mouths of different persons is in itself a distinguishing feature of his mind. It is not every man who can do this, nor every poet. We learn that whatever conclusions Shakespeare arrives at on this subject or on that, he will not hold it in a shrill, eager, intolerant way; he can see things in the round; he can understand another man's point of view; he cannot be what Professor William James styles a "thin" thinker; his way of thinking is essentially "thick." Now to learn this is to learn much. Two men holding antagonistic opinions, if they hold them in the same way, resemble each other mentally much more than do two men who hold identical opinions in different ways. The heads of Poysam the Puritan and Charbon the Papist may be of one build. New presbyter may be very like old priest if both are shrill and intolerant, or like, again, if both are the reverse of "thin" and extravagant in their mode of belief. If we are sure that Shakespeare could see and feel every side of a question we already know a very remarkable characteristic of his intellect.

Though what Browning calls the "spirit-sense," an educated tact, is the surest instrument for the discovery of a dramatist or a novelist in his work, some few canons of discovery can be formulated. There are certain things which, if found, imply the presence of a certain characteristic of the writer's mind. If the dialogue is witty, the author cannot have been devoid of wit. If Falstaff is created, his creator must have had the gift of humour. If Hamlet shows himself a master of irony, Shakespeare must have had it in him to be ironical. And, again, if Perdita, in a phrase of perfect beauty, can make the daffodil flash upon our inward eye, Shakespeare must have felt the beauty of the daffodil. Such certainties as these multiply as we read the plays, coalesce, and form the groundwork of a portrait. And then we know from our experience of life and human nature that some ascertained qualities in a man imply others; we add these to our portrait, and are justified in so doing; if we find evidence of that "open and free nature" of which Jonson spoke, we can infer a liability to those temptations which are proper to a free and open nature. In estimating the significance in relation to Shakespeare's mind of the utterances of his *dramatis personæ*, of course, we try to calculate the angle of refraction. But there are some things of which we can be sure; except by a humorous stumble into good sense, a foolish and slender-witted gentleman will not be made the medium for Shakespeare's wisdom; and a wise man will not often utter what Shakespeare thought folly; the mistakes of the wise and prudent may, indeed, be smiled at ironically, but these are usually detected and exposed in the action of the play, and their exposure is Shakespeare's comment on an error. And this is the case whether his plot follows the story of an Italian *novella* or varies from it, for Shakespeare knew how to adapt a plot to accord with character and how to adapt his treatment of character to suit a plot. Again, Shakespeare evidently felt himself, and he makes us feel, that some of his *dramatis personæ* are evil and some are pure of heart. When Iago describes love as "merely a lust of the blood" we know that he does not express Shakespeare's conception of love, for Desdemona is in the play, and the lie cannot live for a moment in her presence. Thus we gradually accumulate a multitude of details which acquaint us with Shakespeare's ways of thinking and his habitual feelings. "He does not"—to quote the words of Ingram—"mean to affirm all the propositions which he puts into the mouths of his personages, any more than the author of the Book of Job adopted all the utterances of the patriarch and of his friends. But as in the latter case we are little perplexed in separating what is meant to be accepted as truth from what is meant to exhibit the opposition and conflict of thought, so in Shakespeare the difficulty is more hypothetic than real. We can easily discover into what line of thought he throws himself with peculiar spontaneity and heartiness; and we can see what are the types of character and the modes of feeling on which he lets the sunshine of his special favour fall."

Theatre-goers who are familiar with old plays and have seen a hundred actors have often gone to a play of Shakespeare's, not to witness for the twentieth time a performance of *Hamlet* or *The Merchant of Venice*, but to enjoy the Hamlet or the Shylock or the Portia of some distinguished actor or actress. The actor endeavours to present a character of Shakespeare's, and he exhibits something of himself in his conception of the character. "Ah!" we exclaim, "this actor has given us a sentimental Hamlet," or "he has made the melodramatic element too strong," or "he is dignified, but he cannot have perceived the versatility of Hamlet," or "he is proud of his passionate elocution and indulges too much in Berserker rages." And so while losing himself, according to his own ideas and sentiment, in the character which he exhibits, the actor himself emerges, and, having seen him in many parts, we define his individuality in its strength and in its weaknesses. What is true of the actor is true in a far higher degree of the creator of the drama. His individuality emerges through his manner of conceiving and exhibiting the various sorts and conditions of men. We compare dramatist with dramatist as we compare actor with actor, and the essential characteristics of each become more strikingly apparent. We compare the young gallants of Fletcher's comedies with the Orlandos and Benedicks of Shakespeare's comedies, and we come to the conclusion that, however Shakespeare may have delighted in the flash and outbreak of a fiery spirit, he did not regard an ever-bubbling licentiousness or a nerveless lubricity as ordinarily part of the character of a gentleman. We compare the languishing *tendresse* of Fletcher's wronged and sorrowing women with the energy of heart following quick stabs of pain which some of Shakespeare's maidens and wives endure, and we perceive that Fletcher was sentimental and that Shakespeare was passionate in the treatment of women placed in almost identical situations. Are we wrong in believing that Fletcher's nature was of a softer fibre, less sound and sane, more "rathe-ripe, rotten-rich," than that of Shakespeare? Or we compare the persons who are objects of Jonson's indignant satire with those at whom Shakespeare smiles or even laughs outright, and we feel certain that Jonson was a man who enjoyed the lusty wielding of the cat-o'-nine-tails, whereas Shakespeare had often a divine pity for his victims, that of a man who, knowing our infirmities, yet remembers that we are dust. Surely such discoveries as these are as important as the discovery would be of Shakespeare's opinion on the Authority of General Councils or on Sin after Baptism.

In the development of Shakespeare's powers from *Love's Labour Lost* to *The Tempest*, Dr. Lee can find nothing beyond indications that "he began life by being a boy, that he then reached adolescence and middle-age, and that he exemplified in his work characteristics of various periods of human life." Other readers of the plays in chronological order have put on record their impression that they have seen more than this. They say that they notice in Shakespeare's mid-noon a quite unexpected gathering of the clouds; the capacity for writing with real gaiety or easy cheerfulness seems to be somehow withdrawn from him. He seems to look on the world with altered eyes; it spreads before him for a time like an unweeded garden that grows to seed. He writes at perhaps about this date a play of disillusionment, *Troilus and Cressida;* he appears to invent characters whose chief business is to exhibit the seamy side of life; invectives against all the evil that is on the earth, sometimes bitter and cynical, sometimes stormy and thunderous, become frequent. The women of his comedies are not full of laughter like Beatrice, full of exquisite play like Rosalind, but of saintly severity, an Isabella, or, on the other hand, such a wanton as Cressida. The criminal who is a self-deceiver appears as a central figure in comedy—the Angelo of *Measure for Measure.* Thoughts of death are frequent, with images solemn and majestic or full of the hideousness of the grave; thoughts of suicide are occasionally present. And then, as if Shakespeare had said, "I have tried to write comedy, but it will not do! The sunlight of these comedies of mine is getting too pallid and ghastly, like sunlight during an eclipse. To face round upon evil, confront it, explore it, would be better than this"—as if these were his thoughts, he ceases to write comedy; and for several years, with powers concentrated and high-strung, produces tragedy after tragedy. It is quite possible that Shakespeare may have written high-spirited comedies while he suffered acutely; there is an energy diffused by pain which may quicken the power of resistance; it is when the dregs of misery settle in our nature that we are gradually poisoned and the spirit of imaginative mirth suffers paralysis. But a season came when a pure and serene light—not without a touch of pathetic beauty in it—was again shed over Shakespeare's art. At even-time there was light. And yet we feel, or imagine that we feel, a certain personal detachment in the gladness of Shakespeare's latest comedies. They are not light-hearted. The writer smiles sympathetically, tenderly, as Prospero smiled when he uttered the words, "Poor worm, thou art infected!" The ray of evening light comes from a sun that sheds a beautiful illumination, but has lost some of its heat. Shakespeare now seems to see life as a most majestic vision, "harmonious charmingly," and yet

> "We are such stuff
> As dreams are made on, and our little life
> Is rounded with a sleep."

This to not a few readers appears to have been the history of Shakespeare's mental development as indicated by his art, and it impresses them as being far from commonplace.

It must be added that some time before Shakespeare's comedies ceased to be written in the true spirit of comedy occurs the earliest mention of his *Sonnets*. Students of an elder generation—Hallam and Masson and Ingram—understood these poems as expressing Shakespeare's genuine feelings and as alluding to a painful story. The most recent students—Beeching and Bradley and Raleigh—are of the same opinion. Those critics who have attempted to paint a portrait of Shakespeare represent him as a man with a great capacity for joy, but as highly sensitive, and capable of deep and brooding melancholy. In the *Sonnets*, if they do not constitute a body of dramatic pieces the like of which is nowhere to be found, we read that the woman whom Shakespeare loved unwisely but passionately proved false, and that the man whom he cherished with ardent affection betrayed him. His worldly circumstances grew more and more prosperous; that was something to lay hold of; but with what an arid gaze might he not for a time have viewed such material prosperity! How natural that his art before very long should be touched with bitterness.

In such an interpretation we are rather putting things together than making any great ventures of faith. But a venture of faith is often warrantable, is often a part of science, and has often received its justification from evidence afterwards adduced.

Persons who desire to study the portrait of Shakespeare as he is seen in his works may be advised to compare the essays of Bagehot and Leslie Stephen with Professor Raleigh's first chapter and Dr. Bradley's recently-published Oxford Lecture. It is a grief to me to learn from Dr. Bradley that the creator of Launce's immortal Crab did not love a dog. Neither did Goethe; his son threw ammonites, brought with toil from the Hainberg, at the Hamburg mongrels; a poodle took revenge at a later time and drove Goethe out of his theatrical managership. Bacon cannot have been the meanest of mankind, for when Secretary Winwood "did beat his dog from lying on a stool," Bacon quarrelled with Mr. Secretary, and declared that "every gentleman did love his dog." I must postpone the declaration of my conversion to Baconianism until such zealous and learned Baconians as Dr. Theobald and Mr. Stronach prove that Dr. Bradley has maligned our gentle "Shakespeare"—our gentle Shake-speare who bit the hand of Essex that fed him.

IS SHAKESPEARE SELF-REVEALED?

Dr. Lee quotes Carlyle in *Lectures on Heroes* as a supporter of his own views. " I will say of Shakespeare's works generally," declared Carlyle, " that we have no full impress of him there." Carlyle believed that the man was far greater than any or all of his works. It is a pity that Dr. Lee did not carry his quotation one sentence further : " His works were so many windows through which we see a glimpse of the world that was in him." By " the world within him " Carlyle means the man—the " house," which was larger than the " window."

SHAKESPEARE AS A MAN OF SCIENCE

(*Bacon-Shakespeare Controversy*)

His Honour Judge Webb has achieved something remarkable—he has written an entertaining book in advocacy of the Bacon-Shakespeare hypothesis. His vivacity of spirit never flags; he is equal to every emergency; he can explain away the testimony of Ben Jonson with as much ease as he can annihilate the evidence from field-sports of Mr. Justice Madden. He is brilliant; he is dexterous; unhappily, he is not well-informed.

I do not propose to consider the Baconian hypothesis. I do not imagine that serious students will be much impressed by the earlier chapters of Dr. Webb's book, in which they will detect strange errors; but I have found men of ability who are taken aback by the evidence adduced in the chapter "Of Shakespeare as a Man of Science." This chapter I propose to examine; and it is a pleasure, in doing so, to know that the remarkable ability of Dr. Webb assures one that he has made the best of his case. He addresses himself to his argument with a great advantage; duller men (and women) have laboured, and he has entered into their labours. "Bacon," he says, "is the acknowledged author of a vast amount of literature, epistolary, oratorical, historical and philosophical, which has been ransacked for the discovery of *parallelisms* between them and the works of Shakespeare." "Here as elsewhere," he tells us, " the higher criticism has been at work." I have always felt humbled by this awe-inspiring title, " the higher criticism." We shall now see how the higher criticism, here as elsewhere, arrives at its conclusions.

Before coming to close quarters with Dr. Webb's weightiest chapter I may notice a few points of parallelism scattered through other parts of the volume.

" The discussion of ' the Law Salique ' . . . (in *King Henry V.*)," writes Dr. Webb, " displays the learning of a lawyer, and the conclusion that ' the Salique law was not devised for the realm of France,' is identical with the conclusion which is indicated in the *Apophthegms* of Bacon."

Bacon therefore wrote the speech of the Archbishop of Canterbury in *Henry V.*, Act I., scene 2. Unluckily for the argument the speech is simply transferred by the writer of the play from Holinshed's *Chronicle*. I will quote the lines cited by Dr. Webb, and place after them Holinshed's prose :

> " Then doth it well appeare, the Salike Law
> Was not devised for the Realme of France ;
> Nor did the French possesse the Salike Land
> Untill foure hundred one and twentie yeeres
> After defunction of King Pharamond,
> (Idly suppos'd the founder of this Law)."

" This law," writes Holinshed, " was not made for the realme of France, nor the Frenchmen possessed the land Salike, till foure hundred and one and twentie yeeres after the death of Pharamond, the supposed maker of this Salike law."

And the whole long speech of the Archbishop is similarly versified from the *Chronicle*.

" Sometimes," according to Dr. Webb, " the use of a single phrase, like the print of Dirk Hatteraick's shoe, will supply a piece of evidence that decides a question. In the *Advancement* Luther is described as finding in 'discourse of reason the province he had undertaken in his war with Rome,' and Bacon constantly employs the phrase. It is so peculiar that when it was observed in *Hamlet* the critics regarded it as a misprint." A second example is cited by Dr. Webb from *Troilus & Cressida*, and "discourse of thought," he notes, is found in *Othello*.

Unhappily for the decisive piece of evidence, here Dirk Hatteraicks are many. "Discourse of reason" occurs as early as Caxton; it occurs in Sir Thomas More; it occurs in Eden (the examples from Caxton and Eden are cited in the *New English Dictionary*); it is found in Holland's translation of *Plutarch's Morals;* it is found at least four times in Florio's translation of *Montaigne*.

"If Antony says that, 'even at the base of Pompey's statua great Cæsar fell,' the Irving (Irving Shakespeare) annotator admits that Bacon is the only writer that used statua for statue."

The "Irving annotator," if cited correctly, is liberal in admissions, for the form "statua" was not obsolete even when Sir T. Herbert wrote his *Travels*, or when Peter Heylyn published his *History of the Presbyterians*. But it happens that "Pompey's statua" is not found in any text of Shakespeare earlier than Steevens' edition of 1793. The original text is "statue," here as elsewhere, and "statua" was a conjecture of Malone's.

"If Antony is to 'take thought and die for Cæsar,' the Irving (Irving Shakespeare) annotator refers to Bacon's *Henry VII.* as the only authority for the use of the word 'thought' in the sense of anxiety or sorrow."

Surely Dr. Webb does not mean that this sense is peculiar to Shakespeare and Bacon. It is of common occurrence in Elizabethan and earlier English. "Take no thought," is the rendering of the authorised version (Matt. vi. 25) of μὴ μεριμνᾶτε τῃ ψυχῃ ὑμῶν. And in Baret's *Alvearie*, 1580, we come upon Shakespeare's very words: "He will die for sorrowe and thought. *Morietur pro dolore. Conficietur mœrore.*" "I die for thought," says Skelton (*Manerly Margery*). "The old man for very thought and grief of heart pined away and died," writes Holland; and, if it were needful, examples could be multiplied.

The Baconians, and Dr. Webb among them, make much of an error common to Shakespeare, in *Troilus & Cressida*, and Bacon, in the *Advancement*: "Unlike young men," says Shakespeare's Hector,

> "Whom Aristotle thought
> Unfit to hear Moral Philosophy."

And Bacon: "Is not the opinion of Aristotle worthy to be regarded, wherein he saith that young men are not fit auditors of Moral Philosophy." It was of Political not Moral Philosophy that Aristotle wrote thus.

I have not delved the matter to the root and perhaps several instances of the error may have been noticed; but evidently it was current in Elizabethan days, for Mulcaster, the schoolmaster of Edmund Spenser, whose remarkable work on education, *Positions*, was edited in 1888 by the late Mr. Quick, writes (p. 247) as follows: "We use to set young ones to the morall and politike first, and reason, against Aristotle's conclusion, that a young stripling is a fit hearer of morall Philosophie." It would be interesting to trace this error to its source, which is probably mediæval. Mulcaster goes on to explain that Aristotle placed "the Mathematicalles " and " Naturall Philosophie " in a comparatively early stage of education, and reserved the other parts of philosophy " for elder years." Mr. Spedding notices that the same error is found in Malvezzi's *Discorsi*, 1622. It had some origin common to several European countries. The words of Malvezzi's English translator of 1642 are these: " And this opinion of mine is in no way differing from that of Aristotle, who saith that young men are no good hearers of morall Philosophy."

Bacon's reference to himself, after his fall, as in " the base court of adversity," may possibly be, as Dr. Webb seems to suggest, a reminiscence of that " base court " to which Shakespeare's Richard II. descends from the battlements of Flint Castle. Richard, after his manner, plays repeatedly upon the words, into which he reads a pathetic meaning, and Bacon, in the course of the legal proceedings against his friend and patron, Essex, had doubtless been interested in the play, a representation of which had been given as a preliminary to the rebellious rising.

> " Down, down I come like glistering Phaethon,"

exclaims Richard. " And who," asks Dr. Webb, " but the author of *The Wisdom of the Ancients* would have bethought himself of the ' glistering Phaethon ' under such circumstances, and associated the myth of legendary Greece with the surroundings of a feudal castle ? " I cannot answer the question; but I can remind the querist that in writing *Richard II.* Shakespeare had certainly a vivid recollection of Marlowe's *Edward II.*, and that Marlowe makes his Warwick exclaim against Gaveston, not at Flint Castle, indeed, but at the New Temple :

> " Ignoble vassal, that like Phaeton
> Aspir'st unto the guidance of the sun."

Yet Dr. Webb is not one of those Baconians who assert that the author of *The Wisdom of the Ancients* was the author of *Edward II*.

"When Troilus reproaches Hector with sparing the prostrate Greeks, he says:

> "'Brother, you have a vice of mercy in you,
> Which better fits a lion than a man.'

What is the mercy of the lion? Bacon tells us. 'Of lions,' he says, 'it is a received belief that their fury ceaseth towards anything that yieldeth and prostrateth itself before them.'"

A received belief, which may be found in many quarters; but Bacon is here probably thinking of Pliny (I quote from Holland's translation): "The Lion alone of all wilde beasts, is gentle to those that humble themselves unto him, and will not touch any such upon their submission, but spareth what creature soever *lieth prostrate before him.*"

I have selected these parallels, set down in various parts of Dr. Webb's volume, as showing the "higher criticism" on its weaker side. But in the case of the chapter "Of Shakespeare as a Man of Science," I shall not select; I shall notice everything which a reasonable person can suppose to possess importance, everything which Dr. Webb treats in detail rather than in a summary. If Bacon and Shakespeare both observe the fact that "dung applied to the roots of trees doth set them forward," I shall not delay to prove that the fact had been known to others than the poet and philosopher, but my examination of the main contents of this chapter will be exhaustive.

Let me first quote Dr. Webb's statement of what he means to prove:

"The *Natural History* was first published in 1627, a year after Bacon's death. . . . It contains a number of speculations which must be regarded as peculiar and fantastic. What is more surprising, it maintains, as scientific truths, a number of errors which had been all but universally exploded. At the same time, what is equally extraordinary, it anticipates some of the most profound conceptions of modern science. As Shakespeare died in 1616, and as the *Sylva* was not published till 1627, it is plain that the Stratford player could not by any possibility have entered the mysterious wood. And the wonderful thing is this. There is scarce an experiment however mean, there is scarce a speculation however fantastic, there is scarce an error however obstinate and perverse, there is scarce a scientific intuition however original and profound, to be discovered in the *Natural History* that is not also to be discovered in the Plays."

The number of parallels which Dr. Webb has collected or selected from his Baconian predecessors is not remarkable. A larger collection, including many as striking as any adduced by Dr. Webb, has been brought together from Lyly by Mr. Rushton. Lyly's writings were accessible to Shakespeare, as Shakespeare's were to Bacon; but I am not aware that the author of *Euphues* has been yet named as the author of *King Lear*.

What I shall attempt to prove is that all which Dr. Webb regards as proper to Shakespeare and Bacon was, in fact, the common knowledge or common error of the time. The mediæval science of nature was largely derived from Pliny's *Natural History*—its curious lore, true and false, filtered into the general mind through many channels. Doubtless the source of many of the Elizabethan references to beasts and birds and plants and stones was the volume known as *Batman upon Bartholome*, which replaced in 1582 the earlier translation of Glanvilla by Trevisa. In it much is derived from Pliny. My quotations from Pliny are from the translation by Holland, of which the first edition appeared in 1601. *The Secrets and Wonders of the Worlde*, an earlier translation coming through the French is not accessible to me. Many apter and more effective proofs of my position might, I am sure, be obtained by one better provided than I am with old books on gardening, on chemistry, on distillations, on natural history; but I can give something, and perhaps enough, from my modest store of ragged folios and quartos. It is to be expected that in some instances a parallel from Bacon will be closer than others, as in many instances a parallel from Lyly or some other writer will happen to be the best.

"Of all the theories entertained by Bacon," writes Dr. Webb, "the most peculiar is his *Theory of Spirits*." Briefly it is this—that "most of the effects of nature" are produced by "the spirits or pneumaticals that are in all tangible bodies," which spirits are material but invisible. The theory Dr. Webb calls prosaic, but Bacon, writing as Shakespeare, "transmutes it into gold." Bacon speaks of "the spirit of wine," and Shakespeare in *Othello* addresses the "invisible spirit of wine." In *The Tempest*, Alonzo's "spirits" are dulled. Lulling sounds, according to Bacon, conduce to sleep, because they "move in the spirits a gentle attention"; and Jessica is not merry when she hears sweet music, because, as Lorenzo explains, her "spirits are attentive." Bacon tells us that the outward manifestations of the passions are "the effects of the dilatation and coming forth of the spirits into the outward parts"; when Hamlet sees the Ghost, the Queen exclaims:

> "Forth at your eyes your spirits wildly peep."

The "wanton spirits" of Cressida "look out at every joint."

The mediæval theory of "spirits" will be found in the *Encyclopædia of Bartholomew Anglicus on the*

Properties of Things already referred to—a book of wide influence. The popular opinions of Shakespeare's time respecting "spirits" may be read in Bright's *Treatise of Melancholy*, 1586, and Burton's *Anatomy*, 1621, and in many another volume. According to Bartholomew, the spirits are air-like substances; the "natural spirit" in the body arises in the liver, and is a rarefied form of the vapour of the blood; further purified and attenuated in the heart, it becomes the "vital spirit"; made yet more subtle in the brain, it becomes "the animal spirit." This spirit, three in kinds, is essentially one; it is the instrument of the soul, serving as the intermediary between soul and body.

This "spirit" is found not only in animals but throughout inanimate nature. Lodge, in his translation of Seneca, speaks of the "spirit" of lightning left in wine which lightning had congealed (p. 800). Chapman, in his *Bacchus*, speaks of the "spirits" of the odours of wine. And Bright, in his *Melancholy*, naturally has set forth the theory of Bacon, while possibly he was himself influenced by Paracelsus. The "spirit of our bodies" is light, subtile, and yielding, yet it forces the heaviest and grossest parts of our bodies to their several operations; vehement passion either withdraws the spirit from the outward parts or prodigally scatters them on the surface (p. 60); in blushing, for example, the "blood and spirit," first withdrawn, "breake forth again more vehemently" (p. 164). Things inanimate have also a "spirit" in them. "The spirit of our bodies," says Bright (p. 35), "is maintained by nourishments, whether they be of the vegetable or animall kind; which creatures affoord not only their corporall substance, but a spirituall matter also . . . this spirit of theirs is altered more speedily, or with larger travell of nature." The spirit of wine is of all the most swiftly altered and appropriated by our spirits; but everything that we eat or drink is endued with a spirit, for "without this spirit no creature could give us sustentation."

The language of Shakespeare is popular, and connected probably neither with what Bright nor with what Bacon wrote; but if a theory be required, it can be found as easily in a volume which Shakespeare might have read as in a volume published after his death. Bright, indeed, is only carrying into details the current doctrine of the Middle Age.

As to music and its effect upon the "spirits," Bright speaks of it as "alluring the spirites" (p. 241). Burton quotes from Lemnius, who declares that music not only affects the ears, "but the very arteries, the vital and animal spirits"; and again from Scaliger, who explains its power as due to the fact that it plays upon "the spirits about the heart"; whereupon Burton, like Shakespeare's Lorenzo, proceeds to speak of the influence of music upon beasts, and, like Lorenzo, cites the tale of Orpheus.

I do not care to discuss in the pages of a Review the subject in reference to which the expression "expense of spirit" or "spirits" occurs in Bacon and in Shakespeare. Donne (*Progress of the Soul*, stanza xxi.), in the same connection, has the words:

> "Freely on his she friends,
> He blood, and *spirit*, pith, and marrow *spends*."

The thought is of the commonest occurrence in Elizabethan drama; and the expression "expense of spirits" is not peculiar to the writer of the *Sonnets* or the writer of the *Sylva*. Bright in his *Melancholy*, 1586, has the expression on p. 62; again at p. 237;

again at p. 244. It may be found in Donne's *Progress of the Soul*, stanza vi.

Dr. Webb proceeds to notice that the Soothsayer's warning to Shakespeare's Antony, "Stay not by Cæsar's side," etc., may also be found in Bacon. Shakespeare here versifies from North's *Plutarch*, and his Soothsayer's phraseology is that of North, not that of Bacon.

But "the Egyptian Queen, like the Egyptian Soothsayer, adopts the sentiments of Bacon." *The Natural History* lays it down that "the spirits of animate bodies have a fine commixture of flame and an aerial substance"; and in *Antony & Cleopatra* the Queen, on hearing of the death of her lover, exclaims:

> "I'm fire and air! My other elements
> I give to baser life."

Is not man, we may ask in Shakespearean language, made of the four elements? And does not Elizabethan literature afford a "plurisy" of examples (to be still Shakespearean) of the recognition of air and fire as the nobler components of life? The following from Sylvester's *Du Bartas* (second day of first week) may serve as a specimen:

> "For in our Flesh our Bodies Earth remains:
> Our vitall spirits, our Fire and Aire possess;
> And last our Water in our humours rests."

Or this from Chapman's *Andromeda Liberata*:

> "The subtler parts of humour being resolved
> More thick parts rest, of fire and air the want
> Makes earth and water more predominant."

Dr. Webb goes on: "As a corollary to his theory of pneumaticals, Bacon adopts the theory of spontaneous generation. 'Putrefaction,' he says, 'is the work of the spirits of bodies, which are ever unquiet to get forth, and congregate with the air, and to enjoy the sunbeams'; and as examples of 'creatures bred of putrefaction,' he mentions, in another passage, 'the maggot, the weevil, and the moth.' As usual Bacon 'is attended by his double'; 'we can hardly understand the words of Hamlet without a knowledge of the philosophy of the *Sylva*: "if the sun breed maggots in a dead dog, being a god (good) kissing carrion—have you a daughter?—let her not walk in the sun," etc.'"

Now it would be nothing strange if Shakespeare really held the doctrine of spontaneous generation; but here there is not a word to suggest Bacon's theory of the "spirit of bodies" unquiet to enjoy the sunbeams. Shakespeare expresses a popular notion in popular language. "O blessed, breeding sun!" cries Timon of Athens. I will not discuss whether it is the masculine sun, or the feminine moon, or the star Venus, which sprinkleth the dew of generation whereby all things are engendered; Aristotle and Pliny may be consulted on these obscure questions. It will be enough to note that Donne, in 1601 (*Progress of the Soul*, stanza ii.), is, like Shakespeare, the "double" of Bacon:

> "Thee, eye of heaven (the sun), this great soul envies not,
> By thy male force is all we have begot."

And again Donne, in an early satire, written long before Bacon's *Sylva*, described an affected courtier:

> "A thing more strange than on Nile's slime the sun
> E'er bred."

Moffett died in 1604; in his posthumously-published *Theatre of Insects* we are told that beetles "have no females, but have their generation from the sun."

"Bacon," writes Dr. Webb, "maintained a theory of flame which, apparently, was peculiar to himself. He holds that 'flame is a fixed body' . . . and that consequently 'flame doth not mingle with flame, but only remaineth contiguous.'" Here again Shakespeare adopts the theory of Bacon. Proteus explains that one love is forgotten for another even as "one heat another heat expels"; Benvolio remarks that in love "one fire burns out another's burning"; and from *Julius Cæsar* is quoted "as fire drives out fire, so pity pity"; from *Coriolanus*, "one fire drives out one fire."

If Shakespeare's words embody Bacon's "theory of flame," the theory must be not "peculiar to himself," but as old as Tatius and as new as Burton; for in the *Anatomy of Melancholy* (cure of love-melancholy), a book published before Bacon's *Sylva*, we read: "A silly lover . . . when he hath compared her (his mistress) with others, he abhors her name, sight and memory. . . ." As he (Tatius) observes, *Priorem flammam novus ignis extrudit*, "one fire drives out another."

"Nothing," writes Dr. Webb, "in the history of science is more astonishing than Bacon's *Theory of the Celestial Bodies*." Notwithstanding the teaching of Bruno and of Galileo, he maintained that "the celestial bodies, most of them, are fires or flames as the Stoics held." Notwithstanding the teaching of Copernicus he held the mediæval doctrine of "the heavens turning about in a most rapid motion." "But the marvel," says Dr. Webb, "is that the omniscient Shakespeare with his superhuman genius maintained these exploded errors as confidently as Bacon":

> "Doubt thou the stars are fire;
>   Doubt that the sun doth move;
> Doubt truth to be a liar;
>   But never doubt I love."

The Baconian errors are treated by Shakespeare as "the highest types of certainty."

It presses rather hardly upon Hamlet's distracted letter to deduce from his rhyme a "theory of the celestial bodies." Such an ingenious writer as Dr. Webb might as easily have shown that in a letter produced by Polonius to demonstrate the Prince's madness, Shakespeare represented his astronomical ideas as the errors of a madman. But in fact Shakespeare repeats the reference to the stars as fires many times. Perhaps it is better to dismiss Dr. Webb's comment with a jest than to burden my pages with proof that references to the stars as fire and to the motion of the heavens are scattered over the pages of Shakespeare's contemporaries as thickly as the stars themselves. Even Milton's astronomy is in general mediæval, and for him the stars are "fires." Even Sir Thomas Browne, the learned and credulous-incredulous physician of Norwich, writing nearly half a century after Shakespeare (*Vulgar Errors VI.*, chap. v.), mentions the truth of the Copernican hypothesis as in his own day a subject of debate among the learned.

Having endeavoured to show that the style of a passage in *Othello* resembles that of Bacon's *Essay of Gardens*, Dr. Webb writes: "Take again the speech of Agamemnon to the Grecian chiefs in *Troilus & Cressida*:

> "'Checks and disasters
> Grow in the veins of actions highest rear'd,
> As knots by the conflux of meeting sap
> Infect the sound pine and divert his grain
> Tortive and errant from his course of growth.'"

"Here again, even if we hold that the hands are the hands of Esau, we must admit that the voice is the voice of Jacob ; for Bacon tells us that in some plants there is a 'closeness and hardness in their stalk, which hindereth the sap from going up, until it hath gathered into a knot, and so is more urged to put forth.'"

Bacon, however, in the passage from which Dr. Webb quotes with prudent omissions (*Natural History*, 589), expressly denies that "knots," such as he here speaks of, are found in "trees." He is, in fact, treating of nodes, "joints, or knuckles," in "herbs," in "fennel, corn, reeds, or canes," and other plants which he names. Nor does he suggest that these nodes are caused by Shakespeare's "conflux of meeting sap"; on the contrary the sap, as it ascends, "doth (as it were) tire and stop by the way." Neither the phenomenon nor the theory is that of the verses cited from *Troilus & Cressida.*

Pliny's *Natural History* illustrates the next parallel adduced by Dr. Webb between Bacon and Shakespeare. "Letting of plants' blood," according to Bacon, "doth meliorate fruit," but the blood-letting is only to be effected "at some seasons of the year." And the gardener in *Richard II.* "takes the hint," and says :

> "We at time of year
> Do wound the bark, the skin of our fruit-trees,
> Lest being over-proud with sap and blood,
> With too much riches it confound itself."

The parallel is remarkably close ; but the operation and its rules were familiar to the cultivators of trees in Shakespeare's day. Trees have "a certaine moisture in their barkes," we read in Holland's *Pliny*, "which we must understand to be their very blood." The use of the words "blood" and "bleeding" as applied to trees continued for two centuries after Shakespeare's time; perhaps it is not yet obsolete. Dekker in *The Wonder of a Kingdom* (Works iv. p. 230), like Shakespeare, imports the image into drama:

> "(I) would not have him cut so noble a spreading vine,
> To draw from it one drop of blood."

For every operation in husbandry, as may be learnt from Tusser, there is an appointed time, often determined by the waxing or waning of the moon; sometimes even an appointed hour. A fir or pine tree (*Pliny*, xvii. 24) must not have its bark "pilled" during those months "wherein the sunne passeth thorough the signes of Taurus or Gemini"; and, like Shakespeare, Pliny terms the bark the "skin" of the tree. If physicians would "bleed" a mulberry tree, they will do it, we learn from Pliny, at seven or eight o'clock of a morning. It is perhaps worth illustrating from a contemporary author Shakespeare's "being over-proud with sap and blood." "The fittest time of the moon for pruning," says Gervase Markham, "is, as for grafting, when the sap is ready to stir (not *proudly* stirring), and so to cover the wound" (*A New Orchard*, p. 36).

Bacon, as Dr. Webb notices, paid attention to the succession of flowers during the seasons of the year, and suggested that "there ought to be gardens for all the months of the year." And in *The Winter's Tale* the seasons of flowers become types of the seasons in the life of man. The idea of Shakespeare was not a novel one, and, as Hunter observes, had been embodied in heraldic blazonings. Sir John Ferne in the *Blazon of Gentry*, 1596, names the appropriate flowers to typify infancy, puerility, adolescence, lusty green youth, virility (the gillofer and red rose), grey hairs and decrepitude. The parallel between Ferne and Shakespeare is in its idea much closer than that between Shakespeare and Bacon.

In the *Natural History* (of Bacon) we are told that " shade to some plants conduceth to make them large and prosperous more than sun "; and that, accordingly, if you sow borage among strawberries " you shall find the strawberries under those leaves far more large than their fellows." And even so the Bishop of Ely (in *King Henry V.*) explains the large and luxuriate development of the Prince's nature on his emerging from the shade of low company by saying :

> " The strawberry grows underneath the nettle."

True ; but the Bishop of Ely might have known a fact familiar to our old gardeners, and not forgotten in the *Gardener's Labyrinth* of 1608 (part ii. p. 76) : " The strawberries require small labour . . . saving that these are to be set in some shadowie place of the garden, in that these rather desire to grow under the shadow of other hearbes than to be planted in beddes alone." [1]

Bacon remarks that " wheresoever one plant draweth a particular juice out of the earth, that juice which remaineth is good for the other plant," so that " there the neighbourhood doth good." . . . " And the Bishop of Ely (in *King Henry V.*) catches at the idea . . .

> " ' And wholesome berries thrive and ripen best
> Neighbour'd by fruit of baser quality.' "

The idea of Bacon was also " caught at " in prophetic anticipation by Montaigne (as long since noted by Mr. Forbes). In Florio's translation the passage runs thus : " If it hapned (as some gardeners say) that these Roses and Violets are ever the sweeter

[1] *See* Ellacombe's *Plant-Lore*, p. 284, for other illustrations.

and more odoriferous, that grow neere under Garlike and Onions for so much as they suck and draw all the ill savours of the ground unto them," etc. The same practice of placing side by side plants which suck different juices from the earth is spoken of by Lyly in his *Euphues:* "Gardeners who in their curious knots mixe Hysoppe with Time as ayders the one to the growth of the other, the one being dry, the other moist."[1]

"Bacon remarks that 'generally night showers are better than day showers for that the sun followeth not so fast upon them'; and the Bishop of Ely (in *King Henry V.*) refers to the fact ('Grew like the summer grass, fastest by night') as excusing the unworthy night adventures of the Prince."

The fact, if it be one, was known as long ago as the days of Pliny, from whom, indeed, Bacon almost quotes (*Natural History*, book xvii. chap. ii.): "For lands," writes Pliny, "new sowne, and any young plants, injoy more benefit by such shoures in the night, for that the Sun commeth not so presently upon them againe to dry and drink up all the moisture."

In the *Natural History* Bacon suggests that "if you can get a scion to grow upon the stock of another kind," it "may make the fruit greater, though it is like it will make the fruit baser." And even so Polixenes, in arguing with Perdita, continues:

> "You see, sweet maid, we marry
> A gentler scion to the wildest stock,
> And make conceive a bark of baser kind
> By bud of nobler race."

"Scions" and "stocks," of course, crowd into Pliny's pages on "graffing." "All trees that are tame and gentle," he writes, "may well be graffed into

[1] *See* for other illustrations, Beisly, *Shakespeare's Garden*, pp. 105-107.

stocks and roots of the wild . . . contrariwise graffe the wild and savage kind upon the other, you shall have all degenerate and become wild." Neither Shakespeare nor Pliny suggests that the fruit will be "baser." Dr. Webb finds in Bacon a forerunner of Darwin in the doctrine of *The Transmutation of Species ;* and Shakespeare also anticipates Darwin in *The Winter's Tale.* Perdita will have none of the "streaked gillyvors," for

> "There is an art which in their piedness shares
> With great creating nature."

But Perdita is only referring to one of the best known processes of gardening. William Harrison in his *Description of England* (book ii. chap. xx.) wrote long before Shakespeare imagined Perdita : "How art also helpeth nature, in the dailie colouring, dubling and enlarging the proportion of our floures, it is incredible to report ; for so curious and cunning are our gardeners, now in these daies, that they presume to doo in maner what they list with nature, and moderate hir course in things as if they were hir superiors." It would be gratifying to our national pride to suppose that the noble thought of Polixenes —"The art itself is nature"—was the special possession of Bacon and Shakespeare. But that thought was prominent in the teaching of Paracelsus, whom Bacon refuses to honour. Even the art of magic, according to him, is "an art that Nature makes."

And should Baconians ask for a pre-Shakespearean parallel of the closest kind in which the thought that Art is involved in Nature, and itself a part of Nature, is clearly expressed, I can gratify them with a quotation from a volume published at Bale in 1572 : "Auriferæ Artis, quam Chemiam vocaut, Antiquissimi Authores, sive Turba Philosophorum" (p. 26).

" Scitote viri Sapientes, quod ex homine non nascitur nisi homo, nec ex brutis nisi suum simile ; atque ob id dico, *naturam non emendari nisi sua natura*, quemadmodum homo non nisi ab homine emendatur. Ac proinde venerabili *utimini natura, ex ea namque et ars existit et opus ejus fit.* Conjungite ergo masculinum servi rubei filium suæ odoriferæ uxori, et juncti artem gignent, quibus nolite introducere alienum, nec pulverem nec aliam rem, et sufficiat vobis conceptio et verus filius nascetur."

In an " Experiment solitary touching the growth of coral," Bacon describes it as " a submarine plant," and he describes the changes which it undergoes when " brought into the air." Even this lead is transmuted (by Shakespeare) into gold, when . . . Ariel sings

> " Full fathom five thy father lies :
> Of his bones are coral made," etc.

The changes which Bacon describes as taking place in coral when brought into the air are that it " becometh hard and shining red." The connection of Bacon's words with Shakespeare is not obvious ; but such words were in fact accessible to Shakespeare in Holland's *Pliny* several years before *The Tempest* was written. Coral " resembles a bush or shrub in foorme and of itselfe within the water is of colour greene. The berries thereof under the water be white and soft ; no sooner be they taken forth but presently they wax hard and turne red."

" In the *Historia Ventorum* Bacon makes the remark that sometimes the sea swells without wind or tide, and that this generally precedes a tempest. . . . In *Richard III.* this remarkable phenomenon supplies a moralising London citizen with a metaphor for his moral :

> "By a divine instinct men's minds mistrust
> Ensuing danger, as, by proof, we see
> The water swell before a boisterous storm."

Dr. Webb might with advantage have quoted the note of Tollet, given in the Variorum edition of 1821. This is from *Holinshed's Chronicle*, vol. iii. p. 721: "Before such great things men's hearts of a secret instinct of nature misgive them; as the sea without wind swelleth of himself some time before a tempest."

In the second scene of *Macbeth* we read:

> "And whence the Sun 'gins his reflection
> Shipwrecking storms and direful thunders break."

Mr. Lee thinks that this scene may have been "an interpolation by a hack of the theatre." But Dr. Webb declares, "If this be so, the hack of the theatre was Bacon. In his *History of the Winds* he lays it down as an undoubted fact that the sun by the action of its heat is the primary cause of almost all the winds." In a note he adds that Bacon's theory, "if it does not anticipate, contains the germ of the best conclusions of modern science." A passage is quoted also from *Troilus & Cressida* in which the "dreadful spout" called by shipmen the "hurricano" is described as

> "Constringed in mass by the Almighty Sun."

Shakespeare, or Mr. Lee's theatre hack, is not anticipating Sir Robert Ball (from whom Dr. Webb quotes), but is repeating what Pliny and other writers had made a popular belief. In chapter xii. of Pliny's second book we read that "the Sun maketh tempests." Seneca (Lodge's translation 1614, p. 848), in his *Naturall Questions*, explains the phenomenon; "Whence strong windes are caused" is Lodge's marginal note; the sun "reflecting upon the cold ayre" produces these winds according to Seneca; "the Sun is the efficient cause of the winds" (p. 849). The same doctrine is also mentioned in Plutarch's *Morals* ("Opinions of Philosophers," book iii. chap. vii.), the translation of which by Amyot was famous long before Holland gave his translation (1603) to English readers. It was the accepted theory of Shakespeare's day, as set forth in *Batman upon Bartholome*.

> "In the *Atriola Mortis*, Bacon enumerates as signs of coming death: the *motus manuum floccos colligendo*, the *memoria confusa*, the *nasus acutus*, the *frigus extremitatum*, and the *clamor* of the dying man. In *Henry V*. the Quondam Quickly, of all people in the world, translates Bacon's Latin into English, and describes Falstaff as 'fumbling with the sheets,' as 'playing with the flowers' of the quilt, as 'babbling of green fields,' as 'lying with his nose as sharp as a pen' and his 'feet as cold as a stone,' and as 'crying out God, God, God! three or four times before he died.'"

Shakespeare did not need to wait for Bacon's Latin or Holland's English to know the signs of death as they would be described by mine hostess, with a luxury of detail. But it is worth noting that Holland in his *Pliny*, besides observing that "a man may see death in the eyes and nose most certainly," uses Shakespeare's very words, "to keep a-fumbling and pleiting of the bed-clothes." Other signs, he says, are set down by "Hypocrates, the prince and chief of all physicians," which he will not enumerate.

"In the *Natural History* Bacon tells us," writes Dr. Webb, that "hair and nails are excrements," and the Queen in *Hamlet* adopts the extraordinary phrase, and cries out to the Prince:

> "Your bedded hair, like life in excrements
> Starts up and stands on end."

But the "extraordinary phrase" is an ordinary one. In *Soliman & Perseda* we read:

> "Whose chin bears no impression of manhood,
> Not a hair, not an excrement."

And Bishop Hopkins piously writes: "The very hairs of your head are all numbered; God keeps an account even of that stringy excrement."

"Bacon," we read again, "in his *Henry VII.* speaks of a sea of multitude." He has a "sea of matter" and a "sea of baser metals." In *Hamlet* we find "a sea of troubles"; there surely is no necessity, Dr. Webb thinks, "of going far for an explanation of the phrase."

More especially, it may be added, as we find Shakespeare's exact expression, "sea of troubles," in Dekker (Works iv. p. 230), and at a little distance (p. 232) a metaphorical "sea of silver."

Little remains in the chapter of "Shakespeare as a man of Science" which has not been dealt with. From the remaining minor matters I omit but little. Bacon refers to the disease named "the mother," and King Lear mentions the same disease. Yes, for it is mentioned several times (in connection with witchcraft) in the book from which Shakespeare took the names of his evil spirits in *Lear*, and the supposed connection of recent cases of this malady with witchcraft, suggested to the physician Jordan his scientific study, *A Brief Discourse of . . . the Mother*, published in the year in which Shakespeare probably wrote his play. Bacon and Shakespeare speak of the virtues of Carduus Benedictus. The virtues of Carduus Benedictus were celebrated in medical books and herbals of the sixteenth century, and a jest upon the name of Benedick, lover of Beatrice, coupled with a reference to the efficacy of the blessed thistle in diseases of the *heart* (as noticed in *The Gardener's Labyrinth*) suited the lips of the waiting-woman. Bacon mentions mandrake and opium as "soporiferous medicines"; Iago names poppy and mandragora with the drowsy syrops of the world. And Donne, I may add, before Bacon and before *Othello*, in connection with sleeplessness has the line (*Progress of the Soul*, stanza xvii.): "Poppy she knew, she knew the mandrake's might."

It would be waste of time to produce examples from Elizabethan literature of coloquintida, basilisks, salamanders, chameleons, glow-worms, the jewel in the toad's head, and the like which crowd into the pages of Lyly and other popular writers. But I may notice that in trying to produce a Baconian parallel Dr. Webb seems to misunderstand the rather ugly meaning of the word "mooncalf"; it has nothing to do with the "fine young cattle" of Bacon "brought forth in the full of the moon"; and I might beg him to be more exact when he states, in reference to that grave, scientific question of Lear's fool, "Canst tell how an oyster makes his shell?" that Bacon asks, "How the shells of oysters are bred?" Bacon asserts that oysters have no "discriminate sex," asks how they are bred, and adds, "It seemeth that shells of oysters are bred where none were before." But I shall not stand upon points, being willing to make to the Baconians a surrender of the oyster-shell—as generous highwaymen gave back a coin—if they should value it.

That music should be described as "food" is not peculiar to Bacon and Shakespeare. In that delightful volume, Hoby's translation of *The Courtier*, book i., we read: "They (women) have alwaies been inclined to musitions, and counted this (music) a most acceptable foode of the minde." The "dying fall" of the Duke Orsino, to whom music was "the food of love" is, perhaps, misunderstood by Dr. Webb when he tries to identify it with Bacon's "falling from a discord to a concord." The word "fall" in a musical sense is not infrequent in our elder literature. It means a cadence, and in the case of the music played for the Duke, the cadence is given *diminuendo*.

A somewhat striking parallel is pointed out between the Duke's words :

> "O, it came o'er my ear like the sweet sound
> That breathes upon a bank of violets,
> Stealing and giving odour,"

and Bacon's comparison in *The Natural History* of harmony to perfumes and the "smell of flowers in the air." "The breath of flowers," he writes in the *Essays*, "is far sweeter in the air, where it comes and goes like the warbling of music." Dr. Webb makes the parallel yet more striking by adopting Pope's conjecture sweet *South*, a reading which, we are assured by Dr. Furness, no future editor is likely to revive. But the juxtaposition of music and odours is not peculiar, even in Elizabethan literature, to Bacon and Shakespeare. One of Marston's personages "smells a sound" ; one of Jonson's praises the "odoriferous music" ; Donne tells us of a "loud perfume," which "cries" ;

> "Let it like an odour rise
> To all the senses here,
> And fall like sleep upon their eyes,
> Or music in their ear,"

writes Jonson in *The Vision of Delight* (1617) ; the dream which rises as an odour descends as music ; and every one will remember the later words of

Milton in *Comus*, which may possibly be a reminiscence from *Twelfth Night:*

> "At last a soft and solemn-breathing sound
> Rose like a steam of rich distill'd perfumes."

Shakespeare's comparison, however, if we accept the only authoritative text, is of a sound to a sound; the music of instruments to the murmur of a breeze in a garden. Parallels for the passage from Sidney's *Arcadia* have been adduced; critics have not perhaps noticed that in Morley's treatise on music, of 1597, the music-master in the opening of part ii. is in a garden, enjoying the air, "which gently breathing upon these sweet-smelling flowers, and making a whispering noyse amongst these tender leaves, delighteth with refreshing." It is to the whispering of such a breeze that the enamoured Duke compares the strain of his musician. The objections of Dr. Webb to the Folio Text are considered and met by Furness.

I believe that I have now touched on everything worthy of consideration in Dr. Webb's chapter on "Shakespeare as a Man of Science." The whole argument, urged with so much animation and ability by the distinguished translator of *Faust*, seems to me —if Baconians will pardon the expression—an argument *ad ignorantiam.*[1]

[1] Professor Beare—whose authority is high—maintains that the "error" with respect to Aristotle, spoken of on p. 285, is in truth an unerroneous statement of the fact.

ELIZABETHAN PSYCHOLOGY

A CRUDE and popular psychology of the Middle Ages, itself derived in part from elder sources, from Aristotle and Plato, from Hippocrates and Galen, descended to the time of Shakespeare and Bacon, and much that is found in the literature of the Elizabethan period becomes intelligible only through a reference to the philosophy of an earlier period; much also becomes, through such a reference, illuminated with a fuller or more exact meaning.

The elder psychology is set forth in a summary by Bartholomew de Glanville, or, as it is safer to call him, Bartholomew Anglicus, who was living and writing, it is believed, in the century which immediately preceded that of Chaucer. His book, *De Proprietatibus Rerum*, was translated into English by Trevisa, and in the later form, known as *Batman upon Bartholome* (1582), it became a popular natural history for readers of the days of Shakespeare. But as, in our own time, if we open such a volume as Professor William James's *Text Book of Psychology* we shall find a considerable portion of it occupied with physiological inquiry and exposition, so in the Middle Ages it was felt that the study of the mind could not be separated from the study of the body, nor again could this be separated from a study of the four elements, out of which the whole of our globe, with all that lives and moves upon it, was formed by the Creator.

Nor was this all. The study of mind, thus involving the study of earth and its constituents, must needs be extended to a research into the influences of the heavens, of the astrological influences which affect the body and the soul of man, the powers of the stars that govern our conditions, and the play of each sign of the Zodiac upon the part of our frame specially related to it—Aries, for instance, governing the head, Leo the heart, and Pisces the feet. With the macrocosm of the universe the microcosm of man had a correspondence. Thus the science of man became an inseparable portion of a vaster science, which included a knowledge of terrestrial and celestial phenomena. And, finally, over and above all these stood the science of sciences—theology—for man was not only a microcosm corresponding to the macrocosm; he proceeded, in his noblest part, immediately from God, and was made in His image.

If we should now ask an intelligent Sunday School child, "Of how many parts did God make man?" the answer would probably be, "Of two, body and soul." But the child might have been instructed in the tripartite division, and answer, "Of three, body, soul and spirit." Such certainly might have been the answer of a well-taught Elizabethan boy or girl, though instead of "spirit" the answerer might have used the plural "spirits," and he would have understood by "spirit" or "spirits" something that is perhaps different from the vague significance attached to the word "spirit" as distinguished from "soul" by the child of the present day. If we were to proceed with our questioning and ask, "Which of these parts is immortal?" a prompt reply would come from the Elizabethan child:

"The soul."

"And why it alone?"

"Because the body and the spirits are material and are therefore perishable."

As to the origin of the immortal substance which

we name "the soul," there was less certainty. It might, like the body, have been propagated by parents, by the parent's soul if not his body; to use the technical term, it might have had its origin by "traduction." "If," writes Dryden, in the poem *To Mrs. Anne Killegrew*:

> "If by traduction came thy mind,
> Our wonder is the less to find
> A soul so charming from a stock so good;
> Thy father was transfus'd into thy blood."

But the more orthodox answer would have been, "By divine infusion." Sir John Davies, in his poem "On the Immortality of the Soul," considers an objection to the theory of infusion, namely, that if the soul came thus direct from God it could not partake of the sin of Adam. Of course he has his answers drawn from nature, and those drawn from divinity, and gives no uncertain sound in favour of the transfusion theory.

While each human soul is thus of immediately divine origin, some of its powers during our mortal life are dependent on its companion the body; certain of these powers are common to men and beasts; other functions are proper to the soul itself—apart from the body—and distinguish us as human beings from the inferior creatures. With the aid of the body the soul has the power of feeling; it has the power of knowing sensible things when they are present, and this was sometimes named "wit"; and, again, when sensible things are absent, the soul can behold the likeness of them by its faculty of imagination. Feeling, wit and imagination are not peculiar to humanity; they are possessed by brutes. But to man alone belongs "Ratio," reason, by which we discern good and evil, truth and falsehood; and secondly—if a distinction should be made—Intellectus, understanding, by which we apprehend things immaterial, but yet intelligible. Reason may have for its object things that are of this lower earth and of our common daily life; but it has a perception in such things of qualities which are not recognised by creatures inferior to man. Intellect deals with things which are wholly beyond the apprehension of the lower animals, things spiritual and invisible.

Bacon in the *De Augmentis* follows the older psychology in distinguishing between Reason and Intellect, but he does not make his own distinction clear. It may be that he uses the word Intellect as the name of a faculty to which Reason, Imagination and Memory make their reports, and which compares and pronounces upon those reports; at times he uses the word as a generic name including the three faculties which constitute the basis for his great division of human knowledge. He adopted from the Italian philosopher Telesio the doctrine that in man there are two souls—one rational and divine, the other irrational and common to us and the brutes; one inspired by the breath of God, the other springing from the womb of the elements; one an emanation of Deity, the other sensible and produced; one wholly immaterial, the other corporeal but so attenuated by heat as to be invisible; one immortal, the other subject to death. The lower, material soul is a breath compounded of air and fire, receiving impressions readily by virtue of its aerial quality, and propagating its energy by its fiery vigour—"clothed with the body, and in perfect animals residing chiefly in the head, running along the nerves, and refreshed and repaired by the spirituous blood in the arteries." The study of the nature, faculties and operations of the higher soul Bacon would leave in the main to religion; the doctrine concerning the lower, corporeal soul, he held, was a fit subject—even as regards the substance of that soul—for philosophy.

To return from Bacon to the more generally accepted doctrine of the tripartite division into body, soul and spirit, the operation, life or activity of the soul in man was held to be threefold—vegetable, sensible and rational. These three modes of activity are, indeed, often spoken of as if they were three separate kinds of soul; but it seems more correct to speak of them in man as three forms of one life or energy. The vegetable soul is found apart from the other two in plants; they live and increase in size, and multiply themselves by virtue of this soul. The vegetable and sensible souls are found co-operating in animals; they not only live and grow and multiply, they also feel. In man alone are the three souls—vegetable, sensible and rational—found working together.

When, in Jonson's *Poetaster* (Act v, scene 3), Tucca scorns to turn shark upon his friends, and scorns it with his "three souls," he is a sound psychologist. The theory appears and reappears in Elizabethan prose and poetry. Davies in his *Nosce Teipsum* deals, in successive sections, with the vegetative, the sensible, and the intellectual powers of the soul. Donne, of course, could not abstain from versifying the theory, as for example where, in his letter to the Countess of Bedford, he tries to explain the harmonious relation of zeal and discretion and religion, which must co-operate even as

> "Our souls of growth, and souls of sense
> Have birthright of our reason's soul, yet hence
> They fly not from that, nor seek precedence."

And in one of his sermons three relations of man to temporal wealth and worldly goods—the possession and increase in riches, the sense of that advantage and its true uses for life, and last, the discerning the mercy and the purpose of God in the blessing of wealth—are compared to the three souls.

"First," he begins, "in a natural man we conceive there is a soul of vegetation and of growth; and secondly, a soul of motion and of sense; and then thirdly, a soul of reason and understanding, an immortal soul. And the two first souls, of vegetation and of sense, we conceive to arise out of the temperament and good disposition of the substance of which that man is made; they arise out of man himself; but the last soul, the perfect and immortal soul, that is immediately infused by God." In like manner we may, without God's immediate intervention, both possess riches and use riches discreetly; "but the immortal soul, that is, the discerning God's image on every piece, and the seal of God's love in every temporal blessing, this is infused by God alone, and arises neither from parents, nor the wisdom of this world, how worldly wise soever we be, in the governing of our estates."

Before proceeding to say something of the sensible and something of the rational soul, it will be worth while to call attention to a passage of Shakespeare and a passage of Spenser, each of which has perplexed and even baffled the commentators, yet which in truth present no difficulty to one acquainted with the popular psychology of the time, and the fanciful ingenuities based upon that psychology. In the first scene of *King Lear*, Regan, making declaration of her love for her father, says:

"I profess
Myself an enemy to all other joys
Which the most precious square of sense possesses,
And find I am alone felicitate
In your dear highness' love."

How shall we explain " the most precious square of sense " ? Emendations have been proposed and have been adopted by editors ; " spacious sphere of sense " is the reading of Singer ; Mr. Craig interprets the text as meaning " Sense absolute, sense in its perfection."

Let us for a moment leave it unexplained, and pass on to a passage of Spenser's *Faerie Queene*. In the ninth canto of the second book the House of Temperance in which Alma dwells is described. Alma is the soul ; her house or castle is the body. The twenty-second stanza presents the singular architecture of this castle :

> " The frame thereof seemed partly circulare,
> And part triangulare ; O worke divine !
> Those two the first and last proportions are ;
> The one imperfect, mortall, feminine ;
> Th' other immortall, perfect, masculine ;
> And twixt them both a quadrate was the base,
> Proportioned equally by seven and nine ;
> Nine was the circle sett in heaven's place ;
> All which compacted made a goodly diapase." [1]

We may for a moment leave on one side the allusions of an arithmetical kind, seven and nine, for these have perhaps been sufficiently explained by the commentators. But what of the architecture triangular, quadrate and circular ? In 1644 Sir Kenelm Digby published a pamphlet of *Observations* on this stanza, which he had written at the request of a friend. It was reprinted by Todd in his edition of Spenser, at the end of the canto in which the stanza occurs. Were nothing extant of Spenser's writing but this stanza, the enthusiastic Sir Kenelm assures us, " these few words would make me esteem him no

[1] So Dryden (" A Song for St. Cecilia's Day ")—" The diapason closing full in man."

whit inferior to the most famous men that ever have been in any age."

In truth it needs no long commentary to explain the architecture of the Castle of Alma; it needs no more than reference to a passage of Bartholomew Angelicus, a passage which at the same time gives, we can hardly doubt, the true explanation of Shakespeare's "precious square of sense." Following elder authority, Bartholomew declares that the vegetable soul, with its three virtues of self-sustainment, growth and reproduction, is "like to a triangle in Geometrie." The sensible soul is "like to a quadrangle, square and four cornerde. For in a quadrangle is a lyne drawen from one corner to another corner, afore it maketh two tryangles; and the soul sensible maketh two tryangles of vertues. For wherever the soule sensible is, there is also the soule vegetabilis." Finally, the rational soul is likened to a circle, because a circle is the most perfect of figures, having a greater power of containing than any other. The triangle of the Castle of Alma is the vegetative soul; the quadrate—identical with Shakespeare's "square of sense"—is the sensible soul, the circle is the rational soul.

As to Spenser's numbers, seven and nine, possibly the explanation given in the Clarendon Press edition of *The Faerie Queene*, Book II., may be right; the seven is there taken to refer to the seven planets, "whose influences on man's life and nature are mysteriously great"; the nine, says the editor, "is obviously the ninth orb of the heavenly sphere, enfolding all things." But Spenser is speaking of the Castle of Alma, not of the planets or the spheres. The triangle of the vegetative soul and the quadrate of the sensible soul give us the number seven, which sums up the corporeal part of man; but the rational soul is also necessary for man's life, and this, with its two faculties of understanding and will, raises the total number from seven to nine.[1]

The functions of the vegetative soul are, as we have seen, self-maintenance, growth and reproduction. The processes by which these functions are accomplished are four—appetite or " attraction " as Burton calls it, digestion, the retention of what is needed for nutrition, and the expulsion of what is useless or superfluous. Such is Bartholomew's enumeration, and what is substantially identical appears in the verse of Sir John Davies :

> " Here she attracts, and there she doth retain ;
> There she decocts and doth the food prepare ;
> There she distributes it to every vein ;
> There she expels what she may fitly spare."

And in Alma's Castle we are led into a hall where the marshal is Appetite, and to the kitchen where the clerk is named Digestion, whose retainers bear away the prepared food where it is needed, while all that is " nought and noyous " is carried off by its proper conduit to the Port Esquiline.

From the vegetable we pass to the sensible soul. Its seat is the brain ; on its operation depend sensation on the one hand, and motion on the other. When Hamlet pleads with his mother in the closet scene, he cries :

> " Sense sure you have,
> Else could you not have motion ; but, sure, that sense
> Is apoplex'd."

Commentators (and among them the writer of this paper) have interpreted " motion " in this passage as " impulse of desire," a sense which the word cer-

[1] The powers are (1) life, in the sense of self-maintenance, (2) growth, (3) reproduction, (4) the common sense, (5) imagination, (6) reason, (7) memory, (8) understanding, (9) will.

tainly bears elsewhere in Shakespeare. Warburton, with his characteristic dogmatism in ignorance, would read " notion," and Capel explains " sense " as meaning precisely what it does not—" reason." A little knowledge of the mediæval theory would have saved much needless conjecture. Hamlet argues that bodily motion or, it may be, desire—which is another form of motion—implies the activity of the sensible soul, and therefore sense (that is, sensation) cannot be wholly destroyed. But it may be " apoplexed," and here again he uses his words with strict accuracy. " Apoplexia," notes Trevisa in his translation of Bartholomew, " is an evil that maketh a man lose all manner of feeling."

Before going further it is necessary to explain the nature and the function of " the spirits." The whole of animate and inanimate nature is pervaded by a highly attenuated and lively form of matter to which this name was applied. Bacon also uses the word " pneumaticals " in this sense, but he did no more than accept a common theory, and add some conjectures of his own. On the spirits chiefly depend all the active operations within material substances, and the operation of body upon body. They are, says Bacon, " unquiet to get forth and congregate with the air, and to enjoy the sunbeams," and hence arise the phenomena of putrefaction. According to La Chambre the constituents of matter are of three kinds—the gross, the subtle (that is, the spirit) and, connecting these two, the humid. Through the sap plants are nourished by the spirits in the earth. Through food every animal adds to its supply of spirits. They are found in each part of the human body, but the special centre for their development is the liver. The veins, which originate in the liver, are the channels that convey blood through the body, and with this blood is conveyed the spirits, derived from a smoke that rises from the liver. These are, however, only the "natural" spirits, as yet partaking of a certain material grossness. They pass to the heart, and are played upon by the refining influence of the air inhaled by the lungs. Here the natural are transformed into the "vital" spirits. From the heart spring the arteries which transmit, not blood in the strict sense of the word, but a fine aerial substance, or a spirituous blood differing greatly from that which flows in the veins. Of this the vital spirits form a chief—or as some maintained, the sole—element.

"An artery," writes Phineas Fletcher in a note to *The Purple Island* (Canto II.), "is a vessel long, round, hollow, formed for conveyance of that more spritely blood, which is elaborate in the heart. This blood is frothy, yellowish, full of spirits."

The motion of these spirits is the cause of the pulse. From the heart the vital spirits pass to the brain, and being once more attenuated and refined, become the "animal" spirits.[1] Now the chief functions of the animal spirits are two—first, spreading through the nerves which originate in the brain, they convey sensations to the sensible soul and are its agent in producing motion; secondly, they act as the intermediary between man's spiritual and immortal part, the rational soul, and its poor mortal companion, the body. And here it is well to remember that the words "nerve" and "sinew" have in part exchanged their meanings since Elizabethan and earlier times, or rather the application of each word has been narrowed to a single and definite use.

[1] The affable archangel, explaining to Adam (*Paradise Lost*, bk. v. 482-485) the processes of nutrition, uses the words "vital," "animal," and "intellectual" spirits, in place of natural, vital, and animal.

Davies uses the word " sinew " for " nerve," but he also uses the word " nerve " in the sense familiar to us. " Nerves or sinews," writes Burton, " are membranes without and full of marrow within ; they proceed from the brain, and carry the animal spirits for sense and motion." Here " sinew " means what we now call a " nerve." On the other hand, when Prospero declares to Ferdinand that his " nerves " are in their infancy again, and have no vigour in them, the word " nerves " means what we understand by sinews or tendons. Hence, from its double meaning, while a " nervous person " for us means one who is subject to the weakness of nervous excitement or agitation, a " nervous arm " in our elder poetry means what we should call a strong and sinewy arm, and the meaning is not even yet obsolete.

In the function of sense or apprehension which is proper to the sensible soul, two groups of faculties—one outward, the other inward—co-operate. The " outer wit," as it is named in Trevisa's Bartholomew, consists of the five senses. Along the nerves to each sense hasten the animal spirits, which are now named, with reference to their special employment, the spirits of feeling, or " spirits of sense." Thus Davies writes of

> " those nerves, that spirits of sense do bear,
> And to those outward organs spreading go."

Troilus, in Shakespeare's play, thinking of the soft seizure of Cressida's hand, declares that compared with it

> " The cygnet's down is harsh, and spirit of sense
> Hard as the palm of ploughman " ;

that is to say, the subtlest and most tenuous of bodies —the spirit, passing from the brain along the nerves of sensation—seems as hard as the gross and indurated skin of the ploughman's hand. In another passage of the same play the eye itself is named the spirit of sense, but here the meaning is no more than that the eye, as Bartholomew has it, is the subtlest of the outer wits.

The senses make their reports concerning the external objects which have impressed them to the brain. Perhaps those reports do not agree with one another; a marble, which the eye recognises as only one, may be felt by the fingers, if crossed, as two. There is need of some judge to compare and decide between the reports of the several senses. This judge is the inner wit, or inner sense, which Trevisa, translating Bartholomew, names also the common sense. As Bartholomew uses this term "common sense" it has a generic meaning, including under it the inner senses of imagination, reasoning and memory. But different writers employ the term in different ways. With Davies it means the imagination; with Burton it is the kind of reason or judgment which is concerned only with things sensible, as distinguished from the higher faculties of "understanding"; he describes it as the moderator of the other senses—"all their objects are his, and all their offices are his." In the allegorical poem of Phineas Fletcher the meaning is identical with that of Burton. His Common Sense is a Counsellor of middle years and seemly personage—"Father of laws, the rule of right and wrong," who tries the causes submitted to him by the five outward senses. However the term "common sense" may be applied, it was generally agreed that the inner senses of the sensible soul are three—reason, imagination or phantasy and memory. The brain consists of three cells, or ventricles, or wombs—each of these names was in common use—

and in each of these one of the three faculties had its residence; each can, however, pass on ideas to its neighbour faculty. Spenser, agreeing in this with Bartholomew and with Phineas Fletcher, places his Phantastes in the foremost cell, that is in the cell of the brain which is nearest to the forehead. He is a young man, swarthy, of crabbed hue,

> "That him full of melàncholy did shew."

His chamber is "dispainted with sundry colours" in which were writ "infinite shapes of things dispersed thin." But Burton placed phantasy in the middle cell of the brain. The hindmost cell is assigned with little difference of opinion to memory. Certain writers add a fourth cell devoted to the special work of elaborating the animal spirits.

Bacon's division of human studies into history, poesy and philosophy is founded upon the three faculties of the "rational soul," as he calls it, but he would have been more accurate if he had said "the sensible soul." History is connected with memory, poesy with imagination, philosophy with the reason. In a poem by Fulke Greville, Lord Brooke, *A Treatise of Human Learning*, the date of the composition of which it is not easy to ascertain, an account almost identical is given of the centres of human knowledge. Nothing could be more natural —reason and imagination and memory were recognised as the inner wits of the sensible soul, each in possession of a special ventricle of the brain. Of the ventricle appropriated to memory Shakespeare speaks in *Love's Labour's Lost*—ideas "begot in the ventricle of memory"—and in a speech of Lady Macbeth he refers to the second ventricle of reason. She promises that she will so subdue with wine and wassail the two chamberlains of Duncan:

> "That memory, the warder of the brain,
> Shall be a fume, and the receipt of reason
> A limbec only."

The idea that fumes arose from meat and drink, stupefying the brain, is of frequent recurrence; memory, occupying the part of the brain connected with the spinal marrow, is "the warder or sentinel to warn the reason against attack." Such is the explanation of Dr. W. Aldis Wright; but perhaps the following passage from Purchas's *Microcosmus* suggests the true meaning: "The Memorie is a sure *Prison* for such as Reason hath committed to ward . . . or hath not yet leisure to hear." It may be noticed in passing that where Shakespeare in the same speech of *Love's Labour's Lost* mentions the *pia mater*, a membrane which covers the brain—"nourished in the womb of pia mater" are the words—he does not give the term its proper meaning; it signifies with him the brain itself or some portion of the brain, and in each of the other two passages where *pia mater* occurs it is used by Shakespeare with the same inaccuracy.

Those fumes or vapours of which Lady Macbeth speaks are the cause of sleep. Such vapours, as Burton explains, arising out of the stomach, fill the nerves by which the spirits are conveyed. The common sense cannot communicate through the nerves with the external senses, and therefore the external senses cease to operate. The fantasy or imagination, however, remains free, and hence come dreams. "My spirits," exclaims Ferdinand to Prospero, "as in a dream are all bound up"; and in the same play, Antonio, taking up Sebastian's word that he is "indisposed to sleep," goes on, "my spirits are nimble," that is, the spirits can dart along the nerves without encountering the obstruction of vapours

From the sensible soul proceeds, as we have seen, not sensation only but also motion. If we move from place to place it is to obtain some object which we desire or to avoid some object which causes us displeasure. The efficient cause of motion is therefore either reason, or the subordinate of reason, as Burton names it, fantasy, which apprehends good or bad objects. The spirits, commissioned by reason or fantasy, contract or relax the nerves and muscles, which draw after them the joints, and thus we walk, we run, we leap, we dance, we sit.

But the word " motion " comprehends more than this. It includes the motions of the internal parts of the body, such as the passage of blood through the veins; and these are perhaps rather of a vegetable or vital origin than dependent upon the animal spirits. It includes the power of appetite, and appetite is either sensitive, which is common to man and brutes, or intellective, which is possessed by man alone, and which in a well-regulated nature controls and directs the sensitive appetite. Behind this intellective appetite—if it does not, as some hold, belong rather to our immortal part—lies the reason or the common sense; its proper functions are to seek good and to avoid evil in sensible things. In its function of seeking what is desirable, it is named the " concupiscible " appetite; in its function of repelling or evading evil it is named the " irascible " appetite. Hence arise all the affections and passions, or, as they are commonly named, " perturbations " of man. With Shakespeare the word " motion " is used in the two senses—motion with reference to change of place, and motion, an impulse of desire, as in the line of *Measure for Measure*—" the wanton stings and motions of the sense." In more than one passage he seems to make a distinction between "affection" and "passion," and perhaps a line in the *Merchant of Venice* points to what the distinction is:

> "for affection,
> Master of passion, sways it to the mood
> Of what it likes or loathes."

"Affection" here means a man's liking for or disinclination to some object, caused by an external impression on the senses, while "passion"—which results from the affection—signifies the inward perturbation. In Jonson's *Love's Welcome*, written when King Charles I. was entertained at Welbeck in 1633, the Passions—Doubt and Love—enter with the Affections—Joy, Delight and others. The distinction here is not very evident; but perhaps Love and Doubt are more inward—perturbations of the mind—and Joy and Delight more outward and of the senses.

The division of the Passions into two groups—the irascible and the concupiscible—determined the plan of the second Book of Spenser's *Faerie Queene*, that which tells the legend of Sir Guyon, Knight of Temperance. The theme of the Book is discipline in self-control; through the first six cantos the dangers and errors to which the soul of man is exposed through the irascible passions are exhibited in the allegory; in the last six the temptations are those offered by the concupiscible passions, chief among which are the lust for money, the lust for false glory and gross ambition, and the lust for sensual pleasure. The cave of Mammon, the throne of Queen Philotime, the Bower of Bliss, with Acrasia in all her deceiving loveliness, are successively exhibited.

There is, however, another classification of the passions—that founded on their origin and composition. Some are primary and simple; others are mixed or composite. Differences of opinion appear among various writers as to the number and names of the primary passions, but a commonly-accepted doctrine sets them down as four: Pleasure and Pain —the good or evil object being present; and Hope and Fear—the good or evil object being absent, but conceived by the imagination. From these four it was held that all the other passions were evolved by successive minglings and compositions, which grew more complex as the series proceeded in its developments. In that curious piece of dramatic literature, *Pathomachia*, by an unknown author, no fewer than fifteen Affections play their parts. Much speculation existed as to the seat of the passions in the human body. Have they one common centre, or does each passion reside in a special organ of its own? A general, but by no means a universally-accepted, answer was that they reside in the heart. Four female figures, Pleasure and Pain, Hope and Fear, are presented on the pretty title-page of Grimeston's translation of Coffeteau's *A Table of Humane Passions* (1621), while the title itself appears inclosed within a heart in outline. The mode in which the passions are awakened and excited is described with precision by Davies:

"From the kind heat, which in the heart doth reigne,
The spirits of life [the vital spirits] doe their beginning take;
These spirits of life ascending to the braine,
When they come there the spirits of sense do make.

These spirits of sense, in Fantasie's High Court,
Judge of the formes of objects, ill or well;
And as they send a good or ill report
Down to the heart, where all affections dwell,

If the report be good, it causeth love,
And longing hope, and well-assured joy;
If it be ill then doth it hatred move,
And trembling fear and vexing grief's annoy."

Thomas Wright, in his *Treatise on the Passions of the Mind in General*, agrees with Davies in regarding the heart as the dwelling-place of the passions, and so too Timothy Bright, in his *Treatise of Melancholy*. Nevertheless there was a special connection between certain passions and other organs, which aided in a special way the operations of each. Thus the liver was supposed to be in a peculiar degree connected with amorous passion; the gall secreted by the liver was at least an aider and abettor of the passion of anger; what Shakespeare calls "the passion of loud laughter" was connected with the spleen, or the midriff; and the spleen, if distempered—but indeed, of almost every organ this might be said—was the cause of melancholy. The references to these beliefs, and to others of a like kind, are numerous in Shakespeare. The Friar in *Much Ado About Nothing* advises that a report be circulated of Hero's death, and then shall Claudio mourn:

> "If ever love had interest in his liver."

When Hamlet reproaches himself for his deficiency of wrath against his father's murderer, he exclaims:

> "for it cannot be
> But I am pigeon-liver'd and lack gall
> To make oppression bitter."

"Pigeon-livered," for the mildness of doves and pigeons was the result of these creatures possessing no secretion of gall. Maria, in *Twelfth Night*, when she entreats Sir Toby to come and observe the ridiculous follies of Malvolio, cries, "If you desire the spleen, and will laugh yourself into stitches, follow me."

The amorous Duke of Illyria imagines Love enthroned in the whole nature of Olivia; the moment of this consummation will be one

"when liver, brain and heart,
These sovereign thrones, are all supplied, and fill'd
Her sweet perfections with one selfe King."

And in truth he has named the chief organs that govern the life of man and woman—"*those Triumviri*" as Purchas calls them in *Microcosmus*, "the liver, heart and Braine, as a sensible Trinity in this Unity, having under their leading and command three great bands of a Subtill, Swift, Aerie Generation"—the natural, vital and animal spirits—"all of them the bond to unite the Soule and Body, the Chariots of the Faculties, and prime instruments of all bodily actions."

In connection with all the operations of the corporeal part of man—the body, the vegetable and sensible souls, the spirits—and especially in connection with the play of the passions, it should be remembered that, setting aside the rational and immortal soul, men are creatures made of the four elements, and according to the different proportion which the qualities of these elements bear in our composition, we exhibit differences of complexion, and probably of conduct. "Does not our life consist of the four elements?" asks Sir Toby Belch. The elements are, of course, earth, air, fire and water. Their qualities are heat, coldness, dryness, moisture. Fire is hot and dry; air is hot and moist; water is cold and moist; earth is cold and dry. Now as each of the four qualities preponderates in our bodies, and especially in the blood, and as it is combined with other qualities, our temperament is determined. It may be a simple temperament—hot or cold, or moist or dry; it may, on the other hand, be a compound temperament—hot and moist, or hot and dry; cold and moist, or cold and dry. We can hardly hope that any of us should possess the perfect temperament, where each quality bears its due proportion, that temperament named "Eucrasy." It is this perfect Eucrasy which, at the close of *Julius Cæsar*, Mark Antony ascribes to the dead Brutus :

> "His life was gentle, and the elements
> So mix'd in him that Nature might stand up
> And say to all the world, 'This was a man!'"

Now the food which we eat, itself consisting of the four elements, and having their several qualities, is converted by the internal processes of the body into four humours, which have a certain correspondence with the elements, from which they are derived. These primary, nutritive humours are blood, phlegm, choler and melancholy. In what we popularly call "blood" each of these humours is found, and as it courses through the veins each humour supplies nutriment in a peculiar degree to that organ of the body which it is specially adapted to nourish. Thus phlegm, which is cold and moist, in a peculiar degree supplies the brain—itself a cold and moist substance—with the food it needs ; choler, which is hot and dry, feeds especially the lungs ; and so with the rest. A "cool" head, and a "warm" heart, describe only the healthy condition of these organs. As each of the humours preponderates in a man's veins, his complexion—which is often identified with the temperament—is determined ; he is of a sanguine complexion, or it is melancholy, or phlegmatic, or choleric. And, the bodily organs being the instruments of the sensible soul, the thoughts and passions of a man are obviously in a great degree influenced by his complexion.

The doctrine that man is made of the four elements is frequently referred to by Shakespeare. It forms the theme of two connected sonnets, the forty-fourth and forty-fifth, written in absence from the friend to whom his Sonnets are addressed. The dull elements of earth and water cannot leap across the distance which separates him from his friend—that is the theme of the forty-fourth sonnet; the other two elements, air and fire, are gone on embassy to his friend, leaving him mere earth and water:

> "My life, being made of four, with two alone
> Sinks down to death, oppress'd with melancholy,
> Until life's composition be recured
> By those swift messengers return'd from thee."

Thus the doctrine is applied to his purposes in the forty-fifth sonnet. "I am fire and air," cries Cleopatra, when about to apply the asp to her breast:

> "My other elements
> I give to baser life."

The Dauphin's horse in *Henry V.*—for all animals are made of the four elements—"is pure air and fire, and the dull elements of earth and water never appear in him, but only in patient stillness while his rider mounts him." The word "temperament" is never employed by Shakespeare; "temper" fills its place. The small page, Moth, in *Love's Labour's Lost*, loves a little fooling with his solemn and self-conceited master, Don Adriano. The Don would learn from Moth what was the complexion of Samson's love, Delilah. "Of all the four," answers the impertinent boy, "or the three, or the two, or one of the four?"—which is indeed about all that we can conjecture concerning Delilah's complexion, the question giving no less opening to conjecture than those of Sir Thomas Browne's *Urn-Burial*—what song the Sirens sang, and what name Achilles assumed when he hid himself among women. The word "humour" is gloriously abused by Pistol in *Henry IV*. and by Nym in the *Merry Wives*. Ben Jonson comments upon the careless use of the word for some fantastic oddity, and, through his Asper, in the opening of *Every Man out of his Humour*, he gives the correct definition. By a metaphorical transfer Jonson himself, as is explained by Asper, extends the significance of the word from physiology to psychology, and makes this idea a basis for his dramatic representation of character :

> "It may, by metaphor apply itself
> Unto the general disposition ;
> As when some one peculiar quality
> Doth so possess a man, that it doth draw
> All his affects, his spirits, and his powers
> In their confluctions all to run one way,
> This may be truly said to be a humour."

Allusions to the hot, the cold, the moist, the dry temperaments are, of course, of most frequent occurrence in Elizabethan literature. The elements, with their children, known as the complexions, and the five senses appear upon the stage, each appropriately habited, in the moral masque, *Microcosmus*, by Thomas Nabbes. The subject of the masque is not unlike that of the old moralities—the struggle for Physander, who represents (as his name signifies) the natural man, between the powers of good and evil. At the close Physander is accused in the court of Conscience of infidelity to his lawful spouse, Bellanima, the soul. Fire and Air, the active elements, are presented as men in the vigour of youth ; Water and Earth, the passive elements, as women. Choler is a fencer with rent garments ; Blood, a dancer ; Phlegm, an old physician, and Melancholy, a musician, swarthy of hue, attired in black, a lute in his hand. " He is likewise," adds the description of the *dramatis personæ*, " an amorist." Melancholy and love are both connected in a special degree with the liver, and hence with one another; it will be remembered how large a proportion of Burton's *Anatomy* is devoted to the melancholy of lovers.

It remains to say a few words of that part of man which is wholly immaterial—his immortal part, the rational soul. But they may well be few, for as Burton, quoting from Velcurio, puts it, this is " a pleasant but a doubtful subject, and with the like brevity to be discussed." The two chief faculties of the reasonable soul are first, wit or understanding, or intellect (for each of these terms is used), and secondly, will; an understanding occupied not only with particular and material things but capable of comprehending truths that are general, universal, and divine; a will, not merely set in motion by desires of the lower nature, but, when duly informed and illuminated by the understanding, capable of seeking the highest good, which is God Himself. From each of these faculties a habit of life may proceed—from the will, the active life; from the understanding, the life contemplative. Instead of understanding and will, we may, if we please, use the word " intellect " as comprehending both functions, with a distinction between " the intellect speculative " and " the intellect practical." Under these heads subordinate powers may be ranged; thus, the understanding includes a memory, which is not, like the memory of the sensible soul, a perishable thing, but which survives the great change of death, when the reasonable soul enters on its disembodied state.

In *Humour's Heaven on Earth*, by John Davies of Hereford, the ornaments of Psyche (the soul) are Wit, Will and Memory:

> "Her Understanding's power that Power did line,
> Which Heaven and Earth religiously adore;
> And in her will she wore grace most divine;
> But in her memory she Artes did store;
>
> . . . .
>
> Affects and Fantasies her servants were.
>
> . . . .
>
> The outward Senses her Purveyors were,
> To whom the Common Sense was Treasurer."

The Conscience, again, may be regarded as one of the powers of the higher understanding. The images of things sent up by the sensible to the reasonable soul are tested, judged, purified, and when found in accordance with truth are offered by the understanding to the will. But the will of the reasonable soul is something far different from appetite. "The object of appetite," writes Hooker in the first Book of *Ecclesiastical Polity*, "is whatsoever sensible good may be wished for; the object of will is that good which reason doth lead us to seek." The will, illuminated by the understanding, in its own right of freedom chooses good. It cannot directly control the appetites, which move instinctively and involuntarily when the objects of their desire are presented to them; but the will can refuse the gratifications demanded by the appetites. Over the irascible and concupiscible passions the power of the reasonable soul is, or rather may and ought to be, supreme. All these and kindred matters are discoursed of in much detail by Primeaudaye in the Second Tome of the *French Académie*. The doctrine of the reasonable soul was sung by Phineas Fletcher in the *Purple Island*, and by Sir John Davies in *Nosce Teipsum*. Thus Davies puts it:

> "Will is the Prince, and Wit the Counsellor,
> Which doth for common good in Counsell sit,
> And when Wit is resolved, Will lends her power
> To execute what is devised by Wit.

Wit is the mind's chief judge, which doth controule
Of Fancies Court the Judgments false and vaine,
Will holds the royal scepter in the soule,
And on the passions of the heart doth raigne."

Some writers, and among them Samuel Purchas, argue that all the operations of the sensible, and even those of the vegetative, soul are ultimately dependent on the reasonable soul; "Not the Liver, but the Soule, in and by the Liver, sanguifies; as the Heart and Braine are but Shoppes and Tooles for Life and Sense; the Workman is the Soule in these."

But we need pursue these discussions, and the diversity of opinions, no farther. The whole of the little world of man, the Microcosm, has now been mapped out, as it was known to Elizabethan explorers. Explorers they were to some small extent, but in a considerable degree they did no more than repeat what had come down to them with authority from their predecessors.[1]

[1] An excellent resumé of the whole subject will be found in the preface to *A Table of Humane Passions*, by N. Coffeteau, translated by E. Grimeston, 1621; much may also be learned from *The Examination of Men's Wits*, by Huarte, translated by R. C. A full treatment of the psychology of the time is easily accessible in Charron's *De la Sagasse*.

THE ENGLISH MASQUE

"THESE things are but toys," wrote Bacon in his essay on *Masques and Triumphs;* yet he did not think it beneath him, as they came home to the business and bosoms, and the purses, of princes and of queens, to consider how the toys might be made beautiful. But it is to be noted that while Ben Jonson regards the masque as an imaginative "solemnity," a "mirror of man's life which ought always to carry a mixture of profit with it no less than delight," Bacon studies the masque solely from the external point of view, as a show or a spectacle. The costumes, the colours, the lights, the scenes, the odours, the music, the dances interest Bacon. Not one word has he to say of the poetry, and he dismisses the whole subject with the words: "But enough of these toys."

The distinction, however, of the English masque, that which in this particular province compels Renaissance Italy to yield to Renaissance England, is the lofty invention of its poets. Shakespeare in *The Tempest*, Beaumont and Fletcher, Chapman, Marston, Daniel, Campion, Middleton, Browne, Shirley, Carew, Davenant are among those who composed masques. The crowning glory of the species is that Milton wrote in *Comus* a poem which evades the formal laws of the courtly toy. The enchanter's rout of monsters bearing torches may be named, if we please, an antimasque; the brothers and sister at the close dance their "going off"; but there is no company of masquers, no dancing the entry, no main dance, no " taking of the ladies," no revels ; song and spectacle are subordinate to a noble poetical celebration of virgin chastity. And this Puritan masque is the only work of the kind which to-day is inevitably familiar to every lover of English poetry.

The conditions under which the masque existed, the circumstances which determined its character, can be easily comprehended. It was a flower of Italian culture, but grafted on an English stem of the same family. The central point of a highly complex work of art was the dance of the masquers, or rather a sequence of dances—for in what we would term the normal type the " main dance " was preceded by the " entry " and was followed by the " going off." After the main dance—often a novelty ingeniously devised—the masquers ordinarily took from among the spectators partners of the opposite sex, and joined with them in dances of the customary kind, galliards, corantoes, and the like, whereupon a more general " revel " succeeded. The entry was itself preceded by dialogue, spoken or chanted in recitative, in which the masquers took no part. Thus the purport of the whole device was dramatically expounded, and the expectation of the spectators was raised to the height. Between the dances songs were introduced, with the purpose of affording the performers a time of needed rest and of stimulating them to new efforts. But the normal type could be varied in this direction or in that ; there might be two sets of masquers, who, after separate dances, would unite ; the introductory matter might expand into more than an introduction ; songs might be multiplied, so as to take the chief place ; an antimasque might serve as a grotesque or humorous foil to the beauty of the masque ; or there might be a succession of quaint antimasques. The whole performance—song and speech and dance—was set in a framework of magnificent decoration, aided by the elaborate and costly surprises of the mechanist.

To represent the value of money during Shakespeare's life by its modern equivalent, Mr. Sidney Lee multiplies the sum by eight. The average cost of a Jacobean or Caroline masque, which seldom had the honour of a second presentation, was, upon this estimate, equal to £10,000 of our current coin ; but on some occasions it reached or exceeded twice that amount. The masque was essentially an aristocratic form of art. It addressed itself to a cultivated audience, who would be rather flattered than displeased by learned allusion and ingenious allegorical device. In an age when neo-classical influences were predominant it naturally imported much of the mythology of Greece and Rome, and decorated this with Renaissance arabesques. The chief personages in the performance—young persons of noble or gentle birth—were silent executants of intricate dances, and must be elevated by the imagination into something higher than mimes or posture-makers. The art of dancing might indeed be regarded by philosophers as a sacred mystery. Sir Thomas Elyot in *The Governour* had shown how it is the highest ethics reduced to practice, the special virtues of the two sexes being resolved into nobler virtues which unite the finest qualities of either sex ; Sir John Davies in *Orchestra* showed how the whole universe with all its members performs a dance, chaos being so converted into a cosmos. But all men were not philosophers. It was desirable to dignify in every possible way the silent dancers, and this, which could not be attained by the exposition of character, might be effected by imaginative invention, or by an allegory which should present them as symbolising some of those invisible powers of morals or wisdom or beauty or love which preside over human life. The whole device must be joyous; yet it might have a certain seriousness of beauty, it might admit of lofty thoughts, but not of tragic emotions. Its ideal was one of grace rather than of greatness. If anything of horror or of fear were introduced, this must be as a foil to throw out and enhance the brightness of the rest. If comedy should appear, the comic effects would naturally arise from the contrast between the vulgar many and the high-born few.

Again, the masque was an occasional piece. It did not arise through any imperious need felt by the poet to relieve his feelings, or to embody the visions of his imagination. The suggestion came to him from an external quarter, whereupon he set his wits to work. The occasion frequently determined the direction in which his fancy must play, and imposed bounds upon its operation. If the festivity took place at Christmas or at the opening of the New Year it was fitting that the invention should be appropriate to the season. If it was intended to honour a bridal pair, the masque took a hymeneal form, and might conclude with an epithalamium. The inducement to courtly compliments and allusion was of course irresistible:

> "They must commend their King and speak in praise
> Of the assembly; bless the bride and bridegroom
> In person of some god. They are tied to rules
> Of flattery."[1]

Jonson fell below none of his contemporaries in the homage which he paid to royal and noble patrons; but he rose above many of them in a certain dignified ideality, which he could confer even on flattery. The art of the poet of a masque did not lie in the

[1] *The Maid's Tragedy*, I. i.

perfect utterance of his own passionate thoughts and imaginings, but in making the most of an opportunity, in adapting his genius to circumstances, and in heightening the splendour of an occasion.

Sometimes the general idea or an essential pivot of the piece was indicated by a great person, whose will was law. Thus, in the masque personated at the Court on Twelfth Night, 1605-6, the Queen was herself a performer, and it occurred to her sportive fancy that the amusement would be heightened if she and her honourable ladies were to appear as blackamoors. It was not for Jonson to propose difficulties or raise doubts; his duty was to invent a design which should account for the appearance of a troop of blackamoors at Whitehall, and at the same time prove that the daughters of Niger may be surpassing beauties. When after a lapse of three years it was Her Majesty's wish that the twelve daughters of Niger, with four more added, should reappear, but now in the loveliness of English lily and rose, and that their long absence should be ingeniously excused, the problem for Queen Anne's poet was perplexing, but Jonson again taxed his wit and the problem was triumphantly solved.

A central idea was a necessity. If the masque was not to "flicker down to brainless pantomime," the spectacle, the material splendours, must be counterpoised by an inward motive, of which the spectacle should be the embodiment and the interpretation. Thus there was an ideal element in the masque, which in the hands of a true poet might become of chief importance. The harmonising of spectacle and idea was often effected by something of the nature of symbol or allegory. Jonson, as we know from the type-characters or humorists of many of his comedies, had a tendency, although he was a great observer of men and manners, to dramatic abstractions; and it was his mistake to suppose that a load of realistic observations imposed upon an abstraction is enough to create a living person for the stage. Here in the masque was a literary form where his tendency to abstractions helped rather than hindered his art, and where the external paraphernalia could be so arranged as splendidly to set forth the idea.

Besides the invention or general device, controlled sometimes by the wishes of his patron and always to a greater or less extent by the novelties of the mechanist, the poet's contribution to the evening's entertainment was twofold—first, speech in verse or prose for dramatic delivery, and, secondly, song. Thus the masque united a dramatic element, exhibiting itself in speech and action, with a lyrical element, expressing itself in song and the music of violins or wind instruments. The dance might be conceived as an ecstasy or rapture, arising out of the joy of action, speech, and song, too fine for utterance in words. The poet's part in the whole performance may be described as a lyrical drama in miniature. In the decline of the masque sometimes the spectacle overpowered the poetry, as was the case with the *Triumph* by Shirley; more rarely the poetry broke away from the other elements of the composite whole and became supreme, as was the case with Milton's *Comus*. Nowhere are the conditions so clearly recognised and so fully accepted as in the best of Jonson's inventions. He, better than any of his contemporaries or successors, maintains the just equipoise between the various elements of the masque. Arrogant as a man, ambitious as a poet, he is obedient to the laws of his art, has a true sense of ordonnance, and submits, at his best, to the bounding line. The danger was considerable that in the variety of splendid and surprising spectacle unity of idea might disappear; but the happiest of Jonson's efforts, while brilliant and varied in detail, subordinate the splendid details to a single dominant conception.

The spectacle and scenic effects of these Court entertainments must have reacted upon the regular drama, creating a desire for more elaborate stage arrangements and for fuller pomp appealing to the eye. When in Restoration days the public theatre became richer in spectacle, memories of the masque co-operated to produce the new development. The feeling also that female parts were inadequately rendered by youths with uncracked voices was doubtless quickened by the masque. Here were the most noble and beautiful ladies of England appearing with gesture and grace of movement as it were upon a stage. Long before a professional actress appeared in the theatre it must have been felt by persons who had the entrance to Whitehall that such a company as that which Hamlet welcomes to Elsinore lacked certain performers whose presence might become a source of elevating pleasure to all who care for the true interpretation of tragic passion or for the sunniest play of mirth.

The earliest example of the use of the term "antimasque" cited in the *New English Dictionary* is of the year 1613, from Chapman. But the antimasque had come into existence before that date. In the "solemnity," written for the marriage of Viscount Haddington, on Shrove Tuesday, 1608, after the Graces, at the desire of Venus, had played the part of criers for the runaway god of love, suddenly Cupid discovered himself, and came forth armed, attended by twelve boys anticly attired who represented the sports and pretty lightnesses that accompany love. On Cupid's invitation they fell into "a subtle, capricious dance, to as odd a music, each of them bearing two torches, and nodding with their antic faces, with other variety of ridiculous gestures." This was Jonson's first antimasque, which contrasted with the dance of the masquers—signs of the Zodiac, of happy influence for wedded lovers—a dance conducted to the musical ring of hammers of the Cyclopses. Next year Her Majesty, who perhaps had been pleased by the nodding boys, commanded an anti-masque for the magnificent "Masque of Queens." The illustrious queens of history, honoured at the house of fame, were the masquers. The antimasque presented twelve hags or witches, being the powers which are hostile to good fame; some had rats upon their heads; others had evil ointment-pots at their girdles; all bore spindles, timbrels, rattles, and other instruments appropriate to sorcery. Nowhere can witch-poetry more full of spirit be found than in the charms uttered by Jonson's hags of the antimasque. It was the poet's pride that his extravaganza should "sort not unaptly with the current and whole fall of the device." Unlike the antimasques of some of his contemporaries those of Jonson, as his editor Gifford has observed, are not mere diversions, but, however fantastic they may appear, work into the general design and form a part of it.

The occasion of the marriage of the Princess Elizabeth to the Count Palatine, February 1613, gave an opportunity for the splendid rivalry of poets. Jonson had quarrelled with Inigo Jones, and was not in favour; but he could be spared. On the evening of Shrove Sunday Campion's masque of Orpheus and Prometheus was presented by the Lords; on the following evening Chapman's masque of Plutus was successfully given by the gentlemen of the Middle Temple and Lincoln's Inn. The gentlemen of the Inner Temple and Gray's Inn were less fortunate. They came on Tuesday evening by water in illuminated barges; their passage was announced by peals of ordnance, and they landed at the Privy stairs. Their poet was Beaumont; the chief arranger of their masque was Francis Bacon; but so densely crowded was the hall that the masquers found their entry blocked. The King was wearied and sleepy after two nights of the business of pleasure. Bacon prayed His Majesty to endure the performance; to do otherwise would be to bury the masquers quick. "Then," answered James, "they will bury me quick, for I can last no longer." It was not until Saturday that Beaumont's masque of the marriage of Thames and Rhine was presented; when it was printed the dedication of the poet was addressed to Bacon.

Bacon's biographer, Spedding, conjectured that the essay on Masques and Triumphs was, "very likely suggested by the consideration he had to bestow upon this device of Beaumont." A close comparison of the essay with the masques of February 1613 has not only convinced me that conjecture here should give place to certainty, but has also made it apparent that Bacon's criticism consists of little else than indirect commendation of the masque in which he had interested himself, and censure of the rival masque of the Middle Temple and Lincoln's Inn. "All is nothing except the room be kept clear," says the essay; and in truth all was nothing for the unhappy presenters who stood outside the door in the February night. "The colours that show best by candlelight are white, carnation, and a kind of sea-water green with oes or spangs." And in the masque of which Bacon may have contrived the spectacle appear the priests clad in white, the knights splendid in carnation satin with blazing stars of silver, the naiades wearing sea-green taffeta, with bubbles of crystal intermixt with powdering of silver representing drops of water—the oes and spangs of the essay. The masquers dancing to song, the ditty fitted to the device, the graceful action of masquers before they dance their entry, the nymphs, rustics, Cupids, statues moving, the recreative music with sudden changes, which the essay mentions with commendation, are in fact reminiscences from his own or Beaumont's contrivance. Double masques, one of men, another of ladies, says Bacon, add state and variety to the whole; and in Beaumont's verse Iris scoffs at Mercury "for devising a dance but of one sex"; upon which Cupids and animated statues advance and join the nymphs. On the other hand, the tedious antimasque of Chapman is remembered by Bacon only to come under a general condemnation. Alteration of scenes are things of pleasure, says the essay, "so it be quietly and without noise." Can we doubt that the reference in the writer's mind was to the huge rock of the rival masque, which moved "some five paces towards the King, and split in pieces with a loud crack?" On Saturday evening no such explosion disturbed the Royal nerves; His Majesty was pleased, and encored two of the dances; unhappily the performers were unable to obey the command, for one of the "statuas" had undressed.

Jonson's poetry of the masque is found at its best in his folio volume, which was published in the year of Shakespeare's death (1616). After that date prose occupies a larger place, and the humorous dialogue, which sometimes becomes satirical of contemporary follies, expands to almost undue dimensions. The masque occasionally loses something of its special character and approximates to a miniature comedy. From the first, indeed, Jonson could be gay as well as grave; but in the earlier masques the gaiety partakes more of grace, of sprightly fantasy, of grotesque invention in which there is no sting; in the later he appears as a humorous critic of society.

For an example of the earlier manner we may turn to *Oberon, the Fairy Prince*, a masque written in honour of Prince Henry, who in 1610, the year of Jonson's masque, was created Earl of Chester and Prince of Wales, and who died two years later amid the genuine and universal lamentations of the people. In a wild landscape, seen by moonlight, appears a satyr, who summons with the notes of the cornet his companions of the rocks and woods. At first echo alone answers to the call. But at the third sounding a troop of his young and lusty fellows gathers, each from his lurking-place behind the rocks, and with antic gestures, full of mirth and wantonness, they begin their chatter of eager inquiry after the fairy prince. What gifts, what pleasures will young Oberon bring? Will he build us larger caves, or gild our cloven feet, or strew our heads with odorous powders?

> "*1st Satyr.* Bind our crooked legs in hoops
> Made of shells with silver loops?
> *2nd Satyr.* Tie about our tawny wrists
> Bracelets of the fairy twists?
> *3rd Satyr.* Garlands, ribbands, and fine posies,
> Fresh as when the flower uncloses?
> *4th Satyr.* And, to spight the coy nymphs' scorns,
> Hang upon our stubbed horns."

And so with ever-varying imagery the babble of the satyr youngsters proceeds. Suddenly the scene opens, a glorious palace is discovered, before the gates of which lie two sylvans dressed with leaves and armed with clubs, but sleeping soundly at their posts. The boy-satyrs endeavour to tease into their senses these negligent guards; but they are more like "caves of sleep" than sentinels. At length the satyrs try the virtue of a catch:

> "Buz, quoth the blue fly,
> Hum, quoth the bee;
> Buz and hum they cry,
> And so do we,"

accompanying the buzzing song with ticklings in the nose and ear. The sleepers are roused, and, after added sport and song, the interior of the palace is disclosed, with the nation of fays, some bearing lights, some instruments of music, some chanting, while the masquers—knights of the fairy prince—appear, and young Oberon himself advances to triumphant music in a chariot drawn by white bears and guarded by sylvans. "The little ladies (the fays)," says Sir John Finet, "performed their dance to the amazement of all beholders, considering the tenderness of their years and the many intricate changes of the dance, which was so disposed that which way soever the changes went the little duke (Charles) was still found to be in the midst of these little dancers." The dances of the masquers, the measures, corantoes and galliards follow, with choral songs between, until Phosphorus, the day-star, appears summoning the revellers to rest:

> "To rest! to rest! the herald of the day,
> Bright Phosphorus, commands you hence; obey.
> The moon is pale and spent, and winged night
> Makes headlong haste to fly the morning's sight."

Such is the gaiety of Jonson's earlier masques.

If we place by the side of *The Masque of Oberon* a device of ten years later, *News from the New World Discovered in the Moon*, we shall perceive the nature of the change which had given the masque an unexpected development. With the exception of songs introduced in the breathing-time between the dances the piece is written in prose. It is indeed a comedy in little, containing the germ of a very interesting regular comedy, *The Staple of News*, which was subsequently evolved from the idea of this masque. Two heralds enter with the delightful announcement, " News, news, news ! " What happier tidings can there be for the printer, the chronicler and the factor who stand by ? The printer would gladly buy good " copy " for his press, whether it be true or false. The chronicler requires matter to fill ten quires of his great volume, the size of which has already been arranged with the publisher ; since seven in the morning he has sought in vain material for a single page, and, like a faithful chronicler, has even counted twice over the number of candles in the hall. The factor has made it his business to supply the provinces with news. He despatches to the shires his one thousand or twelve hundred manuscript letters each week, with such intelligence as will suit his several classes of customers : " I have my Puritan news, my Protestant news, and my Pontificial news ; " and his present project is to establish such a news agency as Jonson afterwards described in his comedy.

The tidings which the heralds bring is, however, not metropolitan but lunar news. The poet has been to the moon and made discovery of a new world, containing sea and land, navigable rivers, nations, politics, laws, hundreds, and wapentakes. Not as Endymion removed thither, " in rapture of sleep," nor in that odd way of Empedocles, who when he leapt into Ætna, being sear and dry of flesh, was whiffed by the volcanic smoke to the moon, where he lives yet, "waving up and down like a feather, all soot and embers," nor yet on foot, as "one of our greatest poets" (old Ben himself) journeyed to Edinburgh, has the poet reached the moon, but in flight upon the wings of his Muse. And what have been his discoveries? The lunar inhabitants are a silent race, uttering themselves by certain motions to music; even the lawyers there are dumb as fishes. They live, like grasshoppers, on dew; yet these worthy lunatic people are not so very different from the lunatics of earth. Anabaptists are there, and Rosicrucians, zealous women who out-groan the groaning wives of Edinburgh, lovers who sigh or whistle themselves away, and moon-calves very like our fools, and with these the ladies play instead of with little dogs. For there are fine ladies in the moon, who ride in cloud-coaches driven by the wind, and have covert places of assignation in the clouds more secret than the retreats of Hyde Park. Their Tunbridge Wells and Spas lie in certain Islands of Delight, to which they sail in cloud-canoes, of which islands one is inhabited by a race uniting in each individual the male and female sexes. They lay eggs which produce a species of half-feathered fowls, named volatees, that hop from island to island. The whole dialogue here is a piece of Aristophanic humour, a fantastic satire on society, little adapted to invite spectacular display. But presently a covey of volatees enters for the anti-masque, and as soon as their hopping dance is ended the masquers descend from the moon, shaking off their icicles. Subjects they are of the wisest and most learned of English kings, who by contemplation of his virtues have been rapt above the lunar sphere. The satire of Jonson's masque is essentially that of the comedies, but, as becomes an entertainment, is lighter, more fantastic, and less laboured.

The date of one of Jonson's masques—*Pleasure Reconciled to Virtue*—which Gifford was unable to assign, has fortunately been fixed as Twelfth Night, 1617-18, by the *Papers of the Venetian Embassy*, translated by Mr. Rawdon Brown. The chaplain to the Embassy, old Orazio Busino, relates how he waited in the Venetian box, afflicted by the over-crowding and vexed by the free-and-easy insolence of a Spanish gentleman, who, begging humbly for a modest space, secured for himself the most comfortable seat. After an age of endurance, shortened only by the beauty of English faces and the splendour of novel dresses, the masque began. Comus, the god of the belly, entered in triumph ; men disguised as bottles and tuns formed the antimasque, which was followed by an antimasque of pigmies. Presently the herald Mercury announced that all grosser forms of pleasure must pass away, and that, under the influence of a wise and learned monarch, Pleasure shall be reconciled to Virtue. Twelve princes led by Prince Charles formed the troop of masquers ; and Busino records that though Charles excelled all his companions in keeping perfect time and making graceful bows his wind was no good. The dance began to flag, whereupon the King, "who is naturally choleric," became impatient and shouted aloud : "Why don't you dance ? What did you come here for ? Devil take you all ! dance ! " On hearing this, the Marquis of Buckingham, His Majesty's most favoured minion, immediately sprang forward, cutting a score of lofty and very minute capers with so much grace and agility that he not only appeased the ire of his angry sovereign, but, moreover, rendered himself the admiration and delight of everybody. Thus encouraged, the other masquers proceeded to exhibit their prowess with various ladies, ending in like manner with capers, and by lifting, says Busino, their goddesses from the ground. Possibly it was to make amends for his outbreak of temper that King James commanded a second presentation of the masque, on which occasion Jonson added an introductory antimasque — "For the honour of Wales." The loyal, but somewhat vain-glorious and quarrelsome Griffith, Jenkin and Evan—Evan, a Welsh attorney, very litigious in the terms, and out of the terms a poet—are indignant that the scene of the masque should be Mount Atlas, when it might better have been placed in Carnarvonshire. They promise His Majesty a true Welsh reception should he visit the Principality, with plenty of toasted cheese, and the possible distinction added to royalty of a justiceship of the peace. There follows a seventeenth-century Celtic renaissance, for harpers are introduced, and there is a dance of Welsh goats, who are "excellent dancers by birth."

"But enough of these toys." And yet the toys had a grace which was lost in Restoration days. As a motto for what is best in the English masque we might take a stanza of Jonson's own, which is sung with other verses by the great inventor, Dædalus, in that device which the old Venetian chaplain has described:

"Grace, laughter, and discourse may meet,
And yet the beauty not go less:
For what is noble should be sweet,
But not dissolved in wantonness."

The times were at hand when courtiers had to doff their silks and buckle on their armour. The masque perished in the Civil Wars, and, as has been noticed by Mr. Herbert Evans in his excellent volume devoted to this subject,[1] upon the Restoration the attractions of the masque had been transferred to the theatre, at which the King was now a constant attendant.

[1] *English Masques*, Introduction, p. lv.

ELIZABETHAN ROMANCE[1]

To return with intelligent sympathy to a dead literature of pleasure is less easy than to obtain mastery over a literature of thought that has grown obsolete. Thought will always beget thought, even though it should be of a critical or a hostile kind; but a literature of pleasure which has ceased to please seems like salt that has lost its savour and is fit only for the dunghill. The roses of last night's ball, the remnants of last night's banquet—why should we look on them again? Will there not be new-blown roses to-day, with lamps aflash on more fragrant wines and fresher dainties? And yet it is certain that we shall never comprehend aright the lives of our ancestors if we fail to understand their pleasures. It is through these that we wind ourselves into their hearts and their imaginations. And in doing this we enlarge the circle of our own existence; we capture for ourselves strange pleasures, which often are as innocent as they are strange.

The drama of the period of Elizabeth, the lyrical and the narrative poetry, still move us; and here, indeed, is the highest and most characteristic product of the Elizabethan imagination. So far, at least, we live in the minds of our forefathers. Prince Hamlet and Othello, Imogen and Juliet, are with us in the close of the nineteenth century as truly as they were with the frequenters of the Globe or Blackfriars three hundred years ago. Caliban and Ariel, Prospero and Miranda, are creatures of an

[1] A lecture given in the Examination Schools, Oxford, 5th August 1892.

enchanted world over which time owns no sway; they belong to the life of humanity, and are borne onward with the stream of that life from generation to generation. It is not so with the romances of the Elizabethan age; the blossoming-time of the English drama was hardly even the seed-time of the English novel. Not one of these romances, in the true sense of the word, lives; they are prey for the moth and worm, including among these inquisitive searchers of antiquity the human book-worm, who bores his patient way through ancient tomes, and leaves a little pile of dust behind him. The literary specialist may wax enthusiastic over them, but the enthusiasm of the specialist is too often proportioned to the obscurity of his toil; he has departed from the centre and cannot find his way back. The prose works of Greene and Nash have been reprinted in limited issues; a sumptuous edition of the *Palace of Pleasure* appeared a year or two since; but from the chambers of that palace the minstrels and the dancers have departed. One novel, indeed, of Thomas Lodge has had the exceptional honour of a popular reprint; but *Rosalynde* does not live by virtue of any inherent vitality; it lives because it was once read by Shakespeare, and because he found in it material for the most charming of idyllic comedies. Greene's *Dorastus and Fawnia*—in some degree recast—was, not so long ago, hawked about the country among wares of the literary pedlar; a copy sold at the price of sixpence, and embellished with a rude woodcut, was once in my hands. But *Dorastus and Fawnia* seems to have disappeared from the humble market which it adorned. Now and again we are happy enough to meet some lover of literature who is Sidney-struck, and who knows not only what we ought all to know—Sidney's noble *Apologie for*

Poetrie, and the tragic story of his love as told in *Astrophel and Stella*, but also something of that "amatorious poem" (so Milton named it) the *Arcadia*. I confess my own infirmity in having found long days of summer short while I lost myself in that country of courtly shepherds and shepherdesses. One lady of Victoria's days I have met who is familiar with the *Arcadia* from the first to the five hundredth page in folio; who has sighed and rejoiced with Philoclea and Zelmane, with Pamela and Musidorus through all their manifold adventures and amorous soliloquies. But she, I suppose, might be described, in Elizabethan metaphor, as the Phœnix of lovers of literature, perched with her folio "on the sole Arabian tree." The public has not asked for a complete edition of the *Arcadia* during more than a century and a half. And I have not in this matter a word of reproach for the public.

Yet it is certain that this book and others of its kind were the delight of our forefathers. During the hundred years which followed its publication, Sidney's romance was reprinted a dozen times; it was translated into French, Italian, German; continuations were composed; it was modernised so late as 1725. With seventeenth-century readers it was incomparably more in demand than the collected works of Ben Jonson, or even the collected plays of Shakespeare, though doubtless it should be remembered that several of these plays lived their truer life upon the stage. If we find ourselves unable to perceive the grounds of its popularity, this can only be because we are unable to enter into the mind of a former age; and to admit this is to acknowledge an incapacity for the historical criticism of literature.

When the earlier story-tellers of Elizabeth's reign

looked about them for materials wherewith to entertain the public, they found ready to their hand an almost inexhaustible supply of tales, both tragic and mirthful, in the literatures of Italy and France. "In Italy," writes Mr. Symonds, "the keynote of the Renaissance was struck by the *Novella*." The *Novella* was a short tale—passionate, adventurous, romantic; or gay, sportive, sometimes cynical, sometimes obscene; often professing to illustrate a general principle or truth of human life; intended actually, or purporting to be intended, for narration in a social gathering of both sexes, and accepting the limitations imposed by such a condition. In order to give artistic unity to a group of such tales, they were commonly set within a narrative framework, for which the most famous and the most representative of the series of Novelle, Boccaccio's *Decameron*, furnished an admirable model.

In the history of the *novella* in English literature there are two stages—first, that of translation; and secondly, that of imitation. The collection which best represents the former of these stages is Painter's *Palace of Pleasure;* the latter stage is best represented by certain writings of Robert Greene. When Painter's first volume of tales appeared in 1566 (the second followed in eighteen months), he was a man of forty years of age. Born in Kent, an university graduate, some time a schoolmaster at Sevenoaks, he now held the office of Clerk of the Ordinance, under the Earl of Warwick, to whom he dedicated the work. The *Palace of Pleasure* seems to have grown out of a collection of tales, announced during his schoolmaster days under a graver title, which title had also the alliterative tintinnabulum, the *Citie of Civilitie*. More than a score of the earlier tales are from classical sources—Herodotus, Xenophon, Ælian, Æsop,

Livy, Aulus Gellius, Quintus Curtius; and it seems that the designed *Citie of Civilitie* would have been formed in the main from such material. But the schoolmaster passed into the public service; it is more than suspected that he enriched himself with peculation of the public property. He discarded—if we conjecture aright—his more serious design; aimed now rather at the delight of the imagination than at the cultivation of morals and manners; found what he desired in the romantic tales of Boccaccio and in Margaret of Navarre's *Heptameron*, and deemed himself lucky to have at his side a French rendering of the novels of Bandello, to lighten his labour as a translator, although he was not ignorant of Italian, and, in many instances, went direct to the original text.

Some of these tales, however fitted they may be for a Renaissance palace of pleasure, would hardly have been admitted as burghers of a city of civilitie. A moral purpose, however, is strenuously professed by Painter; the tales are represented by their translator as both suited for recreation and in the highest degree edifying. "In these histories (which by another term I call Novelles) be described the lives, gestes, conquestes, and high enterprises of great Princes, wherein also be not forgotten the cruell actes and tiranny of some. In these be set forth the great valiance of noble Gentlemen, the terrible combates of courageous personages, the virtuous mindes of noble Dames, the chaste hartes of constant Ladyes, the wonderful patience of puissaunt Princes, the mild sufferaunce of well-disposed gentlewomen, and, in divers, the quiet bearing of adverse fortune. In these Histories he depainted in livelye colours the uglye shapes of insolencye and pride, the deforme figures of incontinencie and rape, the cruell aspectes of spoyle, breach of order, treason, ill-luck and overthrow of States and other persons. Wherein also be intermixed pleasaunte discourses, merie talke, sporting practises, deceitful devises, and nipping tauntes, to exhilarate your honour's minde." So Painter commends his work to his noble patron, and he promises the reader that it will prove pleasant " so well abroade as at home, to avoyde the griefe of Winter's night and length of Sommer's day, which the travailers on foot may use for a stay to ease their weried bodye, and the journeors on horsback for a chariot or less painful meane of travaile, instead of a merie companion to shorten the tedious toyle of weirie wayes. Delectable these Histories be (no doubt) for al sortes of men, for the sad, the angry, the cholericke, the pleasaunt, the whole and sicke, and for al other with whatsoever passion rising, either by nature or use, they be affected." The *Palace of Pleasure* was, indeed, conceived by Painter as an universal remedy for the ills of human life.[1]

The *Palace of Pleasure* occupies a place of some importance in Elizabethan literature. Its last editor, Mr. Jacobs, has noticed that it is the largest work in English prose that appeared between the *Morte Darthur* and North's *Plutarch ;* but a more just ground of its importance is assigned in the statement that it " introduced into England some of the best novels of Boccaccio, Bandello and Queen Margaret." Painter's prose, if it be copious, is not of pre-eminent excellence. He is, as translator, an honest British workman ; but his translations lose much of the grace, the lightness, the romantic charm of his originals. The book is to be remembered with

[1] For Painter's sources, *see* Mr Jacob's *Analytical Table of Contents*, and the corrections made by Emil Koeppel in his *Studien zur Geschichte der Italienischen Novelle in der Englischen Literatur*, to which volume I here acknowledge my large debt.

honour as the first and, in some respects, the best of a number of books of a like kind; and as, more than any similar collection, a store-house of material and suggestion for the Elizabethan dramatists.

Mr. Symonds has justly observed that the conditions under which the Italian *novella* was produced, and, in particular, the circumstance that it was intended for recitation, gave it from the outset "a dramatic complexion." There was a risk for the English drama in the epic breadth which it inherited from the collective miracle plays; such epic breadth suited well enough with the chronicle history as presented on the stage, but it tempted the writer of tragedy to neglect that passionate concentration which is needful for producing the highest tragic effects. "It was of great importance," says Mr. Symonds, "to the playwright to obtain materials for his plots, which should narrow the dramatic movement, so far as this was possible, to a single point. This was precisely what the Italian *novella* supplied. The most perfectly constructed of Shakespeare's tragedies, *Othello*, follows the tale of Cinthio with very little alteration." A well-jointed framework of incident was furnished by the *novella;* but in the intellectual and spiritual evolution of the tragedy much remained to be developed by the dramatist. The situations were given; the imagination of the playwright was roused and, as it were, challenged to supply the psychological truth which interpreted the situations. I can hardly agree with Mr. Symonds in believing that there was a moment in the history of the English drama when scholarly but uninspired playwrights had a chance of imposing a pseudo-classic manner upon English tragedy and comedy. It may have been so in the history of the court drama, but assuredly not in that of the public theatre. The writers of the pseudo-classic school, such as Sackville and Hughes, never swayed a popular audience. The traditions of the English drama, the temper of the spectators in the rude Elizabethan theatre, secured English tragedy from the sterilising influences of the pseudo-classic manner. But Mr. Symonds is undoubtedly right in recognising the aid given by the Italian *novella* to the romantic movement in the Elizabethan drama. A danger indeed, for the drama was created by these tales of overwrought passion and ingenuities of crime—a danger that the romantic might pass into the fantastic and extravagant; that tragic pity might be replaced by a kind of criminal curiosity and tragic terror by the thrill of almost animal horror. From this danger the English drama did not entirely escape; that it was in great measure preserved is largely due to the sanative influence of its most characteristically English species—the chronicle history of which Shakespeare has left us such glorious examples. The breadth of the historical play, its mass of varied interests acted as a needful counterpoise to the tragic concentration and intensity of the drama derived from the Italian *novella*.

Painter's *Palace of Pleasure* was the first and by far the most comprehensive of a tribe of kindred collections. Before his second volume appeared a young Englishman residing in Paris, Geoffrey Fenton, was engaged on a like task, and in complete independence of Painter. The dedication to Lady Mary Sidney of Fenton's *Tragicall Discourses written out of French and Latin* is dated "At my chamber at Paris, xxii Junii 1567." His collection of novels is derived wholly from Belleforest's Translation of Bandello, and it includes four of those which appeared a little later in Painter's second volume. The central motive of the tales is that theme of sovereign interest to all the poets and narrative writers of the Renaissance—the theme of love; and they are put forth with a special commendation as being historically true. "Neyther do I think," writes Fenton, "that our English recordes are liable to yielde at this daye a Romant more delicate and chaste, treatynge of the veraye theame and effects of love than these Histories, of no lesse credit than sufficient authoritie, by reason the moste of them were within the compasse of memorye." What virtuous grounds of edification or instruction we English are obliged to invent in order to justify a little imaginative enjoyment! We must take our pleasures, if not sadly at least seriously. As a translator Fenton, unlike Painter, is not content to follow his author with painful accuracy. He is caught by the Elizabethan passion for decoration of style, and cannot always deny himself what his contemporaries might have described as "a flourish of fancy." Plain English was not enough to satisfy the state of the time, and accordingly all manner of experiments in decorative prose were being made. A critic of the day—Francis Meres—speaks of those by whom "the English tongue is mightily enriched and gorgeously invested in rare ornaments and resplendent habiliments." Lyly, himself a decorator of prose, speaks with wonder of the eagerness of his fellow-countrymen, "to hear finer speech than the language will allow, to eat finer bread than is made of wheat, to wear finer cloth than is wrought of wool." The "curious file" by the help of which Fenton framed his "passing-pleasant book" is praised by the poet Turbervile. Seven words of Bandello, as a German critic has noticed, form the theme for the following variation by Fenton: "Somewhat in the suburbs of this riche and populus Citie is planted in a pleasant valley, a little village called Montcall, worthie every way to be joyned in neighbourhood to so great a Citie, being invironed at the one side with the fragrant ayre of the fertil feldes al to bedewed with the sondry swete smelles of the incense of Aurora, and on the other side with the loftie hilles, breathing from the mouthe of Zephire the ayre of health, to refresh in time of nede the drowsie tenants of the valley." Aurora and Zephyr in Renaissance times were words having as much magic in them as the names of those modern divinities, "Evolution" and "Heredity" had a few years ago. It is easy to dismiss the Elizabethan de-decorative style and fantastic sentence-building with the word "bad taste." No doubt the taste was bad or at least was crude; plain English was beautified, and beautified, Polonius has told us, in a vile phrase. But to set aside a large tendency of literature with such a summary verdict is to give but a poor account of a remarkable literary phenomenon. The eagerness for decoration betokened a time of inordinate energy, displaying itself in every direction; it was natural to an age possessed by an enthusiasm for beauty, as yet untrained and ready for each new experiment in literary art. Fenton's "Tragicall Discourses" was the first of many translations which occupied him until about his fortieth year. While a strenuous worker in Renaissance literature he was also a strenuous supporter of the Reformed Faith. Graver tasks awaited his elder years. At forty he turned from letters to politics; he was in Ireland with the Arthegall of Spenser's *Faerie Queene*, Arthur Lord Grey de Wilton. When Sir John Perrot in 1585 attempted to divert the revenues of St. Patrick's Cathedral, Dublin, to a new college, afterwards Trinity College, Dublin, Fenton was

Perrot's emissary to the Queen; he acquitted himself to her satisfaction and received knighthood at her hands. He was loyal to the English cause in the distracted country which was for many years his home. Through his mother Fenton belonged to a family illustrious in literature—the Beaumonts. He had the honour of Spenser's acquaintance. And we cannot doubt that with one so ardent as Fenton on behalf of England and the Protestant cause, that was the crowning moment of his life when, standing on the western coast of Ireland, he witnessed the final ruin of the Spanish Armada.

I cannot attempt to notice in detail such collections of stories as Robert Smyth's *Straunge, Lamentable and Tragicall Histories* (1577); Henry Wotton's *A Courtlie Controversie of Cupid's Cautels: conteyning five Tragicall Histories, very pithie, pleasant, pitifull and profitable*; H. C.'s *The Forrest of Fancy*; Barnabe Riche's *Right exelent and pleasaunt Dialogue between Mercury and an English Souldier . . . bewtified with sundry worthie Histories, rare inventions and politic devices*; Bryan Melbancke's *The Warre between Nature and Fortune*; *The Newes out of Purgatorie* ascribed by the unknown author to the popular comedian Tarleton, and like Tarleton's jig "fit for gentlemen to laugh at an hour" or *The Cobler of Canterburie, an Invective against Tarleton's Newes out of Purgatorie, a merrier jeste than a Clowne's Jigge, and fitter for Gentlemen's humours.* The merry jests are not all fit for gentlemen's humours in the nineteenth century, and still less for the humours of gentlewomen. But in the mere recitation of these titles we get some notion of the popularity of the Italian novel three hundred years ago—for all drew upon that common source; and a breath from that world of eager imaginings, passionate curiosity, quaint invention and broad-blown mirth seems to touch our senses.

Two features derived from the Italian models are well exemplified in George Whetstone's *Heptameron of Civill Discourses* (1582), and in the earlier *Flower of Friendship* by Edmund Tilnay—the setting of the grouped tales in a framework of narrative, and the introduction of each tale as illustrating some general thesis or truth of human life, usually some truth or alleged truth connected with love or marriage. In Tilnay's little book, which within three years appeared in three editions, the scene is the house of a certain Lady Julia, where is assembled a company of persons of both sexes. The gentlemen pass the fresh spring hours in open-air amusements: "But Maister Pedro di Luxan nothing at all lyking of such devises, wherein the ladies should be left out, said that he well remembered how Boccace and Countie Baltizar (Count Baldassar Castiglione, author of the *Cortegiano*) with others recounted many proper devices for exercise, both pleasant and profitable, which, quoth he, were used in the courts of Italie, and some much like to them are practised at this day in the English court, wherein is not only delectable, but pleasure joyned with profite and exercyse of the witte." The company pass into the garden; a Queen is chosen and is crowned with a garland of roses; and during two days a learned disputation, illustrated by stories, is held upon the duties of husbands and the duties of wives. Here first, observes Emil Koeppel, we may notice the blending of the influence of two remarkable Italian works—Boccaccio's *Decameron* and the *Courtier* of Castiglione.

Whetstone's *Heptameron of Civill Discourses* is a more elaborate and a more interesting volume than Tilnay's *Flower of Friendship*. In a wood near

Ravenna stands the palace of Philoxenus. The season is winter; and at each yule-tide the hospitable Philoxenus entertains a number of ladies and gentlemen. As with Tilnay, a queen is chosen, and during seven successive days questions relating to love and marriage are discussed, each day's "exercise" giving occasion to one or more tales illustrative of the subject under debate. Having on the first day considered whether the married or the single life be the worthier (and in the company is a German doctor, a misogynist, with a fund of anecdote derogatory to women), the assembly on successive days hold counsel on the inconvenience of forced and of rash marriages, of over-lofty and too base love, and of unions where there is great inequality of age. Finally, the seventh day gives opportunity for a discourse on the excellency of marriage; many sound laws and directions are set forth to continue love between the married; and there is added "the rare historie of Pyrigeus and Pieria, reported by Signior Philoxenus," with "other good notes of regarde." Among the tales given by Whetstone is one—*The rare historie of Promos and Cassandra, reported by Madam Isabella*—which may be accounted among the sources of Shakespeare's *Measure for Measure.*

It thus appears that the Italian *novella* was introduced into English literature by direct translation, and that vigorous efforts were made towards its cultivation. Yet at no time did it really attain to perfection in our country. It was not native to the soil; the art of narrative in English prose was still in its infancy; no skilled, original craftsman, such as Boccaccio in Italian literature, had as yet appeared. To tell a story successfully is to achieve one of the rarest feats of the tongue or the pen. In Elizabethan days success was rendered doubly difficult by the passion, to which I have already referred, for decoration in style. That a narrative should move swiftly and sinuously towards its goal, the garb of language should be close-fitting and succinct. But to move forward was often less important with the Elizabethan romancer than to display the rich and voluminous folds of the robe of speech. The Euphuistic style, with its balancing of clauses, its consonance, its responsions, its alliteration already appears before Lyly's *Euphues* was published in George Pettie's fantastically named book *A Pettie Palace of Pettie his Pleasure* (probably 1576)—a series of well-known classical tales, freely handled by the writer, and, as we might say, transposed from the classical into the romantic, with special stress laid upon the element of love. The tales were old, but the manner of telling them was new, and it is this which gives importance to Pettie's book. "If you like not of some wordes or phrases used contrary to their common custome," he writes, "you must thinke, that seeing we allow of new fashions in cutting of beardes, in long wasted doublets, in little short hose, in great cappes, in low hattes, and almost in al things, it is as much reason we should allow of new fashions in phrases and wordes." The feeling that there were new and splendid possibilities for English prose was natural at the time and was right; but the true development of English prose is in the main due to writers who wrote, not that they might make experiments in decoration, but because they had something to say, and were moved to say it by an energy of feeling which resulted almost involuntarily in beauty, as the curves and strokes of a sword wielded in mortal combat are beautiful and graceful beyond the power of design.

When we say that the *Novella* was not native to

our soil, it is another way of saying that the mind of the entire English people did not and could not go with the *Novella* in sympathetic enjoyment. The Italian novel in England was not only an exotic plant, but an exotic plant which many men feared might prove poisonous in flower and fruit. When Renaissance culture first reached this country, it came not in forms of beauty and pleasure ; it worked in close connection with the religious movement of the time. John Colet lectured in Oxford, interpreting, according to the new lights of criticism, the Epistles of St. Paul. Erasmus was engaged upon his *New Testament* and his *St. Jerome*. More was occupied with serious thoughts of social reform, and even perhaps of a devout liberalising of the Faith. The grave traditions of the New Learning lived on to Elizabethan days, and when the Renaissance movement towards beauty and pleasure entered on its career many men of high intellect and of earnest moral temper regarded certain phases of the movement with mistrust and apprehension. It was probably a year or two after the publication of the first volume of Painter's *Palace of Pleasure* that Roger Ascham wrote thus of translations from the *novellieri* of Italy, pointing expressly, in the opinion of Painter's last editor, at that writer's great collection of tales—the *Palace of Pleasure*. " These," he says, " be the enchantments of Circes, brought out of Italie to marre men's maners in England ; much by example of ill life, but more by preceptes of fonde bookes, of late translated out of Italian into English, sold in every shop in London, commended by honest titles the soner to corrupt honest maners. . . . Ten sermons at Paule's crosse do not so much good for moving men to trewe doctrine as one of those bookes do harme with inticing men to ill living. . . . They open not fond and common wayes to vice, but such subtle, cunnyng, new and diverse shiftes to cary yong willes to vanitie and yong wittes to mischief . . . as the simple head of an Englishman is not hable to invent, nor never was heard of in England before, yea, when Papistrie overflowed all. . . . And that which is most to be lamented, and therefore more needeful to be looked to, there be moe of these ungratious bookes set out in Printe within these fewe monethes than have bene sene in England many score yeare before."

With the fresh tides of pleasure and of passion which flowed in upon English life and English literature in Elizabethan days arose new questions for those whose temper was serious, and who could not be content with a culture which ignored the moral nature of man. Just as to-day, when science has made its triumphant advance, any book professing to deal with the relations of scientific truth and religion—and proposing an accommodation—however superficial—of the two, is certain to obtain a hearing, so in the close of the sixteenth century the interest was great in any literary *eirenicon*, which attempted to reconcile the new joy of life, the new enthusiasm for beauty, the new liberty of passion and the old morality, the temper of seriousness, the devotion to whatsoever things are honourable and of good report in human character and human conduct. A reconciliation of this kind was aimed at by Lyly in his *Euphues*, and it was presented in a novel literary form—a decorated prose, in which the sentences are patterned out and enriched with ornament according to certain rules easy to understand and to apply. Art in prose-writing was a demand of persons of culture, and it was not yet felt that the highest art conceals itself. Here was a prose-style in which every sentence was turned out of the mould as exact in all its ornaments as a piece of our cheap cast-iron. What was the prose of Caxton's *Morte Darthur* compared with the glory of this? The elder English ran on inartificially like ordinary human speech; this prose of Lyly's was like nothing human, like nothing natural, therefore it was so much the more distinctively the product of art. But the detestable style of Lyly was only one of the chief sources of the popularity of his book, which passed through ten editions between its first publication and 1636. The other great recommendation was that it endeavoured to effect a reconciliation between Renaissance culture and the old morality of England. Here was a story which, unlike the "ungracious books" censured by Ascham, was eminently edifying; the hero was a young Athenian; the scene shifted from Naples—"a place of more pleasure than profit, and yet of more profit than pietie"—to London; the author might be presumed to possess acquaintance with the worse and the better side of Italian life and learning; and yet the morals of the book were English morals. Religion, education, literature, manners were seriously handled, and yet with the gleam and brilliance of the newest fashion in prose-writing. Above all *Euphues* treated in an edifying spirit of love; honour was done to woman; honour was done in particular to English matrons and maids; "*Euphues* had rather lye shut in a Ladye's casket than open in a scholler's studie"; and the ladies of England became the patrons and protectors of the author who did them homage. The tale was no old-fashioned romance of knightly adventures; it was an Odyssey of culture, including in that word moral culture; the young men and maidens of whom it told were in fact those of Elizabethan England. We can perceive why the book became popular. Such grace and wit as belonged to Lyly are best seen in his courtly plays; but he is a moral teacher in his prose. The English people has, in each successive generation, some one literary favourite supposed to be the poet or artist who tends most to edification, who safeguards with morality the dangerous pleasure of art, or who sanctifies it with religion. Had volumes of selections and birthday-books been invented to afflict our Elizabethan ancestors, the Lyly birthday-book would have had an unsurpassed sale, and selections from John Lyly would have been given away as prizes at academies and seminaries for young ladies.

Lyly wrote as a superior person, as a reformer of manners, as a reformer of style. Robert Greene was by no means a superior person; he lay open to all the various influences of the time, gave himself away to this and to that, wrote in every style on every subject admitting of imaginative treatment, imitated Lyly, imitated Marlowe, refurbished tales from the Italian, addressed himself to readers of refinement, addressed himself to the vulgar, snatched a hasty popularity, and achieved no masterpiece. His non-dramatic works have been thrown by M. Jusserand, the historian of the Elizabethan novel, into four groups; and the classification is sufficiently comprehensive and correct: his novels proper, or romantic love stories, called by Greene his "love-pamphlets"; his patriotic pamphlets; his "conny-catching" writings, in which "he depicts actual fact, and tells tales of real life foreshadowing in some degree Defoe's manner," with descriptions of low London company and the ways of sharpers, and cut-purses, and women of ill-fame; last, his Repentances, pamphlets in which Greene shadows forth a portion of his own pitiful history, records the errors of his past, and makes feeble resolutions of amendment. Starting on his literary career as a disciple of Lyly, he attempted afterwards the Arcadian pastoral style, the amorous-chivalric style, the classical transformed into the romantic, the grouped tales set within a narrative framework, and whatever other form might lend itself to the taste of the time. His *Morando or Tritameron of Love* is evidently written with a recollection of Boccaccio's *Decameron*. As usual, the scene is Italy; as usual, there is a gathering of ladies and gentlemen; as usual, certain questions relating to love are under discussion; and it is a touch very characteristic of Renaissance days that the discussion should be suggested by a picture that adorns the chamber, a picture such as Titian might have painted, representing the rape of Europa. In *Penelope's Web* we are on the island of Ithaca, where the loyal wife of Ulysses is seen in her chamber, weaving amid her maids. Again the theme of conversation is the never-wearying, never-exhausted theme of love and marriage. The essential virtues of a perfect wife—so Penelope maintains—are three: obedience, chastity, discretion in the use of the tongue; to exemplify which virtues, three tales are told on three successive evenings; the tale of the obedient wife of an Egyptian Sultan, who, by her patient submission to unjust trials, is won back from a wandering passion; the tale of a chaste wife in humble life who gains over to the side of virtue her titled tempter; and the tale of the wife, whose discreet silence procures a kingdom for her husband.

In another of Greene's romances, the story-tellers are Perimides, the blacksmith of Memphis, and Delia, his wife—a poor and laborious, but happy, pair—who after the toils of the day refresh their spirits, when evening comes, with innocent discourse. A copy of the *Decameron* must have found its way to

Memphis, for both Perimedes' tale of the first evening and Delia's tale of the second are derived from that source. In *Euphues, his Censure to Philautus*, the warriors and ladies of Troy siege meet alternately in Priam's palace and in the Greek tents, and tales are told to set forth the character of the ideal soldier or "martialist." *Orpharion* transports us to Olympus, where Jupiter entertains a company of gods and goddesses; Orpheus and Arion are summoned from Hades to beguile the time with tales of cruel maidens or of much-enduring wives.

Ciceronis Amor, *Tullie's Love*, one of the most popular of Greene's prose works, although classical in name is in fact romantic, rehandling, as seems probable, certain motives suggested by Boccaccio. Cicero gives us, in his person, an example of the magnanimity of friendship and of patriotism, which is capable of sacrificing for these high passions even love itself. He is not the Cicero of history nor Shakespeare's Cicero, but an eloquent, amorous, Italian youth, who languishes and faints under the stress of the emotion, which yet in the heroism of his friendship he resolves to overmaster. Perhaps Greene's most fantastic setting for a series of tales is to be found in *Alcida*. The narrator, having escaped from shipwreck on an island off the coast of Africa, finds shelter in the cottage of an old woman, after whom the book is entitled. Once she had been fair, and, for her beauty, was named the Venus of Taprobane; now she is infirm, old and poor, an afflicted mother who has daily reminders of her lost daughters in those sad objects—the pillar of marble, the chameleon-bird, the rose-bush—into which, for their several feminine faults, they had been metamorphosed. The eldest, in her pride and coldness, had played a part as unfeeling as that of Barbara Allen in the ballad;

and see, she is now transmuted to stone, and so must remain for all future time. The second had been frivolous and fickle, and now she is the chameleon-bird, flitting to and fro, and for ever varying its hues. The third had betrayed a fatal secret, the disclosure of which caused the death of her intended husband; Eurymachus lies low beneath the slab, and over his grave bends a weeping rose-bush that once had been the unhappy Marpesia. Greene was named in his day "the Homer of women," and, at one time, it pleased him to style himself "the philosopher of love." While he spent his days and nights in ill streets of London in the company of knaves and trulls, he loved, in his imaginary world of romance and drama, to present visions—let us not call them imaginary—of innocent maidens, of pure and faithful wives, like the afflicted yet unsubdued Philomela, the heroine of one of his best tales. In the end a man's life pulls his imagination after it, and in Greene's latest writings the fair ideals of his earlier romances seldom reappear. To the charity of woman he owed something in his dying hours, and even when he lay in the tranquillity of death. On his death-bed he received from his wronged wife a message which probably called forth his last pathetic letter; and, as his body lay in the mean house in Dowgate, where he died, it was the poor, kind woman with whom he lodged—in whose soul there must have lived some poetry—who laid on his pale forehead and fiery hair a wreath of bay leaves.

M. Jusserand speaks of the most celebrated, the most popular, and the most highly honoured of Greene's novels—that on which Shakespeare founded *The Winter's Tale*—as, in fact, one of the worst. The equity of time may be trusted more than the judgment of any single critic; the general verdict is the true one ; and if any of Greene's romances be read at the present day, by all means let it be *Pandosto.*[1] It is true that we shall find no Autolycus in it to brighten with song and smile the amorous monotony of the pastoral passages ; nor is there any statue-scene, like that in which stage Hermiones compete in beauty with the lines of marble, for Bellaria, the Hermione of Greene's story, dies of grief. But the narrative is told with some skill ; it seldom stagnates in the endless speech-making dialogue, or argumentative soliloquy then in fashion ; and a true feeling for the beauty of country life appears through the conventional forms and colours of the pastoral. There is a charming picture of the finding of Fawnia, as an infant, in the little boat driven by the waves from the Bohemian sea-coast (for in Greene and Greene's source, as in Shakespeare, Bohemia is within hearing of the waves) to the coast of Sicily. The shepherd has wandered down to the sea-cliffs to observe if perchance the sheep were browsing on the sea-ivy ; from the solitary boat he hears the cry of a child, and, wading through the waves, he beholds the babe, ready to die for hunger, but wrapped in a mantle of scarlet, richly embroidered with gold, and having a chain of gold about her neck. "The sheepeheard, who before had never seene so faire a babe, nor so riche jewels, thought assuredly that it was some little god, and began with great devotion to knock on his breast. The babe, who wrythed with the head to seeke for the pap, began againe to cry afresh, whereby the poore man knew that it was a childe, which by some sinister meanes was driven thither by distresse of weather ; marvailing how such a seely infant, which

[1] It has been shown by Karo that Greene's plot is somehow derived from a Polish legend relating to the wife of Duke Masovius Zemovitus, which is found in Archbishop Tcharikovski's Chronicle (printed in Sommersberg's *Rerum Silesiarum Scriptores*).

by the mantle and the chaine, could not be but borne of noble parentage, should be so hardly crossed with deadly mishap." And where, except in a well-known lyric by Greene, is there a prettier eulogy of the shepherd's life than that put into the mouth of Fawnia, when her disguised prince desires to be told what pleasures can countervail its drudging labours? "Fawnia with blushing face made him this ready answere, Sir, what richer state than content, or what sweeter life than quiet? We shepheards are not borne to honour, nor beholding unto beautie, the less can we have to feare fame or fortune. We count our attire brave enough if warme enough, and our foode dainty if to suffice nature: our greatest enemy is the wolfe, our only care in safe keeping our flock: in stead of courtly ditties we spend the daies with country songs: our amorous conceites are homely thoughtes; delighting as much to talke of Pan and his country prankes as ladies to tell of Venus and her wanton toyes. Our toyle is in shifting the fouldes and looking to the lambes, easie labours; oft singing and telling tales, homely pleasures:[1] our greatest wealth not to covet, our honour not to climbe, our quiet not to care."

Greene's most studied piece of pastoral, *Menaphon or Arcadia*, is supposed by his Russian biographer, Storojenko, to be an imitation of Sidney's copious romance, which, however, in 1589, the date of the appearance of *Menaphon*, had not yet appeared in print. It is not easy to discover any decided traces of Sidney's influence, but that of Lyly is apparent throughout; and we should remember that Lyly's and Sidney's were antagonistic influences.

[1] Milton's "And every shepherd *tells his tale*" has been explained by commentators, "counts the number of his flock." I have no doubt that Milton represents his shepherd under the hawthorn as occupied with pleasure, not business, telling a tale—that is a story, like the shepherds of Greene.

The style is excessively elaborate, so heavily cumbered with ornament as to make the reader's task laborious; but according to the manner of not a few Elizabethan romances (a manner, perhaps, derived from the Spanish romance of *Diana*), songs are interpersed, and in these we may find our reward for toiling through the trammelling flowers with which Greene obstructs the path of his narrative.

The history of the pastoral in verse and prose still remains to be written. The field of study is wide and well deserves a worker: the pastoral lyric, the eclogue, pastoral narrative poetry, pastoral drama and masque; the pastoral romance in prose; Italian, Spanish, French, English pastoral; the sources of the pastoral in classical and mediæval literature; its new and vast development in Renaissance times; the modifications it underwent in the seventeenth and eighteenth centuries; its decline and the rise of new ideals—such are the titles of some chapters in the unwritten history. In every age men sigh for a world fairer and calmer than that in which they actually live and move. Sometimes this ideal world is placed in a remote golden age of the past; sometimes, as with Shelley, it is placed in the remote future, when all our dreams of liberty, of social order, of human happiness shall be made real. In the age of the Renaissance, an age of great monarchies, of splendid pomps, of high-wrought artificial manners, of strife, intrigue and violent passions, this region of peace and contentment, of love and beauty and youth was found in an imaginary land of shepherds and shepherdesses, which could be placed in Greece or Spain, or Sicily or France or England, or in No-man's land, as convenience might suggest. The fashion began with the Italian *Arcadia* of Sannazaro, in which there is more of pastoral description than of narrative.

It was developed into romantic pastoral narrative by George of Montemayor in his *Diana*, which served as Sidney's model, and which was translated from the Spanish into English, in 1598, by Bartholomew Young. An author who desired to project his own personality into literature, freed from the obscuring accidents of actual circumstance, had here an exquisite mode of exhibiting his ideal self; he had but to mask as a shepherd, and transport himself into the Arcadia of romance, it mattering little by what geographical name that radiant land might for the occasion be styled. And since shepherds of Arcady, tranquil as were their lives, were by this very tranquillity exposed most of all men to the hopes and desires, fears and pains of love, and since in no other region did amorous sighs and tears so much abound, if the author transported himself to Arcadian pastures and woodlands he was almost invited to transport thither his passions also; he might, if he so pleased, create a veiled and ideal history of the heart and apply all the Renaissance zeal for decoration to the fanciful bedizening of his amorous joys and sorrows. Thus did Montemayor; and thus did his disciple, our English Sidney. It must, accordingly, surprise no reader to find the shepherds and shepherdesses of Arcady accomplished in courtly manners and abounding in courtly compliment; by-and-by we may discover that they are princes and princesses in disguise. The saint-knight of the Middle Ages, the Sir Galahad who beholds the Grail, was now replaced by the shepherd-knight, and the Holy Grail of his devotion was the love of women. The spirit of Sidney's *Arcadia* is essentially aristocratic; the heroes and heroines are royal or noble persons in disguise; the veritable rustics, such as Dametas and Miso and Mopsa, are laughed at throughout for their rudeness and ignorance. The effort in Arcadian pastoral was to retain as much as could be retained from the old heroic romances of the past, but in a modernised form; to unite this with the new semi-classical or pseudo-classical ideals of Renaissance pastoralism; and sometimes to superadd the interest of veiled contemporary biography or autobiography. Thus, in such a book as Sidney's *Arcadia* there was a threefold attraction—that of knightly adventure, which had pleased the elder generation of Elizabethan readers, and which, if somewhat modernised, had an attraction even for the young; secondly, the charm of the new courtly Arcadianism; and last, the fascination of a personal story and personal allusions under the veil. To these we should add in Sidney's case the interest of a new prose style, far less crudely artificial than that which Lyly had adopted from his Spanish model, Guevara; a style somewhat effeminate it is true, with no strong progressive current in it, but winding and wandering with a certain grace and melody, advancing and delaying, but never stagnating. The *Arcadia* to be enjoyed aright should be viewed as a poem; so Milton correctly describes it; so Sidney himself authorises us to describe it by the passage in his *Apologie*, in which he maintains that verse is only an accident and not an essential of poetry. The mediæval romances in verse had been followed by the mediæval prose romance. The Renaissance epics in verse, such as the narrative poems of Ariosto and Tasso, were about to give place to the Renaissance prose epic, in which heroic and pastoral elements were united. The personages of Sidney's romance are ideal personages such as befit a poem. The two heroes are ideal youths of Renaissance chivalry, ideal in their beauty, their valour, their breeding, their nobility of soul. The heroines are ideals of maiden loveliness and maiden perfection of character; one, the type of feminine dignity and heroism; the other, of feminine tenderness and grace. The landscape is the ideal landscape of the poets—"here a shepherd's boy piping, as though he should never be old; there a young shepherdess knitting and withal singing, and it seemed that her voice comforted her hands to work, and her hands kept time to her voice-musick." The whole romance is a piece of homage to the passions of love and friendship as conceived in the days of the English Renaissance, and both are conceived ideally, or, as we might say, heroically. Love is an overpowering, but in its nobler manifestations an exalting influence. The body may faint under the stress of emotion, but the spirit waxes great to endure all trials, all tortures, if only the sacred passion, of which a human being becomes the vessel, can be preserved inviolable. The tangle of adventures is ingeniously ravelled and unravelled, showing a real gift on Sidney's part for romantic narrative. The situations are skilfully devised for bringing to light what Sidney describes as "mysteries of passion." The dialogue suffers from the absence of those limitations and that nearness to reality which produced genuine dialogue on the stage; it consists of a series of *tirades*, and the soliloquy is an interminable *tirade* addressed by the speaker to himself. The pastoral element is twofold: there are the ideal shepherds and shepherdesses who love, and carol, and dance, and address one another in the newest forms of exotic or classical verse; and there are the genuine rustics who furnish rude material for the comic scenes of the romance. Unhappily Sidney's gift for the humorous was hardly richer than that of a serious schoolboy who makes painful efforts to be funny.

It ought not to be difficult for anyone whose imagination has acquired some flexibility through the study of past literary forms and fashions to win his way back to the Arcadia of the Renaissance, and to recover a feeling for its beauty. I cannot undertake personally to conduct, as Mr. Cook's successor, a party of excursionists to Arcady, but I feel that I could, for a while, be happy in one of its cottages. Not many preparations would be required for the journey; a russet coat, a sheephook, a bottle, a bag, a pipe, would be all the needments of a silly swain; only to these should, if possible, be added fine manners and a hopeless passion. Every morning the new-comer should unfold his flocks and lead them to the pasture. In Arcady it would be always spring; the ground would be diapered with Flora's riches, as if she meant to wrap Tellus in the glory of her vestments. Around the woodland amphitheatres many fair trees would flourish—the pine, the myrrh tree, the palm, the citron, and on each of these the "appassionated shepherds" would carve their amorous fancies in madrigal and sonnet. There would be crystalline founts where Diana and her Dryads and Hamadryads might disport themselves in the noontide. From pleasant arbours the shepherds' pipe or lute would sound, and when the shepherds' melodies had ceased, they would fall to copious dialogues of love, or echo from lip to lip their hopes and fears in alternate ditties or eclogues. For my own part, were I in Arcady, I should sigh with longing despair for some banished princess, who had bought her a neighbouring cottage and a flock of sheep; her tresses should be like the honey-coloured hyacinth, her brows like the mountain snows that lie on the hills, her eyes like the grey glister of Titan's gorgeous mantle, her alabaster neck like the whiteness of her flocks, her face, need it be said, like borders of lilies intermixed with roses; and I should swear there is no benign planet but Venus, no god but Cupid, no exquisite deity but Love. My shepherdess princess should be cruel for a long time—cruel as with a heart of flint; many rivals, among them a prince of Africa and a prince of Spain, should pay her homage. As for me, I should shed abundant tears in solitude, walk with wreathed arms, swoon on befitting occasions, and address to myself at night many hour-long soliloquies on love and its griefs. But in the end it should be discovered by a mark on my shoulder, or a golden chain which some old shepherd had kept since my babyhood, that I was the lost son of an emperor, over-lord of my rivals, and I should bear away my princess in triumph to the court of her father, who, I think it probable, would now have recovered his throne in accordance with the prophecy of an aged hermit, confirmed by the oracle of Delphos. Perhaps, with our giant-factoried towns, our volumes of smoke, our mountains of slag and refuse, our struggle between labour and capital, our strife of parties, our strife of creeds, we too, by-and-by, may be obliged to invent, if we cannot in fact create, a twentieth-century Arcadia. Yet, no: the toiler in our great cities, the bending toiler in our fields, if seen and known aright, is, as Wordsworth has said, "far more an imaginative form" than any "gay Corin of the groves."

Through Shakespeare's exquisite comedy of Arden woods we all know something of the ideal shepherds' and foresters' life. And if we set aside Sidney's *Arcadia* there is no pastoral romance of Elizabeth's days which will better reward the reader than the *Rosalynde* of Lodge, on which Shakespeare founded his play. In writing this prose idyl Lodge beguiled the hours of his voyage under Captain Clarke to the Canaries; he describes it as "hatcht in the stormes of the ocean, and feathered in the surges of many perilous seas . . . every line was wet with a surge, and every humorous passion counterchecked with a storm." But, in fact, there is no touch of salt-sea spray clinging to this romance of the fields and woods; it smells of the meadows and groves of Arcady, which, for the occasion, we know by its other name of Arden. Lodge's romance stands in a middle place between the *Tale of Gamelyn*, that early English ballad narrative which Chaucer probably intended to rehandle and put into the mouth of his yeoman-pilgrim to Canterbury, and Shakespeare's *As You Like It*. A comparison of the three forms in which the story is told—the mediæval ballad, the Renaissance prose idyl, and the Shakespearean comedy, will show how all the rough and rude features of his original disappear in Lodge's dainty restoration; how Lodge constructs in the spirit of his own time all the amorous intrigue; and finally, how Shakespeare adds the elements of a wider and profounder humanity, the elements of thought and humour, to what had become a piece of graceful Renaissance fantasy, by his creation of the characters of Jacques, Touchstone, and Audry, and by deepening all the other characters. He best proved his right to accept so much from his contemporary by proving his power to create so much more, and of a kind which lay beyond the compass of Lodge's art.[1]

[1] The title, *Elizabethan Romance*, seemed to exclude the treatment of Greene's autobiographical and "realistic" writings, and that of Nash's *Jack Wilton*, a novel of the picaresque class, and one from which I must confess my inability to obtain more than a very moderate degree of pleasure.

LUBBOCK CITY-COUNTY LIBRARY
50578000085161
Dowden, Edward/Essays modern and Elizabe